My
Google Apps™

Sherry Kinkoph Gunter
Patrice-Anne Rutledge

QUE®

800 East 96th Street,
Indianapolis, Indiana 46240 USA

My Google Apps™

Copyright © 2014 by Pearson Education

ISBN-13: 978-0-7897-5295-6
ISBN-10: 0-7897-5295-6

Library of Congress Control Number: 2014935808

Printed in the United States of America

Second Printing: December 2014

Trademarks

Warning and Disclaimer

Special Sales

For information about buying this title in bulk quantities, or for special sales opportunities (which may include electronic versions; custom cover designs; and content particular to your business, training goals, marketing focus, or branding interests), please contact our corporate sales department at corpsales@pearsoned.com or (800) 382-3419.

For government sales inquiries, please contact governmentsales@pearsoned.com.

For questions about sales outside the U.S., please contact international@pearsoned.com.

Editor-in-Chief
Greg Wiegand

Acquisitions Editor
Michelle Newcomb

Development Editor
Charlotte Kughen

Managing Editor
Kristy Hart

Project Editor
Steve Johnson

Copy Editor
Renee Smith

Indexer
Kristina Zeller

Proofreader
Jessica Cohn

Technical Editor
Vince Averello

Editorial Assistant
Cindy Teeters

Cover Designer
Mark Shirar

Compositor
Steve Johnson

Contents at a Glance

Prologue	What is Google Apps?	3
Chapter 1	Getting Started with Google Apps	11
Chapter 2	Managing Email and Contacts with Gmail	41
Chapter 3	Organizing Your Schedule with Calendar	71
Chapter 4	Storing and Sharing Files on Drive	99
Chapter 5	Creating Documents with Docs	129
Chapter 6	Tracking and Analyzing Data with Sheets	167
Chapter 7	Creating Presentations with Slides	201
Chapter 8	Communicating with Hangouts	241
Chapter 9	Creating Websites with Sites	267
Chapter 10	Archiving with Vault	295
Chapter 11	Exploring Other Google Tools	311
	Index	329

Table of Contents

P   **What is Google Apps?**   **3**

Understanding Productivity Suites and Cloud Computing....4

What Do I Get with Google Apps?....5

Exploring the Benefits of Google Apps....7

1   **Getting Started with Google Apps**   **11**

All About Google Apps....12

    Gmail....14

    Calendar....15

    Doc....16

    Sheets....17

    slides....19

    Hangouts....18

    Sites....19

    Vault....19

    More Apps....20

What Do I Need to Get Started with Google Apps....21

    Do You Have a Domain Name?....22

    What's Your Email Address?....23

    What's Your Favorite Browser?....24

Signing Up for Google Apps....25

    Sign Up for Google Apps for Business....25

Exploring the Admin Console....29

    Add Users....32

    Manage Users....33

    Add Apps....34

    Upload Your Company Logo....35

    Change Your Personal Profile Picture....36

Signing In and Out....37

    Sign In....37

    Sign Out....38

2   **Managing Email and Contacts with Gmail**   **41**

Exploring Gmail....42

    Sign In to Gmail....44

Sign Out from Gmail..44

Switch Between Gmail Features 45

Expand and Collapse the Inbox List 45

Working with Messages 46

Compose a Message 46

Reply to a Message 47

Forward a Message...48

Attach a File to a Message 49

Download a File Attachment 50

Insert a Picture...51

Managing Messages 52

Turn On Tabs...52

Create a New Label...53

Apply a Label 54

Move Messages...55

Delete a Message 55

Archive a Message 56

Mark Messages...57

Remove Spam..58

Managing Contacts..59

Add a Contact 59

Edit Contacts 60

Create a Group 61

Working with Tasks..62

Create a Task...62

Make a New List..63

Email a List 64

Customizing Gmail 64

Add a Signature 65

Set Up an Automatic Reply...66

Switching to Gmail from Other Services....................................67

Move Mail from Another Account..67

Import Contacts...69

3   Organizing Your Schedule with Calendar   71

Exploring Calendar 72

Change Your Calendar View 73

Navigate Between Days, Weeks, and Months 76

Work with the Calendar List 76

Add a New Calendar..78

Scheduling Events and Appointments 80

Schedule an All-Day Event...81

Add an Event...81

Add an Event with Details..82

Add an Event with Quick Add...83

Schedule Time Slot Appointments 85

Edit Calendar Items...86

Working Reminders..87

Set Up a Reminder 88

Creating Tasks..89

Add a Task 90

Turn Tasks On or Off 90

Manage Tasks..91

Sharing Calendars...92

Share Your Calendar 92

Import a Calendar 94

Export Calendars 95

Enabling Mobile Notifications..95

Register Your Mobile Phone 95

4   Storing and Sharing Files on Drive   99

Exploring Drive 100

Navigate Around Drive..101

Change the View...104

Uploading Files and Folders 105

Upload a File..105

Drag and Drop a File 106

Upload a Folder..106

Creating New Files...107

Create a New File..108

Managing Folders and Files 108

Create a New Folder...110

Move Files Between Folders..111

Preview a File 112

Open a File 113

Search Files 114

Sort Files 116

Download a File 116

Sharing Files and Folders 117

Share a File.. 120

Edit User Access 122

Change the Visibility Option 123

Syncing Files 124

Install Google Drive on Your Computer 125

View Google Drive Folder Preferences 127

5   Creating Documents with Docs   129

Opening Google Docs 130

Creating a Document 130

Create a Document from Google Drive 131

Create a Document from Google Docs.......................... 132

Create a Document from a Template............................. 132

Formatting Documents 134

Select Text 136

Apply a New Font and Font Size................................... 136

Apply a Style... 138

Customize and Save a Style.. 138

Create Numbered and Bulleted Lists 139

Use the Paint Format Tool 141

Inserting Content in a Document... 141

Insert an Image 143

Insert a Link 144

Insert a Drawing... 145

Insert a Footnote 147

Insert a Special Character.. 147

Insert a Bookmark 148

Insert a Table of Contents.. 149

Inserting a Table 150

Insert a Table 150

Managing Your Documents 152

Open a Document... 153

View Revisions History... 154

Download a Document... 154

Find Text in a Document... 155

Replace Text in a Document.. 156

Viewing Documents... 156

Collaborating on Documents.. 157

Add a Comment.. 158

Work with Comments.. 159

Using Google Docs Tools 159

Perform a Spell Check... 160

Printing and Publishing Documents.................................. 161

Specify Page Setup Parameters..................................... 162

Print a Document 162

Publish a Document to the Web..................................... 163

Working with Add-ons.. 165

Install an Add-on 165

6   Tracking and Analyzing Data with Sheets   167

Getting Started with Google Sheets.................................. 168

Creating a Spreadsheet 169

Create a Spreadsheet from Google Drive....................... 169

Create a Spreadsheet from a Template 170

Entering Spreadsheet Data 171

Enter Sequential Data... 171

Formatting Spreadsheets... 172

Format Spreadsheet Content... 172

Wrap Text.. 174

Apply Conditional Formatting... 174

Working with Sheets, Rows, and Columns 175

Insert a New Sheet... 175

Work with Sheets.. 176

Work with Rows and Columns... 177

Working with Formulas and Functions.............................. 179

Enter a Formula Manually 179

Copy a Formula 181

Use the SUM Function 182

Inserting Content in a Spreadsheet 183

Insert a Chart.. 183

Insert an Image 185

Insert a Link 186

Insert a Note... 187

Managing Your Spreadsheets.. 187
    Open a Spreadsheet.. 188
    Download a Spreadsheet.. 189
    Edit a Spreadsheet 190
    Specify View Options 190
    Delete a Spreadsheet.. 190
Working with Spreadsheet Data 191
    Sort Data by Column... 192
    Perform an Advanced Sort.. 193
    Apply a Filter 193
Collaborating on Spreadsheets 194
    Add a Comment.. 194
    Work with Comments 195
Printing and Publishing Spreadsheets.................................... 196
    Print a Spreadsheet.. 196
    Publish a Spreadsheet to the Web 197

7   Creating Presentations with Slides   201
Getting Started with Google Slides... 202
Creating a Presentation.. 202
    Create a Presentation from Google Drive 203
    Create a Presentation from a Template............................. 204
Working with Slides 205
    Apply a Slide Layout... 205
    Apply a Slide Background 207
    Apply a New Theme 208
    Add a Slide to Your Presentation 208
    Import Slides from Another Presentation 209
    Organize Slides... 210
    Duplicate Slides.. 210
    Delete Slides... 210
Inserting Content in a Presentation.. 211
    Insert a Text Box 212
    Insert an Image 212
    Insert a Link 213
    Insert a Video 214
    Insert a Line 215
    Insert a Shape 215

Insert a Table 216

Formatting Presentations 217

    Apply a New Font and Font Size............................ 219

    Create a Numbered List 220

    Create a Bulleted List 220

    Use the Paint Format Tool 222

Working with Transitions and Animations 222

    Set Slide Transitions.. 223

    Animate Slide Objects 224

Managing Your Presentations 224

    Open a Presentation... 225

    Download a Presentation....................................... 226

Editing Presentations 226

    Specify View Options 227

Collaborating on Presentations..................................... 229

    Add a Comment.. 230

    Work with Comments... 230

Using Google Slides Tools.. 231

    Perform a Spell Check.. 232

Printing and Publishing Presentations........................... 233

    Specify Print Settings and Preview Your Presentation.. 233

    Publish a Presentation to the Web......................... 234

Delivering Your Presentation... 236

    Create Speaker Notes... 236

    Deliver Your Presentation 237

8   Communicating with Hangouts   241

Exploring Hangouts 242

    Get Started with Hangouts.................................... 244

Adding the Hangouts App 245

    Install the Hangouts App as a Plug-in 247

    Install the Desktop Hangouts App.......................... 247

    Enable the Hangouts App in Gmail........................ 248

    Enable Google+ Premium Features........................ 249

Working with Chat Hangouts... 250

    Start a Chat in Gmail 251

    Start a Chat in Hangouts 252

    Invite a New Contact... 253

Insert a Picture into Your Chat 254

Archive Your Chat 255

Video Conferencing with Hangouts 256

Start a Video Call 256

Answer a Video Call Invite 258

Share Your Screen 259

Open a Chat Pane 260

Open a Google Drive File 261

Play with Google Effects 262

Take a Photo 263

Phone Calling with Hangouts 264

Place a Phone Call 264

9   Creating Websites with Sites   267

Exploring Sites 268

Benefits of Using Sites 269

Tour Sites 270

Building Sites 271

Build a Basic Website 272

Customizing Your Page 274

Add Your Text 276

Format Text 277

Change the Layout 279

Insert an Image 280

Add a Link to Another Website 282

Add a Gadget 283

Adding Pages 285

Page Types 285

Add a Page 287

Add Links to Subpages 289

Reorganize Pages 290

Sharing Your Site 291

Share Your Site 292

10   Archiving with Vault   295

Exploring Vault 296

Adding the Vault App 297

Add the Vault App 297

Assign Licenses 299

Sign In to Vault 301

Setting Retention Rules 302

Set a Custom Retention Rule 302

Set a Default Retention Rule 303

Working with Matters 303

Create a New Matter 304

Add a Collaborator 305

Creating Holds 305

Create a Hold 306

Searching Message Data 306

Search for Data 307

Exporting and Auditing Data 308

Export Search Results 308

Run an Audit Report 309

11 Exploring Other Google Tools **311**

Browsing the Web with Google Chrome 312

Surf the Web 314

Add a Bookmark 316

Pin a Tab 317

Working with Google Groups 317

Enable Google Groups for Business 319

Create a Group 319

Invite People to a Group 321

Start a Topic 321

Find Basic Permissions Settings 322

Understanding Google+ for Business 323

Enable Google+ 324

Create a Google+ for Business Page 325

Other Google Apps to Try 327

Index **329**

About the Authors

Sherry Kinkoph Gunter has written and edited oodles of books over the past 20 years covering a wide variety of computer topics, including Microsoft Office programs, digital photography, and web applications. Her recent titles include *Sams Teach Yourself Facebook*, *Word 2013 Absolute Beginner's Guide*, and *Microsoft Office for Mac Bible*. Sherry began writing computer books in 1992, and her flexible writing style has enabled her to author for an assortment of imprints and formats. Sherry's ongoing quest is to aid users of all levels in the mastering of ever-changing computer technologies and helping users make sense of it all so they can get the most out of their machines and online experiences. Sherry currently resides in a swamp in the wilds of east central Indiana with a lovable ogre, a menagerie of interesting creatures, and a somewhat tolerable Internet connection.

Patrice-Anne Rutledge is a business technology author whose books include *My LinkedIn*, *WordPress on Demand*, and *Sams Teach Yourself Google in 10 Minutes*, all from Pearson Education. She is a long-time user of many Google tools and technologies, including Google Apps, Gmail, and Google+.

Patrice is also the founder and principal of Pacific Ridge Media, a boutique content marketing and social media agency that offers consulting and training for clients worldwide. She is frequently quoted in major media outlets around the world, including CNN, Inc.; Fox News; ABC News; MSN; AOL; Orange County Register; ZDNet; USAA; CareerBuilder; and more. You can reach Patrice through her website at www.patricerutledge.com.

Dedication

Patrice: To my family, with thanks for their ongoing support and encouragement.

Sherry: To my lovable ogre, Shrek, aka Mathew with one T.

Acknowledgments

Special thanks to Michelle Newcomb, Charlotte Kughen, Vince Averello, Renee Smith, Jessica Cohn, and Steve Johnson for their feedback, suggestions, and attention to detail.

We Want to Hear from You!

As the reader of this book, *you* are our most important critic and commentator. We value your opinion and want to know what we're doing right, what we could do better, what areas you'd like to see us publish in, and any other words of wisdom you're willing to pass our way.

We welcome your comments. You can email or write to let us know what you did or didn't like about this book—as well as what we can do to make our books better.

Please note that we cannot help you with technical problems related to the topic of this book.

When you write, please be sure to include this book's title and author as well as your name and email address. We will carefully review your comments and share them with the author and editors who worked on the book.

Email: feedback@quepublishing.com

Mail: Que Publishing
ATTN: Reader Feedback
800 East 96th Street
Indianapolis, IN 46240 USA

Reader Services

Visit our website and register this book at quepublishing.com/register for convenient access to any updates, downloads, or errata that might be available for this book.

Google Apps Dashboard

In this prologue, you learn about Google Apps—the cloud-based office suite that helps people to connect and get things done.

→ Understanding productivity suites and cloud computing
→ Exploring types of Google Apps accounts and apps
→ Discovering the benefits of Google Apps

What Is Google Apps?

The name Google is synonymous with the Internet. In fact, it's so commonly associated with the Web, that its very name is now an official verb recognized by major dictionaries (Merriam Webster Collegiate Dictionary and Oxford English Dictionary, as of 2006). When someone tells you to "google it", it means to look up something online using the extremely popular Google search site, www.google.com. Over the years, Google has grown from a search tool to include a successful web-based email service (Gmail), specialized tools and features like Google Maps and Google Earth, acquired online sensations like YouTube, and launched its own web browser (Chrome), just to name a few of Google's developments.

Google has a history of trying new technologies and products, and today Google has expanded to offer an ever-evolving series of web-based applications, called Google Apps. Targeting businesses, schools, and organizations, the applications offer essential services to bring people on your team together and equip them with tools to get things done.

Understanding Productivity Suites and Cloud Computing

You can use Google Apps to perform a variety of productivity tasks, the same kind of tasks you do with other desktop office programs—emailing, creating documents and spreadsheets, scheduling appointments, and more. Productivity suites—like Microsoft Office and WordPerfect Office—have been around a long time, helping us work better and faster at home, the office, or on the road. Typically, productivity suites, also called office suites, include word processing, spreadsheet, email, and presentation programs. In order to use these programs, you (and everyone else in your office or network) have to have the software installed on your system, or you at least have to have an app that allows you to read and work with the different file types for each program. Needless to say, the cost of installing and licensing all this software, plus paying the experts often needed to help administrate the programs on a network, is an expensive part of doing business.

With the advent of cloud computing, however, things are changing in the realm of office suites. Rather than buying and installing programs on your own hard drive, you can now access data and programs over the Internet. Cloud computing is growing in popularity, and companies are quickly taking advantage of all the innovations. Cloud services, such as Google, offer not only storage space on their giant network of servers but also access to web-platform apps—programs that run in an Internet browser rather than from your computer's hard drive. In other words, you can open the program from the Web instead of your own computer. Plus, you're not limited to using a computer to use the web apps; you can use any device that connects to the Internet and utilizes a screen in performing tasks. This includes tablets and smartphones.

Google Apps are a boon to companies and groups, large and small. Say you own a small company of 3 to 10 employees and you want everyone to work on documents at the same time. With Google Apps, employees can work on the documents and chat about them as a group—all without spending thousands of dollars and hours on administering a server and purchasing software. It's the ideal collaboration setup.

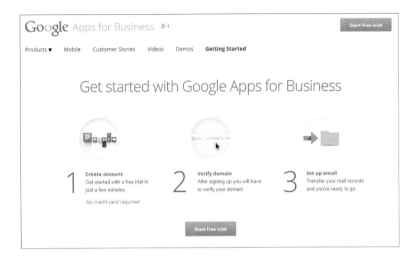

What Do I Get with Google Apps?

Anyone can set up a free Google account and utilize the free consumer products, including Gmail (email), Google Groups (Internet groups), and Picasa (photo organizing). But to tap into the essential business services and all the collaborative products, you must sign up for one of three types of Google Apps accounts:

- Google Apps for Business

- Google Apps for Education

- Google Apps for Government

At the time of this writing, Google Apps for Education is offered free for K-12 schools, universities, and colleges. All you need is a unique domain name to sign up. The Business and Government accounts charge a fee, and also require a unique domain name to sign up. Ready to find out how much? $50 a year (per user) or $5 a month (per user). If you include the Vault app with advanced security and retrieval features, the cost is $10 a month (per user). As you can see, the Google Apps office suite is very economical!

No Domain Name? No Problem!

You can sign up for a domain through the Google Apps sign-up process. Google has partnered with several domain registrars to help you establish a domain name for your organization.

When you sign up for Google Apps with your domain name, everyone in your organization gets a custom email address; access to word processing, spreadsheet, and presentation apps; a shared calendar system; tools for building and adding to your website; and more. Here's a list of the main productivity Google Apps:

- Gmail
- Calendar
- Drive
- Docs
- Sheets

- Slides
- Hangouts
- Sites
- Vault

That's not all—Google is constantly adding more apps and you can always shop for them from among the categories listed on the Google Apps Marketplace web page. You'll find a huge array of apps available, including AdWords, Analytics, Blogger, and Voice.

Exploring the Benefits of Google Apps

There are many benefits to tapping into the power of Google Apps. Whether you're a larger company or a very small organization, you're sure to find Google Apps incredibly reliable and easy to use; it'll be a boon to your bottom line. Here's what Google Apps can do for you:

- **Save Money**—Forego costly business startup and expansion costs that you incur with server and software expenses.

- **Easy Email**—Get a web address and customized email for your company and employees. Google uses your domain email alias for your messages, so users see your domain as the sender/receiver, even though your email account is managed with Gmail. Plus every user in your organization gets email accounts with Google Apps.

- **Docs for Everyone**—Creating documents, spreadsheets, and presentations in the cloud rather than on a hard drive makes it easy to access, work remotely with, and share files. You can use Google Docs, Sheets, and Slides with any operating system, including Windows and Mac. Storing files on Google's Drive app makes it easy to share them.

- **Manage Schedules**—Google's Gmail and Calendar apps work together to help you and your team track appointments, schedule dates, send requests, and receive notifications. You can connect Gmail to your smartphone and always have your schedule and reminders wherever you go.

- **Security and Backup**—With Google Drive, you always have cloud storage, plus easy access to shared folders and files. Google makes sure your data remains safe. Your Google account includes up to 30GB of storage for each user across all the apps combined, and you can grow that as needed for a small additional cost.

- **Work Remotely**—With cloud-based computing, everyone in your organization can access apps and files from wherever they are—as long as they have an Internet connection and a device to connect with.

- **No IT Maintenance**—Stop spending money on IT maintenance; Google Apps doesn't require any and keeps software updated. Plus, Google's own IT staff is ready to help at any time.

- **Website Creation**—If you don't already have a website, Google offers an app (Sites) to help you create one, plus you can incorporate your account into Google Sites so you can edit your web pages from any device. With Sites, you can also create shared workspaces for your team, making it easy for everyone to find information and documents.

- **Video Conferencing and Messaging**—Set up video meetings with as many as 15 participants from wherever they are, which enables you to connect face-to-face even if you're not in the same room, or you can open up viewing-only for as many people as you want. You can conduct a quick call or ongoing dialog communication, message with text and pictures, and work on a document all at the same time.

- **Go Green**—Moving your team's activity to cloud computing not only saves money and time but also helps you spend less on energy costs, employee travel, office materials, and more.

This is just the tip of the proverbial iceberg. Are you ready to learn how to put everything Google to work for you? Then let's dive in!

Try It Before You Buy It!

Google Apps offers a 30-day free trial, no credit card required for sign up. You can choose a free trial when signing up for an account. Simply have your domain name verified and transfer your email records, then you're good to go!

**Google Apps account
Admin console page**

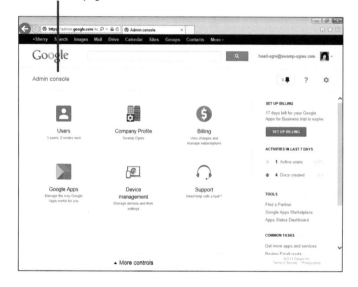

In this chapter, you learn about the Google Apps themselves and how to signup for an account:

→ Discovering the benefits of using Google Apps
→ Previewing what the main apps do
→ Finding out what you need before you get started
→ Walking through the signup procedure
→ Learning your way around the Admin console
→ Exploring a few ways to customize your account
→ Learning how to sign on and off

Getting Started with Google Apps

Cloud technology is sweeping the globe, and businesses, schools, and other organizations are taking advantage of the opportunities it offers. Cloud-based services use the Web as a platform for applications and offer users space on their servers to store all types of files, usually for a fee. People are quickly finding out that using web-based applications and storing data online is much easier and more cost effective than desktop computing solutions. The beauty of cloud technology is it frees you from having to be in the same space to work together and you don't have to worry about maintaining software and servers.

Google has introduced a line of web-based apps for businesses, institutions, and other organizations, called Google Apps. Your first step to understanding Google Apps is figuring out what they are and what they can do for you. After you've decided they're right for you, signing up is easy and fast.

All About Google Apps

Google Apps is a productivity suite, also called an office suite. Designed especially for businesses, non-profits, institutions and other organizations, Google Apps offer unique collaboration tools and apps for conducting all kinds of work, all accessible from online. Here's how Google Apps can help you:

- **No software or hardware costs**—Cloud services like Google Apps do not require software installed on each computer or device that accesses them. You don't have to worry about licensed installations and making sure every user on your team has the correct software. This also means you don't have to worry about network or web servers, hiring technical support and consultants or other IT resources. Your only cost with Google Apps is a monthly or yearly subscription.

- **No upgrades**—You no longer have to worry about keeping everyone configured with the latest software upgrades. Google Apps upgrades their apps automatically without interruption in service. You can be sure everyone is using the latest app every time they log on.

- **More collaboration between users**—Google Apps simplifies working together, allowing people to see changes to documents in real time without the annoyances of out-of-sync edits. Everyone has access to documents at the same time, and changes appear immediately within a document.

- **More reliability**—You can expect greater reliability with your Google Apps uptime—the percentage of time that the service is available. Google Apps boasts a 99.9 percent system availability, so you don't have to fret about your people not having system access.

- **Secure and private**—Because you're storing your data online with Google Apps, your files are always available and easy to find. Unlike desktop systems where you always need to worry about backing up data to be prepared for hard drive crashes, or lost or stolen data, cloud storage means the files are available and accessible. Plus, Google uses the best auditing industry standards to keep data secure and private.

- **Constant support**—Google offers a wide array of software support, including discussion boards, forums, and help centers that are constantly updated. In addition, 24/7 customer support is available via phone, email, or self-service online chat.

It's Not All Good

Who Should Not Use Google Apps?

Google Apps might not work for every business, organization or team. Although situations vary widely, some of these downsides might prove unsurmountable to using Google's productivity suite:

- No Internet connection—Without access to the Internet, you cannot participate in cloud computing because everything's hosted away from your computer. Unreliable Internet connections or extremely slow connections can also hinder users a great deal.

- Security issues—No data is 100 percent safe, even in the cloud, so there is always risk in trusting hosting sites, Google included. Hijacked passwords also pose a threat, so password education and protection is tantamount to keeping your team safe online.

- Change is difficult—If your group's use of other office software, like Microsoft Office, is too ingrained, switching to a new platform might prove difficult, despite the cost savings.

- Too much investment in other solutions—If you've already invested a great deal of time and expense into your current productivity suite, which works fine for your budget and setup, switching might not be economically viable at this time. However, if you're experiencing ongoing costs, then you definitely need to look into cloud computing with Google Apps.

Cloud computing offers you and your team many advantages over desktop suites, cost being a big part of the appeal. Can you imagine not having to spend money for continual software upgrades, licensing, and support? Or rid yourself of the headaches of dealing with your IT infrastructure, exchange servers, and other hardware issues? What about the added functionality of being able to collaborate instantly on all your work projects, scheduling, and communication efforts? Or how about the advantage of managing your files from one spot using any computer, tablet, or mobile device? If all of this sounds appealing, then Google Apps is just right for you!

Let's take a look at each of the major apps in more detail.

Gmail

Gmail is Google's very successful email service. Gmail has been around as a free advertising-supported email service since 2004 and has grown into the most widely-used web-based email provider on the Internet. The regular free account requires the use of the @gmail.com email address domain, while Gmail for Google Apps allows you to customize your email address to use your organization's domain name.

You can also use Google's powerful search tools to look through your email messages to find what you're looking for, including filtering and searching for labels and documents. Gmail's inbox also lets you see who's online with you and connect via voice, text, or video chat. If you use a different email client, such as Microsoft Outlook or Apple Mail, you can use it with Gmail, too.

View email in your Gmail inbox

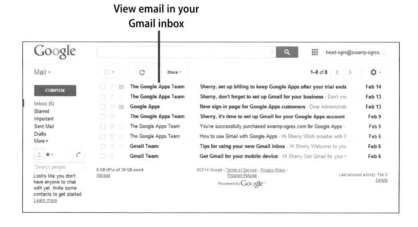

Regular Gmail versus Google Apps Gmail

Regular Gmail users receive 15MB of free storage per account, and can purchase additional storage to suit their needs. As a Google Apps user, you get 30MB of data storage for all the apps, including email, for each user on your account, plus customized email addresses! If 30MB isn't enough, you can always purchase more.

Calendar

Not only can you keep track of your own personal appointments using the Calendar app, you can also synchronize it with the rest of your team, scheduling meetings, conferences, events, and more. A perfect tool for organizing your daily activities, Calendar works seamlessly with your computer, tablet, and mobile device. You can attach files to events to make sure everyone has updated materials. You can share your calendar with others, as well as publish it on your website and set up reminders to help you remember upcoming meetings and events.

View your schedule with Calendar

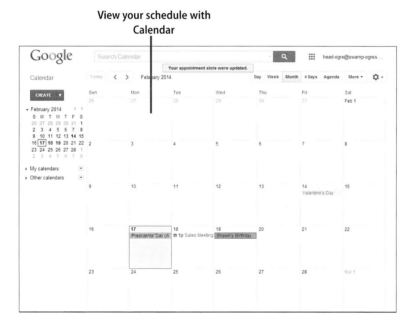

Drive

Google Drive is your go-to storage solution in the cloud. You can save your files to Drive and access them from anywhere, making it the perfect backup system. Rather than take up precious room on your computer's hard drive, for example, you can store your work online, including the docs, sheets, and slides you create with other Google Apps. You can upload photos, videos, and other files, and organize them into folders. Your data is always safe and accessible. You can also allow others to view a file or folder.

View items stored on
your Drive

Docs

Docs is Google's word processing app. You can use it to create documents of all kinds. Whip up letters, reports, memos, and other types of text publications, and store them online. Like any other word processing software, you can create and edit document files, import and export content, control formatting to create the look you want, and make them print ready. Because you store documents online, you can easily share them for review and collaboration, email them, and more.

Use Docs to create text
based documents

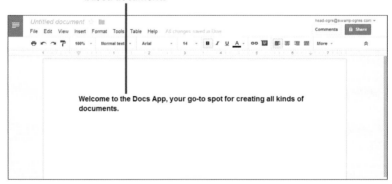

Sheets

Google Sheets is a spreadsheet app designed to help users work with numerical and other organizational data. Like any other spreadsheet program, Sheets lets you automate calculations in tables of data, write formulas and functions, create charts, and more. If you're used to using other popular programs, like Microsoft Excel or OpenOffice Calc, you'll find a similar interface in Sheets, with columns and rows intersecting to form cells for data entry.

Crunch numbers with
Sheets

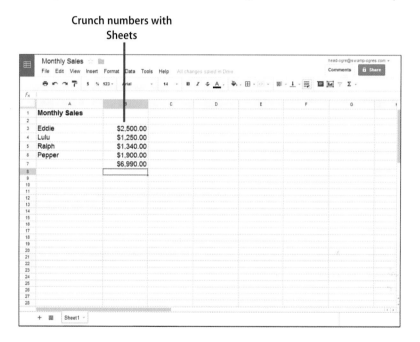

Slides

Slides is Google's presentation app for creating all kinds of visual slide shows. You can quickly assemble slides to create presentations to share online. You can add text, photos, and video clips to create professional slide shows to convey an idea, message, or entertain. If you've worked with other presentation programs, like Microsoft PowerPoint, then you'll find it easy to switch over to the interface and tools in Slides.

Design slide show
presentations with Slides

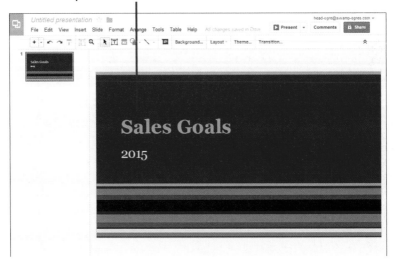

Hangouts

Use Google's Hangouts app for messaging, voice, and video meetings online. Hangouts replaces Talk and Google+ Messenger as Google's instant messaging and video conferencing platform. With Hangouts, you can hold conversations with two or more users, plus you can save conversations, share photos and documents, and more. You can connect with any device, such as a tablet or smartphone, and even initiate video calls from Gmail.

Use Hangouts to video
conference online

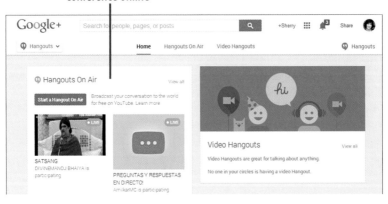

Sites

Make your own custom workspace site for your entire team to interact and find data, or create a web page to share with customers. The Google Sites app lets you create structured wiki and web pages. For example, you can create a site as a one-stop spot for everything related to a project that allows users to grab the latest documents, calendars, and file attachments. Thankfully, you don't need to know HTML coding to get started. Building a site page is much like creating a document. Plus you'll find lots of templates to use to help you get started.

**Make your own project
website with Sites**

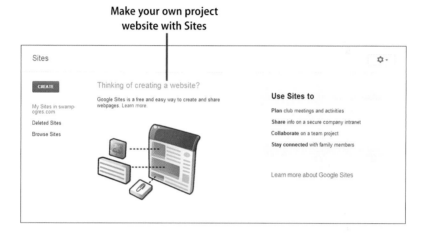

Vault

Vault is an optional app purchase with Google Apps that you can use to help with archiving, e-discovery, and user activity reporting. What is e-discovery? It's a set of administrator tools to search incoming and outgoing email messages—which is often a requirement for businesses for legal reasons—and keep email and chat messages stored securely. For example, a business can legally be required to turn over all the emails concerning a particular topic or employee. With Vault, the information is stored and searchable, making it easy to find. At this writing, Vault is only available for Google Apps for Business users.

Add e-discovery
capabilities with Vault

More Apps

There are additional apps available on the Google site, and more are being added all the time. Check the Google Apps Marketplace page (www.google. com/enterprise/marketplace) anytime you want to browse other apps. You can use the site to review top apps, browse among special categories, or conduct a search for a specific kind of app.

Shop for more apps in the
marketplace

What Do I Need to Get Started with Google Apps?

Google offers its productivity suite in several editions, and the one you signup for depends on what type of organization you are. Here's the price breakdown:

- **Google Apps for Business**—$5 per user per month, or $50 per user per year

- **Google Apps for Education**—Free for grades K-12, colleges and universities

- **Google Apps for Government**—$50 per user per year

Party of One?

Are you the only employee? Google Apps is just as useful to you, especially if you work with different clients in different locations. You can conduct online video calls, share documents, and schedule meetings with other people in your social or business network.

Want to know what you're getting with an Google Apps account? Most of the main apps are available in each edition (Vault costs extra); here's what else is included:

- 30GB Gmail and Drive storage (for each user)

- Custom email addresses for your domain

- Unlimited users (you can add as many as you need)

- 24/7 customer support

- Video chat, calendar, and document editing

- Business controls and security

- 99.9 percent uptime guarantee

If you're signing up for a Google Apps for Education account, these additional points apply:

- No ads for faculty, staff, or students

- Other staff and volunteers might see ads

- 30GB storage per person across all the products

Other than determining whether you are a business, educational institution, or government entity, all you need is a domain name, email address, a secondary email address, and your favorite web browser.

Free Trial!

Don't forget, Google offers a 30-day free trial of Google Apps so you can try it before you commit to it. At the end of the trial period, you can start your paid subscription.

Do You Have a Domain Name?

Google Apps requires a domain name to associate the apps with and you need to verify you are the owner or administrator. A domain name is a unique name for your website, often looking something like this: mycompany.com. Your domain name marks your unique site and is used in the URL (Uniform Resource Locator) you type into the browser's address box to display your web page.

Domain name

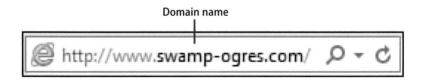

A domain name is required as part of your Gmail customization. The verification process helps Google ensure that only your organization uses the domain for emailing and other tasks. To verify the domain during signup, you need access to the domain's DNS (Domain Name System) settings (which are available from and managed by the domain host), need to know the server that hosts your site, or must have a Google Analytics account for your domain. Google enables domain services for your domain name, but your account still remains with your original domain host.

Must I Use My Primary Domain?

No. You can register a new domain name just for Google Apps, thus making a secondary domain. You might consider this route if you want to leave your existing website as it is, without bothering any of the resources you have associated with the site. However, this means your customized Google Apps email address is attached to the new domain rather than the existing website. Thankfully, you can work around this issue by adding the original domain to your account via the Domains tool found on the Admin console. After you have created your account, click the More controls link at the bottom of the dashboard to find the Domains tool.

If you don't have a domain name, you can purchase one during signup from Google's registration partners. It's incredibly easy to do so, and the cost is very reasonable. As part of creating a new domain name, Google checks the name you choose against all the other registered names. If you choose a name that's already in use by someone else, you'll have to come up with another name or variation.

Google's domain registration package includes a yearly fee, protects the domain against unauthorized transfer, and automatically configures it to work with Google services. It's up to you to manage the settings for your DNS going forward, such as setting any functionality options required for your particular organization.

Do I Need a Web Page?

You don't have to have an actual web page associated with your domain name; you just need a domain name to create your Google Apps account. You can use Google Sites to help you create a simple page if you want to make one later.

What's Your Email Address?

During the signup process, Google asks you for a primary email address, such as my_name@mycompany.com. This email address becomes your login name for your Google Apps account. This is the email address others will see, so choose one that clearly identifies you as it relates to your organization.

You also need to add a secondary email address to use in case you forget your login information and need Google to email it to you again. The secondary email address should be outside of your Google Apps domain, like the email address you currently use.

What's Your Favorite Browser?

If you're concerned about being able to use Google Apps on a Windows, Macintosh or Linux system, don't worry. Google Apps is platform independent, so it works with any system. All you need to run Google Apps is an updated web browser. There are many web browsers to choose from. Here are a few popular ones, one of which you probably use:

- Internet Explorer (Microsoft)

- Safari (Apple)

- Opera

- Firefox (Mozilla)

- Chrome (Google)

Internet Explorer

Update Your Browser!

Make sure you and others in your work group update to the latest version of your web browser before you signup for Google Apps. Users can optimize their Google Apps performance when using the latest browser edition.

Signing Up for Google Apps

You can signup for a Google Apps account from any browser window. Much like any other signup process you encounter, Google asks you for pertinent information, like name, address, and so on. Just fill out the forms as prompted. The following steps show you how to signup for Google Apps for Business, but signing up for the other types of Google Apps editions work pretty much the same way.

Upgrade to Google Apps for Business

If you have an existing Google account from previous versions of Google Apps, you can upgrade to Google Apps for Business and take full advantage of all the business tools. From the Admin console page, click Company Profile, click Profile, and click Upgrade to Google Apps for Business.

Sign Up for Google Apps for Business

These steps show you how to sign up for Google Apps for Business. Signing up for the other types of Google Apps editions work pretty much the same way; there are just some slight variations in the forms you fill out.

1. In your browser's address box, type www.google.com/a and press Enter/Return.

2. Click the Get Started button.

Not a Business?

If you're signing up as a school, college, university, government affiliation, or nonprofit group, you can start at the same Google Apps for Business page (www.google.com/a), but click the Google Apps for Education or Google Apps for Government links. You'll follow a similar sign up process shown in these steps, but you'll need to verify domain name ownership. If you're a registered nonprofit group, use the Google Apps for Education path.

3. Enter your first name, last name, and your current work email address in the About you section of the form.

4. Fill out your business information, including name, number of employees, country, and phone number.

5. Click the Next button.

6. Specify whether you want to use an existing domain name or purchase a new one. From here out, the sign up procedure varies based on your choice. If you're using an existing domain name, go to the next step. If you're creating a new name, skip to Step 8.

7. Enter your domain name and click the Next button. Skip to Step 23.

Verify Your Domain

If you have an existing domain name, you must verify it. Google gives you instructions on how to do so starting with a welcome email that includes a link you can follow to verify your domain.

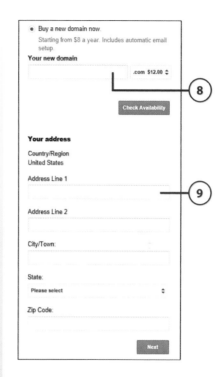

8. Enter the new domain name you're creating and click the Check Availability button to see if it's available. If not, try another variation.

9. Enter your address information and click the Next button.

10. Enter the email address you want to create for your Google Apps account.

11. Enter a password and retype it to confirm it.

12. Enter the word verification.

13. Select the agreement check box. Optionally, you can opt to receive special announcements, special offers, and such; select the top check box to do so.

14. Click the Accept and Signup button.

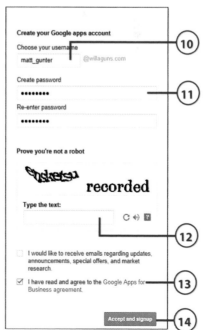

15. Review the purchase plan for your domain and select the terms and services check box.

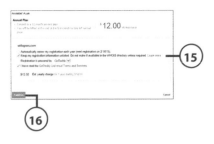

16. Click the Continue button.

17. Review your purchase and select the acknowledge check box.

18. Click the Continue button.

19. Fill out the billing profile form and click the Continue button.

20. Set up your payment options, entering your credit card or bank information and click the Submit and Activate My Account button.

21. Google takes you to your Admin console page where you can set up your account by adding more users or take a tour of the administration tools.

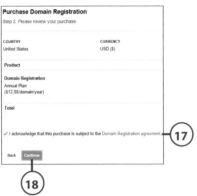

Continue Setting Up?

To go ahead and add more users to the account, click the Add Users link on the Admin console page, or to check out the layout of your Admin console, click the Tour of Admin Console link. To skip these tasks, click the Next Step button, and click the Close Set Up button.

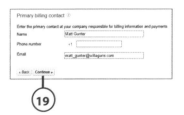

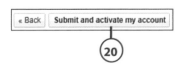

>>>Go Further
USING THE SETUP WIZARD

Your new Google Apps account offers a variety of options to help you get set up and running at full steam. You can access these options using Settings options. Simply click the Settings button (looks like a gear or cog) and click Setup, Take a Tour, or Take a Marketplace Tour.

If you click the Setup option, Google opens a setup wizard that walks you through steps for activating new services. You can always skip the details for now or exit the wizard entirely. You can return to it at any time and resume your learning. You also have the option of taking a video tour or joining a scheduled webinar. Starting with a Welcome page, you can progress at your own pace, learning about features as you go along.

Exploring the Admin Console

The Admin console page, also called the dashboard, is your go-to spot for administrating tasks for Google Apps for you and your team. Google takes you to the Admin console after you complete the signup process, but you can sign in anytime by typing google.com/a/yourdomain.com in your browser's address box, substituting your own domain name, of course.

Bookmark your Admin console

Bookmark It

It's a good idea to bookmark the page so you can easily navigate to it in a flash. Use your browser window's tools to save the page as a bookmark or favorite.

Notifications button — Help button — **Settings button**

Look for any announcements and alerts using the Notifications button, which is shaped like a bell. Click the button to view all notifications. To the right of the Notifications button, you can find the Help and Settings buttons. Use them to find help with tasks or change settings.

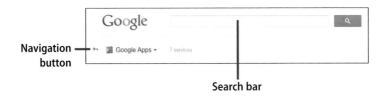

Navigation button — **Search bar**

You can use the universal Search bar at the top of the page to conduct a search. As you open different tools, you can use the Navigation button at the far left corner of the page to return to the Admin console.

Usage and activities stats

The console's right pane offers a quick look at usage and activities stats, plus more tools and common tasks.

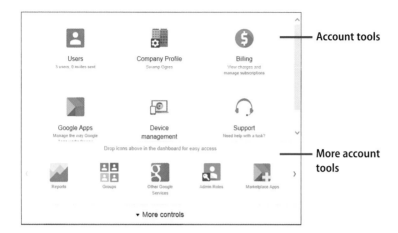

The control icons, or tools, on the Admin console page are for managing apps and users. You can drag them around the page to rearrange them. To add more controls, you can click the More Controls link and drag icons from the bar to the dashboard to add them to your main administration tools.

Here's what you can do with the default tools already on the console:

- **Users**—Add more users to your domain. You can also reset passwords and view activity logs.

- **Company Profile**—View and personalize your Google account, such as adding a company logo, time zone setting, and more.

- **Billing**—Access tools for managing your billing, payment plans, and sub-scription renewals for the account.

- **Google Apps**—Manage how Google Apps works for your team. You can enable and disable individual apps and customize the settings for how each app works.

- **Device Management**—Manage devices that connect with the account, such as smartphones and tablets.

- **Support**—Find help through online chat, phone, or email support.

From the Admin console, you can carry out administration tasks for your Google Apps account and however many users you have assigned to it. You can use the console page to activate services, configure features, add more users or reset passwords, check billing, and more. Whether you're the only user or administrating a large group of users, the Admin console page is your launching pad for taking care of your organization's Google Apps account.

Add Users

To add users to your account you assign them a unique email address. You can choose to invite users to work with you by sending out an email invitation, add users manually, or add a bunch at once using a CSV file upload (Google provides a tutorial). The steps here show how to add them manually.

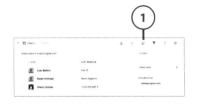

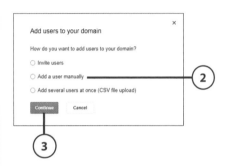

1. Click the Users icon on the Admin console page and click the Add More Users button.

2. Click the Add a User manually option button.

3. Click the Continue button.

4. Enter the user's name and the primary email address you want to assign. Google sets a temporary password for the account.

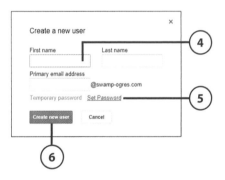

5. Click the Set Password link if you want to set a password for the account and enter a password and retype it to confirm it. Optionally, select the Require User to Change Password at Next Sign In check box.

6. Click the Create New User button.

7. Optionally, you can choose to email the sign in instructions to the new user, or you can print them out.

8. Click the Done button to finish, or click the Create Another User button to add more users.

Manage Users

From your list of active users, you can click a username to view that person's Information page, which includes tools for editing the profile, resetting a password, assigning groups, and viewing a user license.

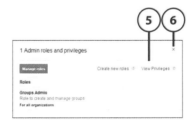

1. To add administrative privileges from the user's information page, click the Admin Roles and Privileges link.

2. Click the Manage Roles button.

3. Select a role for the user. If you select Super Admin, for example, the user is assigned the same administrative tools and privileges as the original account owner.

4. Click the Update Roles button.

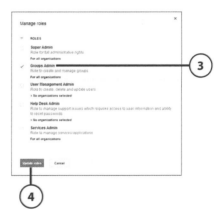

5. Google assigns the role. Optionally, if you want to customize which controls the user can manage, you can click the View Privileges link.

6. Click the Close button (x) to exit.

What's on the Information Page

The user's Information page keeps track of how much allotted storage space they've used, when they were last logged on, and how many documents they created. You can scroll down the page to view settings and click a setting to make changes.

Add Apps

You can easily add apps and services to your account from the Admin console page. You can quickly view additional services Google offers, as well as link to the Google Apps Marketplace to shop for more.

1. Click the Get More Apps and Services link.

2. Click the Add It Now button to add a listed app or service.

3. Click the Shop Now button to shop for more apps.

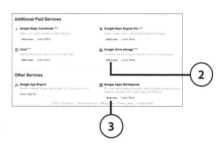

4. Scroll through the apps and pause your mouse pointer over an app to learn more about it. To add it, click the Install App button.

5. Select the agreement check box..

6. Click the Accept button to add the app to your account..

7. Click the Close button (x) to exit.

View More of the Marketplace

To view a bigger window of available apps, visit the Google Apps Marketplace page; type www.google.com/appsmarketplace in your browser's address box. You can shop by business categories on the full marketplace page.

Upload Your Company Logo

Ready to replace the generic Google account logo with something more suited for your organization? Before you upload a logo, make sure it utilizes the PNG or GIF file format, and is sized at 143 x 59 pixels. The upload won't work unless the logo matches these parameters.

1. Click the Company Profile icon on the Admin console page and click Personalization.

2. Click the Custom Logo option button.

3. Click the Choose File button.

4. Navigate to the logo file you want to use, select it.

5. click the Open button.

6. Click the Upload button.

7. Optionally, select the Show This Logo in All Sites That Users Create check box.

8. Click the Save Changes button.

9. Click the Close button (x) to exit.

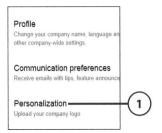

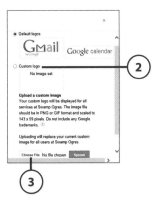

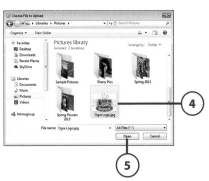

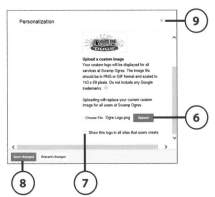

Change Your Personal Profile Picture

You can easily change the profile picture in the upper-right corner of the Admin console page. Your profile picture is displayed throughout your apps, such as Gmail, and is helpful to identify you when interacting with others online.

1. Click the drop-down arrow next to your profile picture on the Admin console page.

2. Pause your mouse pointer over the image and click Change Photo.

3. Click the Select a Photo from Your Computer button.

4. Navigate to picture file you want to use, select it.

5. Click the Open button.

6. Google uploads the file; drag the corners to crop the picture the way you want it.

7. Click the Set as Profile Photo button.

8. Your image is now part of your profile.

Change More Profile Details

You can continue editing your personal profile by clicking the View Profile button.

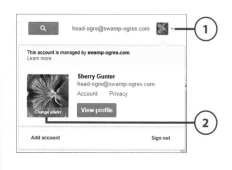

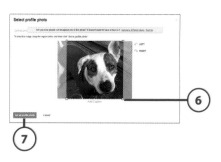

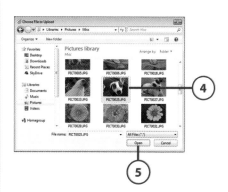

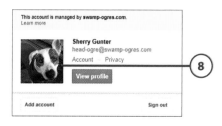

Signing In and Out

One of the big benefits of using Google Apps is the ability to use it from any computer, tablet, or smartphone. As long as you have an Internet connection, you can sign in (also known as log in) to Google Apps. Like most web accounts, you need to use the Sign in page in order to access Google Apps. You can also sign out (also known as log out) when you no longer want to work with your account.

Sign In

If you've signed out of your Google Apps account, or closed the browser window, you can easily find your way back again.

1. In your browser's address box, type www.google.com/a/your-domain.com (substituting your own domain name of course) or accounts.google.com and press Enter/Return.

2. Enter your password.

3. Click the Sign In button.

Sign In As Another User

If you're sharing a computer, another user can also sign in to their account from the Sign in page. Simply, click the Sign In with a Different Account link, enter the user's username and password, and click the Sign In button.

Bookmark It!

You can speed up your sign in process if you bookmark the Sign in page so you can quickly return to it without having to type in the URL. Look for a bookmark or favorites feature on your browser to help you save your favorite websites.

Sign Out

When you finish working with your Google Apps account, you can sign out.

1. Click the drop-down arrow next to your profile picture.

2. Click the Sign Out button.

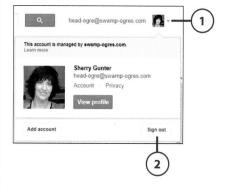

Gmail for
Google
Apps

Email messages,
contacts, and
more

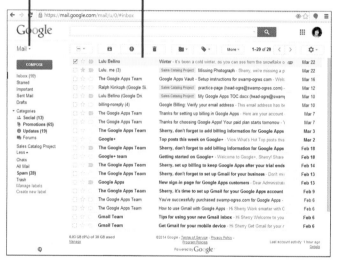

In this chapter, you learn all about Google's Gmail app and how to use it to communicate with others via email:

→ Exploring the Gmail interface
→ Discovering how to compose and send email messages
→ Managing your Inbox with labels
→ Seeing how easy it is to add contacts to build an address book
→ Finding out how to use the Tasks feature to make to-do lists
→ Customizing your email messages with signatures
→ Importing contacts from another source
→ Learning how to move mail from another account

Managing Email and Contacts with Gmail

More than 2.5 billion people use email services today, and more than 500 million of them count on Gmail to handle all their messaging needs. You can use it to send and receive email messages and connect with people around the world. If you aren't already a Gmail user, or you're transitioning from another email service, or you've just signed up for Google Apps for Business/Education/Government, it's time to find out how to make Gmail work for you.

Exploring Gmail

Gmail has been around since 2004. Some would argue Gmail is the backbone of Google apps. Available for free, a regular Gmail account is advertising-supported, which means users see ads on the Gmail page as they work with email tasks. A regular Gmail account also offers 15GB of storage, spread across Gmail, Drive, and Google+ Photos. As a Google Apps for Business/Education/Government user, the advertising is removed and the amount of storage is increased. You and each user in your organization gets 30GB of storage (spread across Gmail, Drive, and Picasa Web Albums).

As part of your email service, Gmail offers its powerful search technologies to look through messages, top-of-the line spam filtering, seamless synchronizing with smartphones and tablets, and easy contact management. You can attach files, filter messages, and organize your email using labels.

The Gmail interface is pretty straightforward. The primary Inbox and default labels (like Sent Mail or Drafts) and system categories are listed on the far left side of the page. Messages appear in the middle of the page with the latest emails at the top of the list. Also along the top of the page are some additional tools for moving through and managing messages..

Inbox and system labels

System categories   Message list

You can click a message in your list to read it. When you open a message, it appears in full. More tools appear at the top of the page to perform tasks such as archiving, labeling, or deleting the message.

Message   Tools

In addition to emailing, you can use Gmail to create and keep an index of contacts, creating a digital address book. Once you enter a contact, it's easily available for future messages.

Contacts page   Pop-up people widget

You can also keep track of important things you need to do using Gmail Tasks. You can specify due dates, add notes, and check items off your list as you complete them. The items in Tasks synchronize with Google Calendar, so due dates automatically appear on your calendar as soon as you create the tasks.

Sign In to Gmail

You can use the Gmail icon to open Gmail and log on, or you can navigate to http://mail.google.com/a/yourdomain.com, substituting your own domain name, of course.

1. Click the Apps icon and click the Mail icon to open the Gmail page.

2. Enter your password.

3. Click the Sign In button.

Sign Out from Gmail

You can sign out when you finish using the Gmail app.

1. Click the profile picture.

2. Click the Sign Out button.

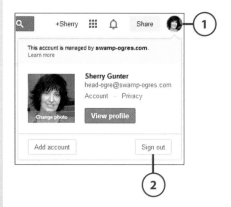

Switch Between Gmail Features

Gmail includes three main features: Mail, Contacts, and Tasks. You can switch between them using the feature drop-down list in the top-left corner of any Gmail page. The name of the button changes based on which Gmail feature you're using.

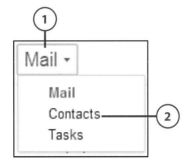

1. Click the feature drop-down button.

2. Click a feature (Mail, Contacts, or Tasks) to open it.

Expand and Collapse the Inbox List

You can control what you see in the Inbox list by expanding and collapsing the categories, tabs, and labels listed there.

1. Click an expand arrow to next to a heading to expand it.

2. Click a collapse arrow to collapse the heading.

Show More or Less

You can also click the More arrow to expand the Inbox list display, or click the Less arrow to show less of the display again. You can also hide the Chat/Hangouts area entirely; click the Hangouts icon at the very bottom of the Inbox pane to hide it.

Working with Messages

Basic emailing tasks include composing new messages, replying to and forwarding messages, and learning how to work with file attachments. Gmail offers several additional tools you can use to help you compose messages, including formatting options you can apply. You can also insert a photo, links, smiley icons (known as emoji), and send invitations using the tools found in the message window.

Compose a Message

The only thing you need to create a message is the email address of the person you're messaging. You can email multiple users or just a single recipient.

1. Click Compose on the Mail page.

2. Enter the person's email address. To continue adding more addresses, just press the Spacebar key or the comma key and type in the next address.

3. Enter a subject for the message.

4. Enter your email message.

5. Optionally, click the Formatting button to display a toolbar of formatting controls you can apply to your message text.

6. Click the Send button.

Using Existing Contacts

If the person is already in your list of contacts, you can just type in their name and Gmail displays the contact name; click the name to insert it as your recipient.

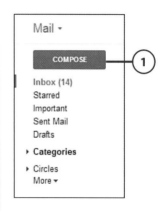

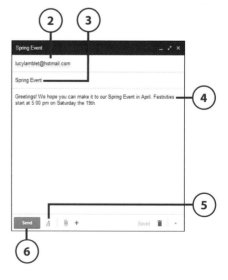

>>>Go Further

USING CC AND BCC

The term carbon copy is a remnant of the days in which you had to use a sheet of carbon paper inserted between two sheets of paper in a typewriter to make a copy of a memo or letter. To Cc someone on a message, click the Cc link and enter their email address in the Cc field.

To blind carbon copy is to send a copy of the message to another user without the original recipient knowing or seeing the other person's inclusion. To Bcc someone, click the Bcc link to display the field and enter the recipients.

Reply to a Message

When you use Reply, Gmail sends a response to the sender, but if the message was originally addressed to multiple users, the Reply All command sends the response to everyone referenced on sender's list (the To field).

1. Open the message to which you want to write a reply.

2. Click the Reply button or click the Reply link in the message text box.

3. Enter your reply in the text box.

4. Click the Send button.

5. Gmail sends your message and adds the reply text to the conversation. (The original message is displayed on top with the reply message underneath.) Click the Back to Inbox button to return to the main Gmail page.

Drafts

If you exit a message window without sending the message, Gmail places the message in the Drafts category in the Inbox list. To view it again and work on it some more, click Drafts, and click the message. To remove it entirely, select the message's check box and click the Discard Drafts button.

Sent Emails

Gmail keeps a copy of all the messages you send. You can find them in the Sent category in the Inbox list.

Forward a Message

You can forward an existing message to a new recipient. When you forward a message, a FW: prefix is added to the subject title, which stands for Forward.

1. Open the message you want to forward.

2. Click the More drop-down arrow.

3. Click Forward.

Sent mail

Drafts

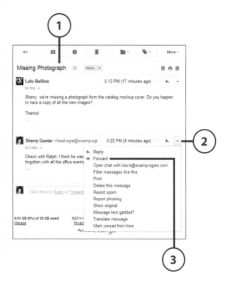

4. Enter the address of the person to which you want to forward the message.

5. Enter the message text you want to add.

6. Click the Send button.

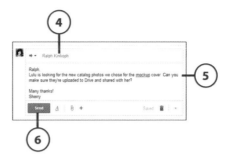

Attach a File to a Message

You can attach files to your emails to send to others. Attachments can be pictures, documents, spreadsheets, slideshow presentations, and so on.

1. Compose a new message as you normally would.

2. Click the Attach Files button.

3. Navigate to the file you want to attach and select it.

4. Click the Open button.

5. Click the Send button.

Increased Message Size

File attachments increase the overall size of your email message. This is something to consider if you know the recipient's email service sets limits to how much data is allowed. Some files are obviously bigger than others, with picture files often being the largest.

Download a File Attachment

You can open attachments you receive from others and save them on your computer or save them to Google Drive. Messages with attachments are identified by a tiny paper clip icon next to the message date.

1. Open the message containing the file attachment.

2. Pause your mouse pointer over the attachment to display two options: Download or Save to Drive. Click the option you want to apply.

3. If you choose Save to Drive, you can optionally specify a folder to move the file to, if needed. Make a selection and click the Done button. If you choose to download the file to your computer, it's automatically placed in your Downloads folder.

It's Not All Good

Use Caution

Always be mindful about viewing attachments, particularly from unknown sources. Computer hackers commonly use file attachments as a way to distribute viruses and malware. If you trust the source, you can open the downloaded file. If not, stop and run a virus check using your computer's virus protection software.

Insert a Picture

You can add an image to send along within an email message. When you do this, the photo is an embedded image; it's not treated as a file attachment.

1. Compose a new message as you normally would.

2. Click the Insert Photos icon (pause your mouse pointer over the + icon in the message window to view more tools).

3. Click the Choose File button (the button name might vary between browsers).

4. Navigate to the file you want to attach and select it.

5. Click the Open button.

6. Click the OK button to insert the image into your message. You can finish the message and send it when you're ready.

Insert Files and Links

You can also use the tools in the new message window to insert files and links into your message body. For example, you might send a colleague a link to an article. Simply click the appropriate tool and follow the directions in the dialog box.

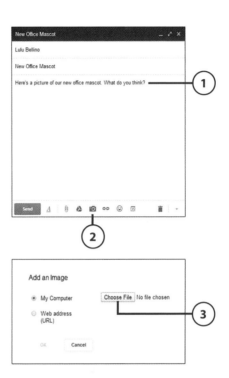

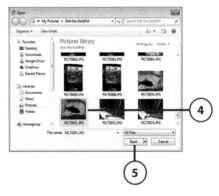

Managing Messages

It doesn't take long for messages to pile up in your Inbox. You can move messages around to special tabs and assign labels to help you keep them organized and keep your Inbox lean and manageable. Gmail doesn't use a folder system like other email services. Rather, labels are applied to help identify messages, much like tags. For example, you might label emails pertaining to an office project as Sales Catalog or Budget Report. You can then choose to view all the emails with a particular label assigned.

Turn On Tabs

Gmail's default tabs—Primary, Social, Promotions, Updates, and Forums—can help you sort messages, such as those from a social media site or advertisements. Tabs are not displayed by default. You must turn them on using the Settings page.

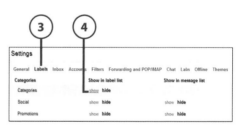

1. Click the Settings button.

2. Click Settings.

3. Click the Labels category.

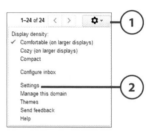

4. Scroll down the page to view Categories and click the Show link to turn on the default tabs.

5. Click the Inbox.

6. Gmail displays the tabs in the label list area.

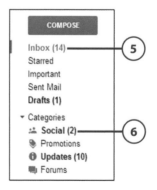

Inbox List or Message List

You can choose to display the tabs in the Inbox pane, in the Categories label list, or you can turn them on so they show up in the message list area of the page. You can also control which tabs appear and which are hidden. You can also use the Settings page to control the appearance of other items in your Inbox pane, such as hiding the Spam category. The labels and categories on the Settings page toggle on or off.

Create a New Label

You can create labels to help manage email. Labels are tags you can apply to group messages together, such as Sales Catalog or Department Meetings.

1. Click the More link in the Inbox pane.

2. Click Create New Label.

3. Enter a name for the label.

4. Click the Create button.

5. Gmail adds the label to the Inbox pane.

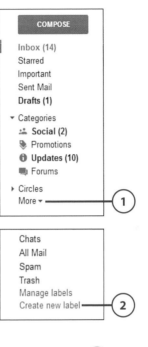

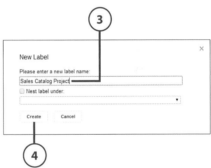

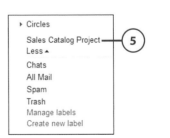

Apply a Label

You can use the Labels drop-down menu to assign a label to a selected message. You can assign labels from the message list area or when you open a message to read it.

1. Select the check box next to the message you want to label.

2. Click the Labels button.

3. Select the label check box you want to assign.

4. Click Apply.

5. Gmail adds the label to the message header.

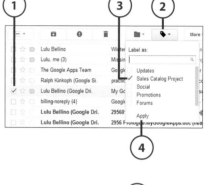

Using Multiple Labels

You can use multiple labels if a message can fall into several categories. For example, if you subscribe to a trade newsletter, you might tag the messages with a unique label. If one of the messages relates to an upcoming project, you can tag it with the project label, too.

Move Messages

You can organize messages into tabs by clicking and dragging them, then dropping them in the tab where you want the message to go. You can also use the Move To feature to help you move emails, as shown in these steps:

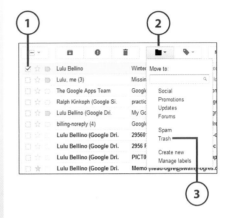

1. Select the check box for the message you want to move.

2. Click the Move To button.

3. Click a label to move the message to the designated category.

Delete a Message

You can delete messages from your Inbox and place them in the Trash category. Any messages listed in Trash are automatically deleted after 30 days.

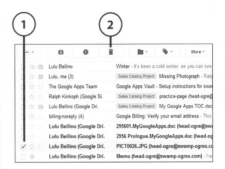

1. Select the check box next to the message you want to delete.

2. Click the Delete button to place the message in the Trash category.

3. To view messages ready for permanent deletion, click the Trash category in the Inbox list.

4. Select a message in the Trash list and click Delete Forever to permanently remove it.

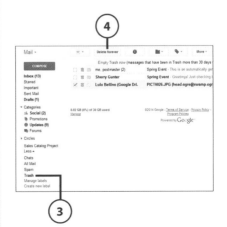

Drag-and-Drop It

You can quickly move messages around and drop them into which categories or tabs where you want them to go. For example, to remove a message, you can drag it and drop it into the Trash category, or to move a message out of the Trash, drag it and drop it into the Inbox.

Archive a Message

The archiving feature in Gmail removes messages from your Inbox but keeps them stored as part of your account so you can look through them later. Archiving is a great way to clean up your Inbox without permanently removing messages you need to keep.

1. Click the message (or messages) you want to archive.

2. Click the Archive button.

Finding Archived Messages

To locate an archived message, you can use the Search box at the top of the Gmail window, or you can look through your messages in the All Mail category. To do so, click the More button at the bottom of the Inbox list and click All Mail.

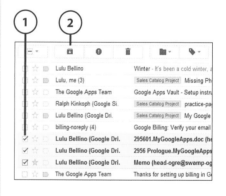

Mark Messages

You can use Gmail's tools to mark messages, such as marking a read message as unread, or adding a star to mark the message as important.

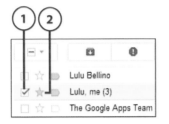

1. Select the check box next to the message you want to mark.

2. Click the star column next to the message to assign a star.

3. To mark a message as read or unread, click the More button and click Mark As Read or Mark As Unread.

Viewing Stars

To view all of the messages to which you have assigned stars, you can click the Starred category in the Inbox list.

>>Go Further

CHANGE STARS

By default, Gmail is set up to show just one type of star: yellow. You're not stuck with just a yellow star. You can use different colors for stars, or different icons entirely. From the Gmail page, click the Settings button (looks like a gear or cog) and click Settings. Scroll down the General tab settings until you find the Stars heading. Three presets are listed: 1 star, 4 stars, or all stars. Click the 4 stars preset, and select the stars or icons you want to use. Drag icons from the Not in Use list into the In Use list until you have the four icons you want to use. Click the Save Changes button at the bottom of the page when you finish. The next time you want to assign a star, click the Star column, as usual, and keep clicking to rotate through the available stars you selected.

Remove Spam

Google's Gmail includes a spam
filter, but you can help it recognize
additional spam email by pointing it
out when you find it in your Inbox.
When you activate the Spam feature,
it moves the message to the Spam
category.

1. Select the check box next to the
   message you want to move to the
   Spam category.

2. Click the Report Spam button.

3. Click the Spam category (if the
   category is not displayed in the
   Inbox, click More).

4. Select the message or mes-
   sages you want to remove; click
   Delete Forever or Delete All Spam
   Messages Now.

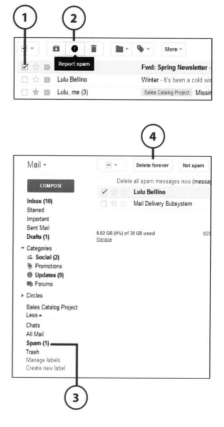

Check for Non-Spam Messages

It's a good idea to periodically
check the Spam category from
time to time just in case something ends up there that's not
actually spam.

Unmark Spam

If you find a legitimate message
mixed in with your spam, you
can remark it and return it to the
Inbox. Select the message in the
Spam list, and click the Not Spam
button.

Managing Contacts

The Contact Manager tool helps you organize and access people you communicate with the most. Acting like an online address book, you can use Contacts to build an index of people and include as much or as little information about each as you want. Typically, a contact's information includes their name, an email address, phone numbers, address, job title or company. You can switch between Business and Standard forms when filling out contact details; the latter includes a field for entering the person's birthday, whereas the former includes fields for a work phone.

People Widget Pop-up

When you add contacts to the Contacts page, the Gmail People widget appears anytime you pause your mouse pointer near a contact name across the Google apps. The People widget displays a pop-up box with contextual information about the contact, including links to emailing, calling, and chatting with the contact. To pursue an additional task, such as viewing recent emails from that person, click the link in the people widget pop-up box.

Add a Contact

Creating a new contact in your address book is as simple as filling out a form. As soon as you start filling out the fields, the Contacts Manager automatically saves your work.

1. Click the Gmail feature drop-down button.

2. Click Contacts.

3. Click the New Contact button.

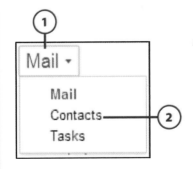

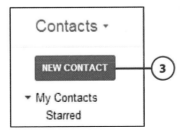

4. Fill out the form fields to create the contact, starting with the contact's name.

5. Click the Go to My Contacts button to go back to the Contacts page where the new entry appears in the list.

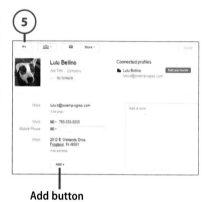

Change and Add Fields

To change which fields appear on the contact form, click the More button and click Business or Standard. You can also add fields, such as birthday or nickname, to your form. Click the Add button on the new form page and click the field you want to add.

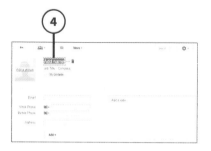

Add button

Edit Contacts

You can make changes to the information for a contact, such as update a phone number or address. To do so, simply revisit the contact's form.

1. Click the contact you want to edit on the Contacts page.

2. Make any changes needed to the information.

3. Click Save Now.

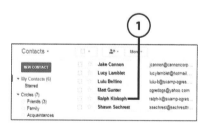

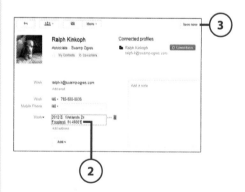

Delete a Contact

From the Contacts list, select the check box next to the contact you want to remove. Click the More button and click Delete Contact. If you accidentally delete the wrong one, click the Undo link.

Create a Group

You can organize your contacts into groups to make it easier to email everyone at the same time. For example, you can set up a group for your coworkers and send out a memo to everyone in the group.

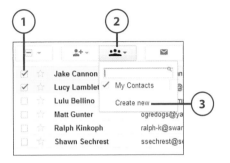

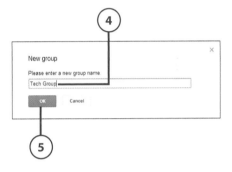

1. Select the check boxes next to the contacts you want to add to a group.

2. Click the Groups button.

3. Click Create New.

4. Enter a name for the new group.

5. Click the OK button.

>>Go Further

GOOGLE+ CIRCLES

Google+ users have a different name for groupings of people, called circles. If you're a Google+ user, Circles is also available to you in Contacts Manager. You can create all kinds of circles and share information with the people in a particular circle.

To assign a circle to a contact you enter using the contact form, click the Add and Invite button after you start filling in form details. You can then choose from your preset circles, such as Friends, Family, Acquaintances, Following, or Coworkers. You can also choose to create a new circle.

You can tell groups from circles in the contacts list based on a tiny circle icon next to the circle name.

Working with Tasks

You can use Google Tasks in Gmail to help you keep track of things you need to do. You can use Tasks to make lists, jot down notes, or assign a due date utilizing your Calendar app. Google Tasks opens into a small window and displays your tasks as a list with check boxes you can use to mark tasks as complete. You can also perform a variety of actions on your tasks, such as email a list, print a list, or sort your tasks by due dates. You can create different lists and manage their hierarchy by moving tasks up and down the list or making tasks subordinate to other tasks.

More Tasks in Calendar

The Tasks feature in Gmail is the same one you use in Google Calendar. You can learn more about this feature in Chapter 3.

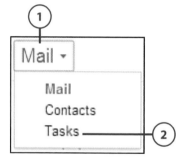

Create a Task

You can enter tasks directly in the Tasks window. After you add a task, it appears in the list.

1. Click the Gmail feature drop-down button.

2. Click Tasks.

3. Enter the task you want to record.

4. Click the Edit Details arrow.

5. Add any additional details about the task, such as a due date or notes about the task.

6. Click the Back to List link.

7. Click the Add Task icon.

8. Click Close (x) to exit.

Make a New List

Tasks starts you out with a default list labeled with the user's name. You can create more lists and switch between them using the Switch List button.

1. Click the Switch List button in the Tasks window.

2. Click New List.

3. Enter a name for the list.

4. Click the OK button.

5. Tasks creates the new list where you can start to add tasks. Click the Close button to exit or click the Switch List button to switch to another list.

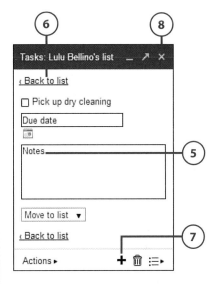

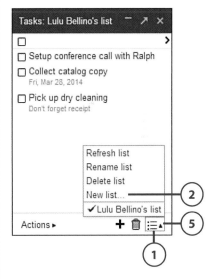

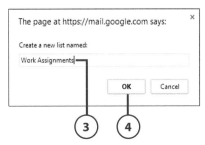

Email a List

You can email your list to another user. For example, you might email a shopping list to your spouse or a to-do list to a colleague. When you activate this feature, Gmail inserts the list into the message body of your email.

1. Open the list you want to send from the Tasks window.

2. Click the Actions button.

3. Click Email Task List.

4. A message window opens with the list inserted into the message body. Enter an email address.

5. Click the Send button.

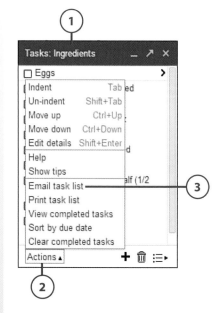

Customizing Gmail

You can customize the way you work with Gmail using a variety of options. For example, you can set up a signature that appears automatically at the bottom of every message. Most of the customizing options are found through the Settings page. The Settings page offers several tabs for controlling how various features work.

Add a Signature

A signature is preset text that is automatically inserted at the bottom of every message you create and send. You might use a signature that includes your company name and website, or a favorite quote. Signatures include a dashed line to separate them from the rest of the message text.

1. Click the Settings button.

2. Click Settings.

3. Scroll down the General tab to find the Signature section and enter your signature text.

4. Format the text, as needed.

Not All Formatting Is Viewable

Not all email readers can display formatting, so keep this in mind as you're thinking about adding a lot of formatting to a signature or a message. Your best bet is to keep it simple.

---

5. Scroll to the bottom of the page and click the Save Changes button.

6. The next time you click the Compose button, the new message window includes the signature automatically.

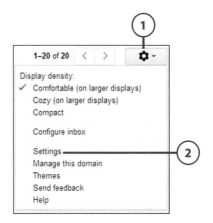

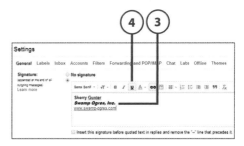

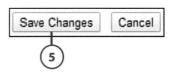

Set Up an Automatic Reply

If you're planning on being away from your work for a vacation or several days off, you can set up Gmail to send an automatic reply to messages you receive while you're away. You can also control who receives an automated message.

1. Click the Settings button.

2. Click Settings.

3. Scroll down the General tab to find the Vacation Responder section and click the Vacation Responder On option.

4. Specify a date range for the time you're away: start date and end date.

5. Enter a subject heading for the reply message.

6. Enter your reply message text and format it, if needed.

7. Select the check boxes to specify whether to send the reply to people from your contacts or people in your domain.

8. Click the Save Changes button.

Turn It Off

To turn off an automatic reply, simply revisit the Settings page and click the Vacation Responder Off option.

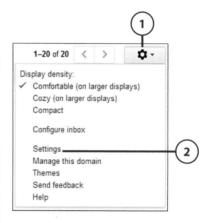

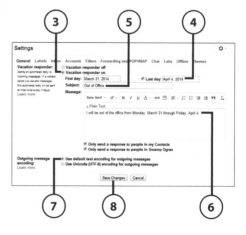

Switching to Gmail from Other Services

You can import your emails and contacts from another email provider and use them in your Gmail account. Gmail is compatible with email services such as Yahoo! Mail, Hotmail, or AOL. You can also import your emails and address book from other email programs, such as Microsoft Outlook.

Move Mail from Another Account

You can use Gmail's Mail Fetcher tool to help you connect two accounts and import your messages. When you use this tool, it downloads all your old emails as well as checks the other account frequently for new email messages.

1. Click the Settings button.

2. Click Settings.

3. Click the Accounts tab.

4. Under the Check Mail from Other Accounts (Using POP3) section, click Add a POP3 Mail Account You Own.

5. Enter the email address of the account.

6. Click the Next Step button.

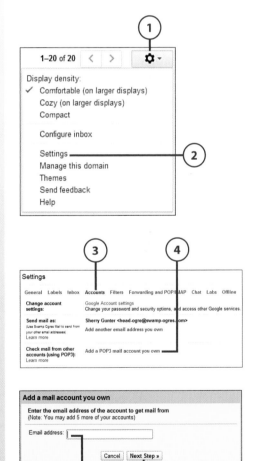

7. Enter your password.

8. Check the other settings to make sure everything's correct.

9. Click the Add Account button.

10. Click the Yes I Want to Be Able to Send Mail As option to enable the feature for sending email from the account from within Gmail.

11. Click the Next Step button, verify the information and click the Next Step button.

12. Gmail verifies you as the account owner by sending an email verification. Click the Send Verification button to continue.

13. When you receive your email with the confirmation code, return to this window and enter the code into the text box

14. Click the Verify button to complete the process .

Change Your Reply

After you add an account, you can send email as the original Gmail account user or as the added account user. To do so, click the From drop-down arrow in the new message window and select the name you want to use.

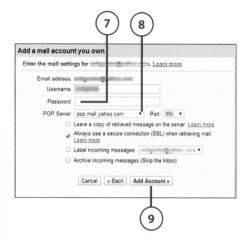

Import Contacts

If you use another program, such as Microsoft Outlook, you can export your address book as a CSV file and import it into Gmail.

1. Click the Gmail feature drop-down button.

2. Click Contacts.

3. Click the More button.

4. Click Import.

5. Click the Choose File button.

6. Navigate to the file you want to import and select it.

7. Click the Open button.

8. Click the Import button to add the contacts.

Duplicates?

If you end up with any duplicate contacts, you can remove them. Select the ones you want to delete, then click the More button and click Delete Contacts.

Export Your Contacts

You can also export your own Gmail contacts into a CSV file to share with another program you use. From the Contacts page, click the More button and click Export to get started.

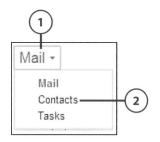

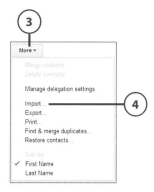

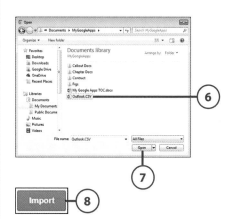

View your schedule with Google Calendar

In this chapter, you discover how to tap into the power of Google's Calendar app to maintain your busy schedule:

→ Exploring the Calendar app layout and basic features
→ Scheduling events and appointments
→ Working with reminders
→ Creating tasks to help you manage things you need to do
→ Sharing your calendar with other users
→ Registering your mobile phone to receive text notifications

Organizing Your Schedule with Calendar

Google offers a wonderfully useful app to help you keep your schedule organized—Calendar. You can use the Calendar app to mark appointments on a digital cloud-based calendar that you can access from any computer, tablet, or mobile device. You can keep track of appointments, meetings, and events. You can easily share your schedule with other, assign pop-up or email reminders, and more. If you're working with a team, you can tap into the smart scheduling feature that helps synchronize meeting times for everyone's schedules.

Exploring Calendar

Time-management software has been around for quite some time now, help-ing people stay on track with their busy lives. Time-management programs go hand in hand with productivity suites, and Google Apps includes one, too. Google's Calendar app is beautifully simple in its construct and truly powerful in its scheduling capabilities, and as soon as you start using it, you'll wonder what took you so long to discover it. When you first open the Calendar app, a blank calendar awaits you. This is your primary calendar and you can use it however you want. Fill it with all the important items you need to manage in your daily life.

Navigation buttons   **View options**

Mini Calendar   **Schedule area**

You can easily navigate between days, weeks, and months, and quickly change your view of your schedule. The top of the Calendar app features but-tons to navigate between views, access settings, and view the current date. The left side of the screen shows a navigable mini calendar you can use to jump to dates, along with a list of all of the calendars you use (such as project calendars, other team member's calendars, and so on). You can expand and collapse the calendar displays in the left pane. The middle of the screen dis-plays your actual schedule. You can easily add appointments and events and view details about scheduled items.

To find your way to the Calendar app, just click the Calendar link in the top Navigation bar. If you don't see the Navigation bar, you can also click your

Apps icon and click Calendar. The app starts you out with an empty calendar, but you can add other calendars specific to things you want to do, like a calendar for a work or school project to share with other team members. You can also view other users' calendars. By adding calendars to your list, you can overlay them on your own and see when people are free or busy, or what activities they have planned. You can easily turn off your view of other calendars when you just want to focus on your own.

Calendar list   Apps icon

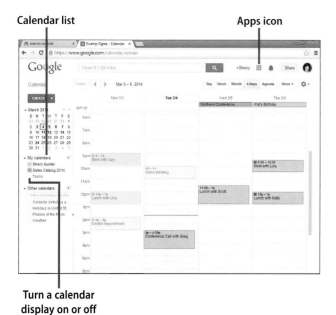

Turn a calendar
display on or off

Change Your Calendar View

You can switch between views to change how you look at your schedule.

1. Click the Day button to display your daily schedule divided into hourly increments, which are then divided into half-hour increments.

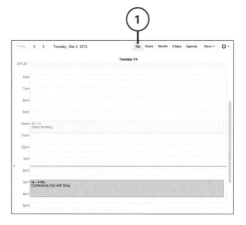

Where Are All-Day Events Displayed?

If there's an all-day event assigned to the day, like a birthday or holiday, it appears at the top, just under the date in Day view. If you're viewing your schedule by week, events appear at the top of the date column. If you're viewing by month, all-day events appear at the top of the date square.

2. Click the Week button to display your schedule as a 7-day week with each column representing a day.

3. Click the Month button to display your schedule a month at a time where you can see each day of the month listed as a grid of dates, much like a wall calendar.

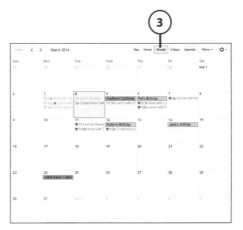

4. Click the 4 Days button to display four days of your schedule, starting with the current date and the three following days.

Customize Your Days

You can customize the 4 Days view, if you need to, to more or fewer days. Click the Settings drop-down arrow (which looks like a little cog or gear icon) and click Settings. Next, scroll down the General tab page and click the Custom View drop-down arrow and make a selection. Click the Save button at the top or bottom of the screen to save the new setting.

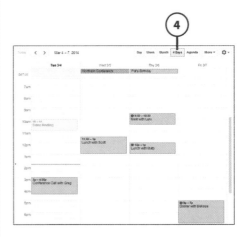

5. Click the Agenda button to change to Agenda view, which displays all the items on your schedule in a list format, which is perfect for printing out and taking with you or handing off to someone.

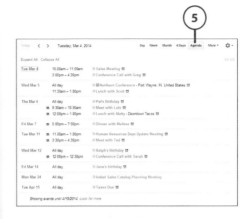

>>>Go Further
SPEAKING OF VIEWS, CHANGE YOUR INFORMATION DENSITY

If the display of calendar information on your screen is an issue, you can adjust the density of space for calendar elements. This feature can help improve your viewing experience if you use a smaller screen, such as a tablet, or prefer a smaller browser window. Basically, the setting affects how much space you see around the calendar buttons, labels, and list items. You can choose between three different settings:

- **Comfortable**—The least dense setting

- **Cozy**—Slightly denser

- **Compact**—The most dense setting

To change your density settings, click the Settings button (the cog-like icon in the upper-right corner of the Calendar app), and select a setting. If you don't see an immediate change, your browser window is most likely smaller than the selected density option allows.

Navigate Between Days, Weeks, and Months

You can quickly and easily navigate between days, weeks, and months on your schedule using the navigation arrow buttons at the top of the calendar, or the mini calendar on the left.

1. Click the Next Period button to move forward in your schedule; depending on your view, the schedule displays the next day, week, or month.

2. Click the Previous Period button to move backward in your schedule; depending on your view, the schedule displays the previous day, week, or month.

3. Click a date in the mini calendar to navigate to that particular date.

4. Click the Today button to return to the current day.

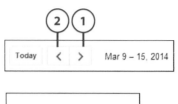

Work with the Calendar List

The left side of the Calendar app is a pane displaying a navigable mini calendar and a list of all your calendars, called the Calendar list. You can expand and collapse the items displayed here and control which calendars appear in the main viewing area.

1. Click the Collapse (down arrow) icon to the left of a calendar group, including the mini calendar, if you want to collapse it.

2. The group is collapsed to just its name.

3. Click the Expand (right arrow) icon to the left of a name to expand a group.

4. Google displays all the items associated with the group.

5. Click a box next to a particular calendar (the box appears filled with a color when selected) to view it. You can view more than one calendar at a time.

6. Click a filled box next to a calendar name to hide it (the box is empty when deselected).

7. Pause your mouse pointer over a calendar name and click the drop-down arrow to the right of the name to open a menu of options.

Delete a Calendar

If you have a calendar you no longer need to keep, you can delete it. Click the drop-down arrow to the right of the calendar name and click Calendar Settings. Scroll to the bottom of the page and click the Permanently Delete This Calendar link. Follow the prompts to remove the calendar. Note: You cannot delete your primary calendar; you can delete only other calendars you add.

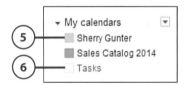

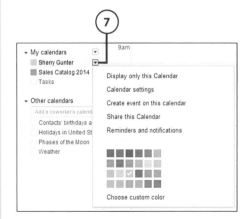

Add a New Calendar

The left side of the Calendar app displays your calendars. You can add new calendars to the list and view them separately or in conjunction with other calendars.

1. Click the drop-down arrow to the right of My Calendars.

2. Click Create New Calendar.

3. Fill in details about the calendar, including assigning a name and whether you want to share the calendar with others.

4. Click the Create Calendar button.

5. Google adds the calendar to the My Calendars list. To view it at any time, click the calendar's box.

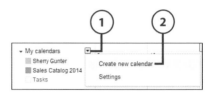

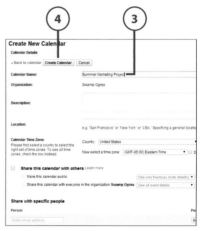

Viewing Two or More Calendars at the Same Time

You can view more than one calendar by clicking the box for each calendar you want to add to the display. Google overlays each calendar so you see all the scheduled items from each in one single calendar view. Pretty handy!

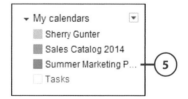

>>>Go Further

ADDING FRIEND'S CALENDARS, COWORKER'S CALENDARS, AND SPECIAL CALENDARS

You're not stuck with just the calendars you create. You can also add calendars from other sources. You can add other team members' calendars to your list, making it easy to coordinate schedules. You can also add a friend's calendar who isn't part of your Google Apps team. You can subscribe to interesting calendars Google offers, such as sports calendars, holiday calendars, birthday calendars, and more.

To add a coworker's calendar, make sure the Other calendars group is expanded on the calendars list, click inside the Add a Coworker's Calendar box, and enter the user's name. (This box says Add a Friend's Calendar if you're not using Apps for Business.) Click the full name to add their calendar to your list. You can also click the Other Calendars drop-down arrow and click Add a Coworker's Calendar. Google opens a box for you to enter the user's email address. If the person doesn't have a calendar account, you can invite them to make one.

To subscribe to other calendars, click the Other Calendar's drop-down arrow and click Browse Interesting Calendars. This takes you to a page offering a variety of holiday, sports, and other interesting calendars. You can peruse the offerings and even preview a calendar before deciding to subscribe to it. If you find something you like, click the Subscribe option. You can revisit this page to unsubscribe to special calendars, too. When you finish with the Interesting Calendars page, click the Back to Calendar link to return to your own calendar page.

You find out how to import calendars from other formats later in this chapter.

Scheduling Events and Appointments

You can add events and appointments to your schedule to help you manage your time. With some time-management software, events and appointments are distinctive items you add, but with Google Calendar the term "events" encompasses both. You can add all-day items, like a conference or birthday, or you can designate specific appointments in your schedule to items like meetings, doctor appointments, and places you need to be at a certain time.

You can also use a variety of techniques to add events. You can add them directly onto the calendar. Simply,click the Create button to utilize the Quick Add feature, or use the feature from the calendar list. After you add items, you can click and drag them to move them around the calendar or edit them using a detailed form.

All-day events appear at the top of the day

Appointments appear in designated time slots

Schedule an All-Day Event

All-day events take up the whole day on your calendar, such as birthdays and anniversaries. The fastest way to add an all-day event to your calendar is to type directly onto the calendar.

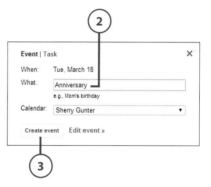

1. Navigate to the date you want to add an event to and click it (Month view) or click the top of the day (Day, Week, or 4 Days view) to open an event.

2. Enter a name for the event.

3. Click the Create Event button.

4. The event appears at the top of the day's schedule, or, in the case of Month view, at the top of the day square.

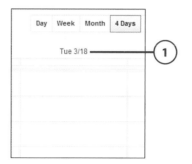

Remove It

To delete an event, click it and click the Delete link. It's immediately removed from the calendar.

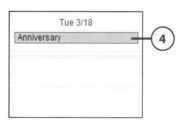

Add an Event

Any item you want to specify a time for on your calendar is considered an event.

1. Navigate to the date and time slot where you want to add an event and click it to open an event.

2. Enter a name for the event.

3. Click Create Event.

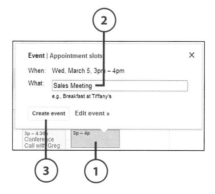

4. The event is immediately added. If you need to adjust the time, you can drag the top or bottom edge of the event block to change the start or end time, or you can drag the entire appointment to a new location.

Remove It

To delete an event, click it and click the Delete link. It's immediately removed from the calendar.

Add an Event with Details

If you want to include details about an event, you can use the form page to fill out additional information, including description info, color-coding to help distinguish it from other items, reminder details, availability options, and file attachments.

1. Click the Create button to open an event form page.

2. Enter a name for the event.

3. Specify the date and time range for the event.

4. Optionally, select the All Day check box.

5. Use the Event details tab to fill out location, description, and other details.

6. Click the Save button.

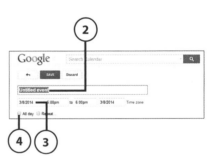

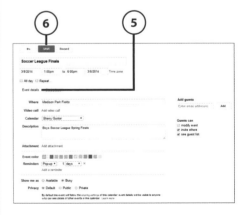

>>>Go Further

INVITING GUESTS AND COORDINATING SCHEDULES

You can invite others to your events and send out an email. Guests can then respond to the invite. You can invite other people on your Google Apps team, or you can invite people from outside the group. All you need is an email address to send an invitation. In the Edit Event form, enter the email address for the person you want to add in the Add Guests area and click the Add button. You can keep adding more guests, as needed.

If your guests share their calendars with you, you can use the Find a Time tab on the form page to look for a meeting time that works for everyone. Click the Find a Time tab to view everyone's schedule for the appointment time.

When you are ready to send the invitations, click the Event Details tab again and click the Email Guests link. A special box opens with the email addresses entered and subject filled in; enter a message and click the Send button.

When you finish editing event details, click the Save button when you to return to the calendar. Google might display a prompt box concerning inviting people outside of your group; just specify Invite External Guests.

Add an Event with Quick Add

Another fast way to add an event is to tap into the power of Google's Quick Add feature. Quick Add attempts to figure out what you type and insert it properly into your calendar, such as "Lunch with Lisa 12pm Saturday" or "Jane's Birthday Saturday."

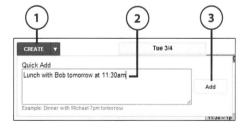

1. Click the Create button.

2. Enter the information you want to add, such as "Dinner with Bob tomorrow at 7pm."

3. Click the Add button.

4. Quick Add immediately inserts the information into your calendar. To view details about the event, click it to display its pop-up box.

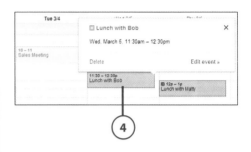

It's Not All Good

Rules for Using Quick Add

Before you think the Quick Add feature is magically reading your mind, there are a few rules that govern how it works. Here's what to watch out for when typing in your entries:

- If you enter a time without a date, Quick Add chooses the earliest date based on the time. So if you type "Dentist at 3pm" and it's 8 o'clock in the evening when you create the event, Quick Add puts the event on the next day's schedule.

- If you don't specify an end time, Quick Add automatically marks the event as an hour-long appointment.

- If you don't put a start or end time in the entry, Quick Add thinks you want to create an all-day event.

- If you need to specify a range of time, Quick Add recognizes formats written as "12-3" or "45 minutes."

- If you want to designate a time zone, Quick Add recognizes their abbreviations, such as EDT (Eastern Daylight Time) or CST (Central Standard Time).

- If your event details include a name or location with a time or date name, such as Monday Blues Café at 7pm Friday, it confuses Quick Add and it tries to schedule the event on Monday. Be sure to put quotation marks around the name to alleviate the confusion, such as "Monday Blues Café."

Schedule Time Slot Appointments

If you use Google Apps for Business, you can add an appointment block and specify the time and length. This method is useful for dividing slots of times for reserved purposes, such as teachers allowing students to book tutoring times from a block of time, or a department head scheduling performance reviews. The fastest way to do this is to type directly onto the calendar.

Limited Editing

Unlike other events you add, when you use appointment slots to create time blocks directly on your calendar, you cannot tap into the same editing options as adding events using other methods. If you're looking to add more details, use another method.

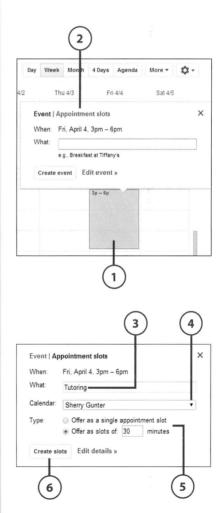

1. Navigate to the date you want to add an appointment and click the time slot where you want it noted. If the appointment is longer than an hour, you can click and drag the amount of time required.

2. Click the Appointment Slots link.

3. Enter a name for the appointment.

4. Optionally, select a different calendar from the drop-down list.

5. Click Offer as a Single Appointment Slot or Offer As Slots of 30 Minutes.

6. Click Create Slots.

7. Google adds the item to your schedule. You can click the appointment to view details.

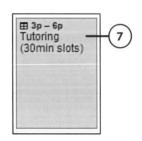

Another Option

Yet another route for adding events is to click the drop-down arrow next to the calendar name on the calendar list and click Create Event on this calendar . This opens the form page for filling out details.

Edit Calendar Items

If you need to make changes to the details of a calendar item, such as changing its time or location, you can edit the event. Using the form page, you can change details, such as color-coding appointments or changing the item to a repeating event.

1. Click the item on the schedule.

2. Click Edit Event to open the form page.

3. Edit the details as needed.

4. Click the Save button.

Delete It

You can also use the form page to delete an event. Click the Delete button to permanently remove it.

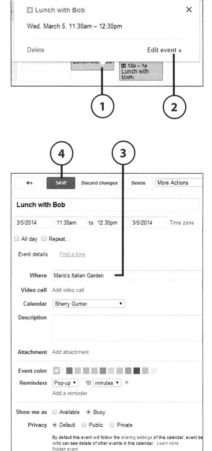

Color Code It

One way to distinguish types of appointments is to assign colors. For example, you might assign personal appointments different colors than work-related appointments. Click the appointment on the calendar and click the tiny drop-down arrow to the left of the appointment title to display a color palette. Click the color you want to assign.

Working with Reminders

You can use reminders to help you remember upcoming events on your schedule. You can specify a pop-up reminder, which pops up as a box on your screen at the predetermined time telling you about the event; you can set an email reminder that sends you an email message about the event; or you can choose to utilize both reminder options.

By default, a 10-minute pop-up reminder is added to every new event you create, unless you specify otherwise. You can immediately tell which event has a reminder assigned by looking for the alarm clock icon when you pause your mouse pointer over the event on your schedule.

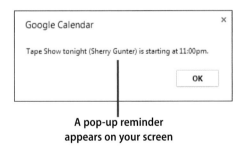

**A pop-up reminder
appears on your screen**

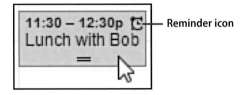

Reminder icon

Set Up a Reminder

To add or edit a reminder, you can use the event's form page.

1. Click the item on the schedule where you want to add or edit a reminder.

2. Click Edit Event to open the form page.

3. Scroll down to the Reminders settings, click the Reminders drop-down arrow and click Pop-up or Email.

Delete It

If you prefer not to add a reminder, you can remove it from the event's form page. Click the Remove Reminder button, which looks like an x.

4. Set how many minutes, hours, day, or weeks you want for the reminder.

5. Click the Save button.

Add Both!

You can choose to add both a pop-up and an email reminder. After setting the first reminder, click the Add a Reminder link and set up the second type of reminder.

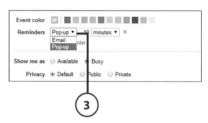

Creating Tasks

You can add tasks to your calendar to help you keep organized and on track with the things you need to get done on a schedule. Tasks are added to their own calendar, called Tasks, and you can find it in the calendar list as soon as you add your first task. Like any other calendars you add, you can turn the Tasks calendar on or off to overlay onto another calendar or view it on its own.

The Tasks calendar also displays a list pane on the right side of the screen displaying your task entries, along with a set of tools at the bottom of the pane to help you work with tasks. In Google language, they call this pane the Tasks gadget. The Tasks feature is also available in Gmail.

You can use the Task pane to review your list, move items up and down the list to prioritize them, and change details about the task. You can mark tasks as complete, or delete them from the list. You can also make new lists and move tasks from one list to another.

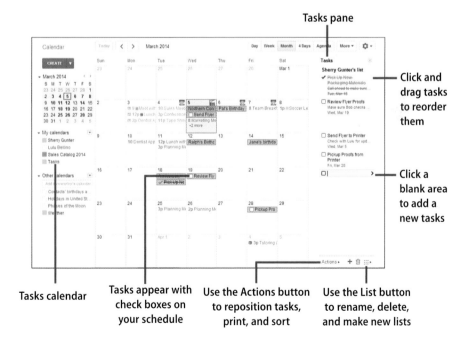

Tasks pane

Click and drag tasks to reorder them

Click a blank area to add a new tasks

Tasks calendar

Tasks appear with check boxes on your schedule

Use the Actions button to reposition tasks, print, and sort

Use the List button to rename, delete, and make new lists

Add a Task

You can add a task with a click in one of two special areas in your calendar: either switch to Month view to add a task or click at the very top of a date (where the all-day events appear) in Day, Week, or 4 Days view.

1. Navigate to and click the date where you want to add a task in Month view, or click the All-day event area at the top of the date.

2. Click the Task link.

3. Enter a title for the task.

4. Enter any details about the task, such as a description.

5. Click the Create Task button to add the task to the calendar date.

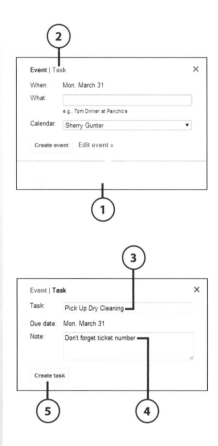

Add More New Tasks

After you create a Tasks calendar, you can use the Tasks pane to add new tasks. Click a blank area of the pane to start a new task, or click the Add Task button at the bottom of the pane.

Turn Tasks On or Off

You can view tasks on their own, without the rest of your calendar details. This might help you focus on areas in your schedule where you know you have upcoming due dates.

1. Click the Tasks drop-down arrow on the calendar list.

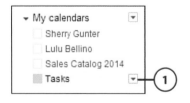

2. Click Display Only This Calendar.

View Tasks with Another Calendar

To overlay the tasks onto another calendar, such as your primary calendar, simply select the calendar's check box (the box next to the calendar name).

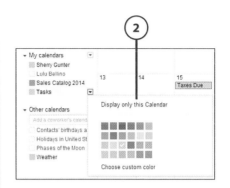

Manage Tasks

You can use the Tasks pane to review and manage your tasks.

1. Click the Tasks box in the calendars list to display the Tasks pane.

2. To mark a task as complete, select its check box.

3. To remove a task from the list, select it, and click the Delete task icon.

4. Select the task and click the edit details arrow to change details about the task. Make changes to the details, as needed, and click the Back to List link.

Toggle It On or Off

Selecting or deselecting the check box next to the Tasks calendar name actually toggles the Task pane on or off. You can also click the pane's Close button (x) to close the pane.

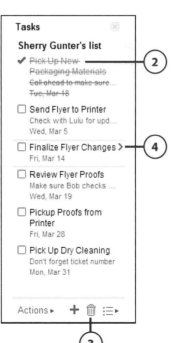

Print Your List

To print the list, click the Actions button at the bottom of the pane and click Print Task List, and click the Print button.

Sharing Calendars

Google calendars are made for sharing, whether you share by allowing others access or by swapping calendar files. For example, you can share your calendar with everyone on your team or just a select few. When thinking about sharing options, there are several privacy settings to consider. One option is to make the calendar public, which means anyone on the Internet can view it. Another option is to make the calendar available only to other users in your organization. A third option is to share it only with designated people.

You can also import other calendars and export your own as another way to share your schedule. Google supports the iCal or CSV file formats, which allows you to import calendars from programs like Microsoft Outlook or Yahoo! Calendar. You can also do the reverse and export your calendar data to other formats.

Regardless of which sharing options you pursue, Google makes the process relatively easy and painless.

Share Your Calendar

You can find all of the calendar sharing options located on the Share This Calendar tab of the Calendar settings page. You can perform these steps on each calendar you want to share, including your primary calendar as well as additional calendars you create and maintain.

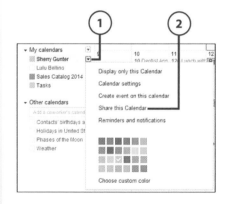

1. Click the drop-down arrow next to the calendar you want to share in the calendar list.

2. Click Share This Calendar.

3. Select the Share This Calendar with Others check box.

Keep It Private

If you don't want to share your calendar with anyone, deselect the Share This Calendar with Others check box and click the Save button to exit the form.

4. Choose whether to make the calendar public or share just with your organization by selecting the appropriate check box and selecting whether to hide details or show details from the drop-down list.

5. Click the box below the Person heading and enter a user's email address to share only with people you designate.

6. Click the drop-down arrow under Permission Settings and select what actions you want to allow the user to perform on your calendar.

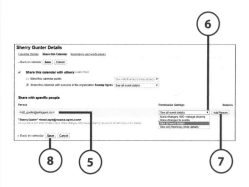

7. Click the Add Person button.

8. Click the Save button.

Specify Permissions Settings

Use the permission settings to control whether a person is allowed to make or not make changes to your calendar items and view your free and busy periods. To change permissions, click the drop-down arrow and make a selection.

Import a Calendar

If you're migrating from another
time-management application, you
can import a calendar into Google
Calendar. For example, you can
import a Microsoft Outlook calendar or Yahoo! Calendar into Google
Calendar. Before you import, first
save the original calendar as an
iCalendar file format (.ics).

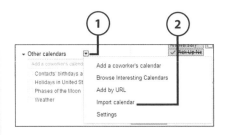

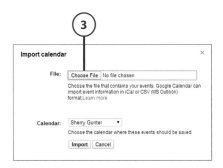

1. Click the Other Calendars drop-
   down arrow.

2. Click Import Calendar.

3. Click the Choose File or Browse
   button (you're browser may vary).

4. Navigate to the file you want to
   import and select it.

5. Click the Open button.

6. Optionally, click the drop-down
   arrow and choose which calendar
   you want to import to.

7. Click the Import button.

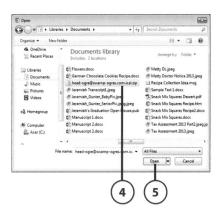

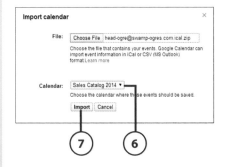

Export Calendars

When you activate the Export feature, Google automatically downloads a zip file of all your calendars in bulk, each one saved as an .ics file in the compressed folder.

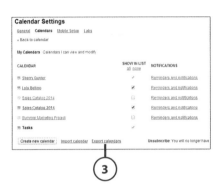

1. Click the My Calendars drop-down arrow.

2. Click Settings.

3. Click the Export Calendars link to download and save the calendars as a compressed file.

Enabling Mobile Notifications

You can register your mobile phone to work with Google Calendar, receiving notifications such as reminders about events coming up on your schedule. This is handy if you're away from your computer or tablet and still need to receive reminders about important events. Google supports most carriers, so chances are your mobile phone works with Google Calendar. Just remember, Google doesn't charge for sending SMS (Short Message Service) texts, but your carrier probably does.

Register Your Mobile Phone

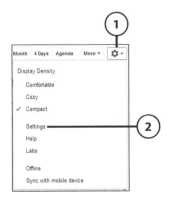

1. Click the Settings button.

2. Click Settings.

3. Click the Mobile Setup tab.

4. Specify your country from the drop-down list.

5. Enter your mobile phone number.

6. Click the Send Verification Code button.

7. Check your phone for the text message from Google containing your code and enter the code in the verification code box.

8. Click the Finish Setup button. Google sends another message verifying your registration.

9. Use the Reminders and notifications tab, which appears automatically after you register your mobile phone, to specify what types of SMS texts you want Google to send you; select the SMS check box for each notification you want.

10. Click the Back to Calendar link to return to your calendar screen.

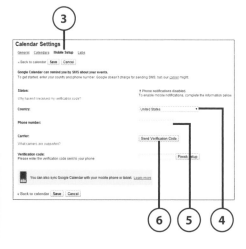

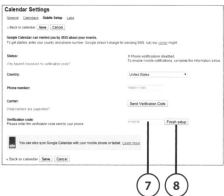

Finding the Google Mobile Calendar

To access your Google Calendar from a mobile phone, type http://calendar.google.com/a/yourdomain./m into your browser's address box.

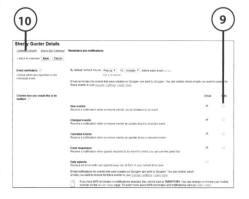

Use Google Drive to store and share files in the cloud

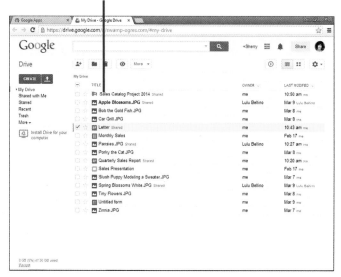

In this chapter, you learn how to utilize Google Drive to store and share files in the cloud:

→ Exploring Drive's interface and learn what features it offers

→ Finding out how easy it is to upload files and folders

→ Learning how to create new files from within Drive

→ Discovering tools and procedures for managing your files and folders online

→ Collaborating with others by sharing your files and folders

→ Installing Google's Drive folder on your computer and syncing your files between your PC or Mac and your online cloud storage

Storing and Sharing Files on Drive

A key part of cloud computing is storage—rather than store files on your own computing device, you can upload them to Google's online servers instead. With this scenario, you can access your files from any computer, tablet, or mobile device as long as you have an Internet connection. With Google Drive, you can store documents, photos, music, videos, and so on, all in one convenient place. Drive goes beyond just storage, though, allowing real-time synchronizing of documents. Lets find out what exactly you can do with Google Drive.

Exploring Drive

Drive is a file storage and synchronization service that gives you a place to keep all your files, rather like a virtual hard drive. Introduced in 2012, Drive is an essential part of Google's office suite. If you use other online storage services, such as Dropbox, OneDrive (formerly SkyDrive), or iCloud, you're already familiar with the conveniences of using the cloud to save your files. Cloud storage is a brilliant concept and here's why.

- You don't have to worry about where to store your files.

- You don't have to wonder how much storage space your hard drive has left.

- You can quit trying to keep up with what's on what flash drive or CD/DVD.

- You don't have to worry about running out of storage space and having to delete data to make room for more.

- You always have a backup of your files in case your own hard drive crashes.

Unlike the limited storage on most computers and mobile devices, you can tap into Google's giant data centers filled with thousands of servers dedicated to online file storage.

Google Drive works a lot like your computer's hard drive, using a folder system to organize and store files. You can create new folders, create subfolders inside of other folders, move files from one folder to another, and so on. Google Drive syncs with your computer and mobile devices, so if you make a change to a file from one device, it automatically shows up when you or someone on your team accesses it from somewhere else.

Google Drive on first use

First Time Access

The first time you access Google Drive, it may ask you if you want to install Drive for your computer. This feature lets you synchronize files automatically between your computer and cloud storage, giving you a place to manage the files even if you're offline. You can learn more about his option later in the chapter, but for now you can choose to skip it.

Google Drive can handle more than 30 different types of files, which means you don't have to have the applications installed on your computer in order to use the file. You can view and share pictures, videos, documents, and other file types directly—no need to send email attachments, just pass along a link to the file.

Google Drive is also integrated with Google Docs, Sheets, and Slides, making it incredibly easy to create new content directly from Drive. You can also install Drive on your computer so you can access and synchronize your Drive files from a folder on your hard drive.

Navigate Around Drive

You can access Drive by clicking the Drive link on the Navigation bar, or by clicking the Apps icon button and clicking Drive. The first time you access Google Drive, it's pretty empty until you start adding files and making folders. Take a moment and acclimate yourself to the various onscreen elements.

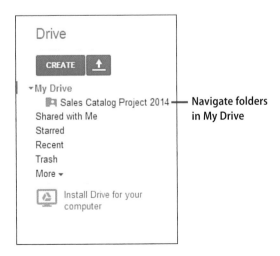

Navigate folders in My Drive

The left side of the page displays all of your folders, acting as your navigation tool for moving in and out of folders, and filtering your view of files.

Select a file to view more tools

Files list

The middle of the page displays the files each folder contains. You can sort the list, change the way in which files appear, delete files, and more. When you select a file, more tools appear to help you work with the file, including sharing it with other users, moving the file to another folder, and previewing the file. Each file in the list has a tiny icon indicating what type of file it is, such as a document, picture, or slide show, for example.

Upload files and folders

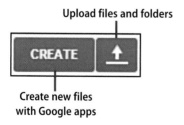

Create new files with Google apps

You can use the Create button located in the upper-left corner of Drive to start new files and folders, and the Upload button next to it to upload files from your computer to Drive.

Search box

Use the Search box across the top of the page to help you look for files among all of your folders. You can search for keywords to find the file you're looking for.

Details and Activity button

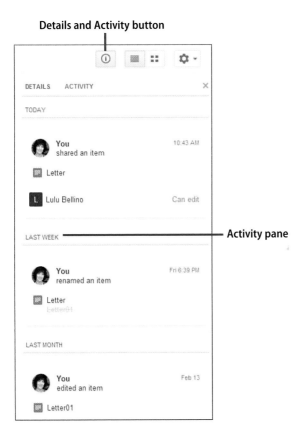

Activity pane

You can also display an Activity pane that gives you details about your recent online sessions with Drive. This includes information such as file deletions, file uploads, shared data, and other file-related activities. You can toggle this pane on or off by clicking the Details and Activity button.

Change the View

You can switch between two views of your files: List view and Grid view. List view, which is the default view, displays your files in a list. Grid view displays your files as thumbnail previews, allowing you to see your content without having to open the file. If the file is more than one page, the thumbnail shows an icon representing the file type. Folders appear as folder icons in Grid view.

1. Click the Switch to Grid button to display your files as thumbnail previews.

2. Click the Switch to List button to display your files as a list.

What If I Need Help?

Any time you need some extra help with using Google Drive, visit the Help Center. Click the Settings button (the small cog-like graphic) and click Help. This takes you to Google's Help Center and displays the Drive help topics.

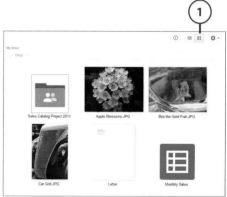

Settings button

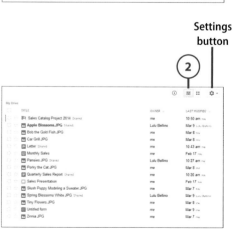

Uploading Files and Folders

Ready to start uploading some files? It's incredibly simple. You can perform a manual upload by dragging files directly to Google Drive or you can upload with the help of a dialog box to navigate to the file's location. You may find one method works better for you than another.

Another option is to upload a folder, in which case everything in the selected folder is uploaded, including the folder name, and added to Google Drive.

Upload a File

Uploading only takes a few seconds or so, depending on the file size and your Internet connection speed.

1. Click the Upload button.

2. Click Files.

3. Navigate to the file you want to upload and select it.

4. Click the Open button.

5. The file uploads to Drive, and the Upload Complete window opens.

6. Click the Close button (x) to exit.

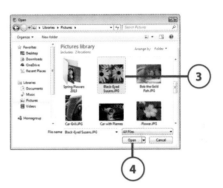

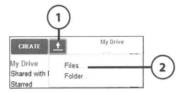

Upload Multiple Files

You can upload more than a single file at a time. Windows users can press and hold the Ctrl key while clicking files, and Mac users can press and hold the Cmd key while clicking files.

Drag and Drop a File

Although the easiest method, drag and drop does require some room to maneuver between onscreen windows: the browser window and the open folder window or desktop. You might need to resize your browser window to accomplish this task successfully.

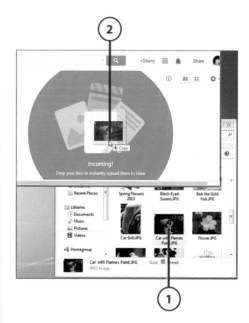

1. Drag the file from its location.

2. Drop it on the Drive page.

3. The file uploads to Drive and the Upload Complete window opens.

4. Click the Close button (x) to exit.

Drag Multiple Files

You can also drag multiple files to upload. Windows users can press and hold the Ctrl key while clicking files, and Mac users can press and hold the Cmd key while clicking files. Then you can drag them as a group.

Upload a Folder

Uploading a folder is as easy as uploading individual files, but with a different dialog box to help you.

1. Click the Upload button.

2. Click Folders.

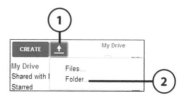

3. Navigate to the folder you want to upload and select it.

4. Click the OK button.

5. The folder uploads to Drive and the Upload Complete window opens.

6. Click the Close button (x) to exit.

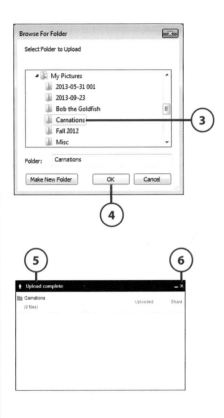

Enable It First

You may need to enable a Java applet before trying to upload a folder. Just click the Enable Folder Upload option when you click the Upload button.

Drag and Drop It

You can also use the drag-and-drop technique to upload folders. For example, if the folder you want to upload is sitting on your computer's desktop, you can simply drag it over the browser window and drop it into Drive.

Creating New Files

You can create new files directly from Drive using the Google Apps. For example, you can start a new document file with Docs or a spreadsheet file with Sheets without having to open the apps separately. The Create button offers several preset apps to choose from, plus any others you might add:

- **Folder**—Create a new folder.

- **Document**—Start a new document file with Google Docs.

- **Presentation**—Start a new presentation file with Slides.

- **Spreadsheet**—Create a new spreadsheet file with Sheets.

- **Form**—Create all kinds of forms, such as surveys, quizzes, and other information with Google Forms.

- **Drawings**—Create and edit drawings with this app.

You can add more apps to the list as needed; just click the Connect More Apps link at the bottom of the Create menu.

Create a New File

To create a new file to store on Drive, you can use the Create menu and choose the type of file you want to build. Depending on which app you choose, an additional browser window opens for you to create the new file.

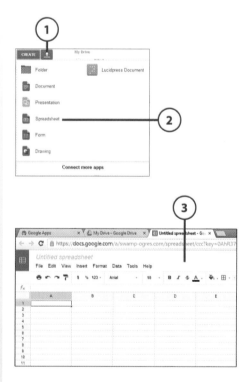

1. Click the Create button.

2. Click an app.

3. A new browser tab opens for the app where you can create a new file.

Managing Folders and Files

The more files you add, the more you'll need to keep them organized. Drive starts you out with several preset filters you can use to change how you view your files. You can add more folders as you go along to help manage your work. For example, you might create a work folder you share with your team to collect and collaborate documents for a particular project.

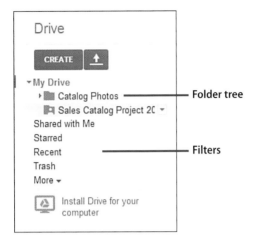

The folder tree on the left side of the page is where you can display or hide folders by expanding or collapsing the view simply by clicking the arrow icon next to the folder name. Along with organizing folders, you can also filter your view of folders and files. The left pane includes several preset filters. Here's what you can find listed by default:

- **My Drive**—This is your primary folder. Use this filter to display everything you add and sync within this main folder. If you install Google Drive on your computer, you can synchronize its content with everything on My Drive.

- **Shared with M**e—Use this filter to display all the folders and files shared with you.

- **Starred**—Use this filter to display items you mark with a star .

- **Recent**—Use this filter to list all recently opened files in reverse chronological order.

- **Trash**—Use this filter to delete files you no longer want to store on Drive.

Click the More button to view additional filters: All Items (shows everything) and Offline (helps you access files when you're offline).

To activate a filtered view of your files, just click the filter name.

In addition to filtering your view, you can apply a variety of file management techniques to your cloud content. For example, you can add and delete folders and files, rename them, mark them with stars to bring attention to certain items, preview files before opening them, search through and sort your files, and download files onto your computer.

Install Drive for Your Computer

Also in the left pane is a link for installing Google Drive on your computer. You can learn more about this feature later in this chapter.

Create a New Folder

You can create a new folder in Drive anytime you want to further organize your cloud storage. You might create a folder just for pictures, for example, or another for home budgeting files. You can add as many folders as you need.

1. Click the Create button.

2. Click Folder.

3. Enter a name for the folder.

4. Click the Create button.

5. Drive adds the folder as a sub-folder to the My Drive folder. To view the folder's contents, click the folder name.

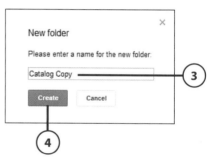

Adding Subfolders

You can also create folders within folders. To do so, select the folder to which you want to add a sub-folder, click the Create button and click Folder. Name the new folder and click the Create button. Drive lists the new folder subordinate to the folder you designated. Subfolders in the left pane can be expanded to view their contents or collapsed to hide their contents. Just click the arrow icon next to the folder name to expand or collapse the folder.

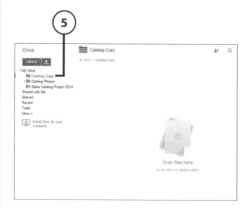

Right-clicking Shortcuts

You can right-click folder or file names to view a shortcut menu that offers quick access to the same commands found on the main menus.

Move Files Between Folders

Moving files is a breeze. You can drag them around Drive and drop them in a folder, or you can use the Move To dialog box as shown in these steps:

1. Select the check box for the file you want to move.

2. Click the Move To button.

3. Select a folder from the list in which to place the file.

4. Click the Move button to move the selected files to the folder.

Create a Folder As You Go

If you haven't yet created a folder for the file you're moving, you can do so from the Move To dialog box. Click the Create New Folder link, type a folder name, and click Create. The new folder is immediately added to the list in the Move To box. Now you can select the new folder name and click Move to move a file.

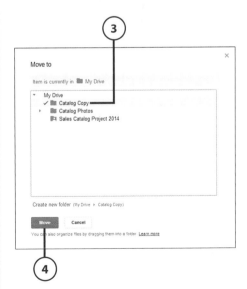

Rename Folders and Files

The fastest way to rename a file in the Drive is to right-click the file name and click Rename. This opens a dialog box where you can type a new name. You can also find the Rename command on the More menu (which only appears when you select a file).

Preview a File

You can preview a file before opening it using the built-in viewer. This tool is great for perusing files, like a group of photos, before committing to opening the file. The viewer supports more than 40 file types, including image files, video files, and Microsoft Office files such as Word and Excel.

1. Select the check box for the file you want to preview.

2. Click the Preview button to open the built-in viewer and display the file.

3. Click a navigation arrow to view the next file in the list.

4. Click the Close button (x) to exit.

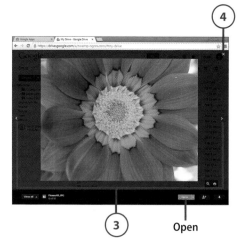

Open

More Tools

The viewer window offers several tools you can use. You can view all the files in the selected folder, for example, or print the file. You can click the Open button in the preview window to open the file.

Open a File

You can open a file from the files list and view it in its own window. For example, if you open a document file, Google Docs opens and displays the file; if you open a spreadsheet file, Google Sheets opens and displays the file. If you open a non-Google Apps file, the preview viewer window opens instead.

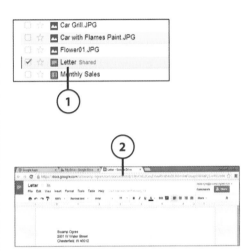

1. Click the name of the file you want to open.

2. The file opens in its own tab.

Delete Files

Deleting files you no longer need helps you free up storage space. When you delete files with Drive's Trash feature, the files are stored in the Trash list until you permanently delete them. It's good practice to empty your Trash list regularly.

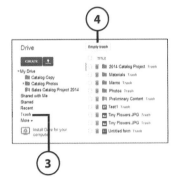

1. Select the check box of the file you want to delete.

2. Click the Remove button to move the file to the Trash list.

3. Click the Trash filter.

4. Click the Empty Trash button to permanently remove all the listed files.

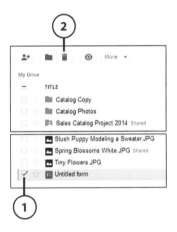

Reclaim It!

To retrieve an item found in the Trash list, select the check box next to the file's name and click the Restore button.

Delete Just One

To remove just one item from the Trash list, select its check box and click Delete Forever.

Search Files

To search for a particular file or files, you can type keywords into the Search box and conduct a search of your Drive files. If you need to specify some search criteria, you can use the Search drop-down menu.

1. Type the keyword or words you want to search for in the Search box.

2. Click the drop-down arrow to specify search criteria.

3. Specify the criteria for narrowing your search.

4. Click the Search button or press Enter/Return.

5. Any matches display in the results list.

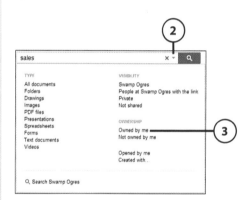

>>>Go Further
USING SEARCH OPERATORS

Search operators are special characters or formats you can type to find just the right file you want to locate. Predefined search operators are commonly used in many types of searches, including Google searches. You can use the following operators to help you fine-tune your search for content on Drive:

"quotes"	Find an exact phrase
OR	Find files with at least one of the words, such as Apples OR oranges
-	Locate and limit document matches with multiple word combinations, such as figure -skating
to:	Locate documents shared to someone, such as to:melissa@gmail.com
from:	Locate documents shared from someone, such as from:melissa@gmail.com
type:	Search by document type, such as type:image
owner:	Search for documents by owner, such as owner:bob@gmail.com
title:	Locate documents based on title, such as title:"Sales 2014"

Sort Files

You can use the sort drop-down arrows at the top of the Owner and Last Modified columns in List view to sort your list of files. You can sort files by several different options.

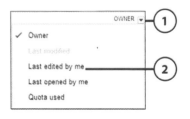

1. Click the drop-down arrow next to the column you want to sort.

2. Specify a sort criteria.

3. Drive sorts the list accordingly.

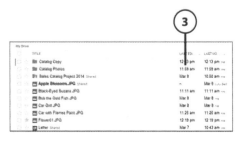

Download a File

You can move a file from Drive onto your computer by activating the download command. You can export up to 2GB at a time.

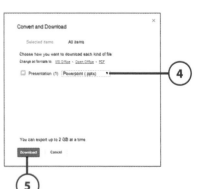

1. Select the check box for the file you want to download.

2. Click the More button.

3. Click Download.

4. Specify how you want to download the file. You can specify a file format, if needed.

5. Click the Download button..

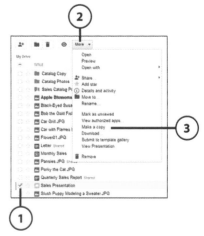

>>>*Go Further*

NEED MORE DRIVE STORAGE?

Google Apps for Business/Education users automatically receive 30GB of storage for each person on the account. This doesn't include files you create with Docs, Sheets, or Slides. The 30GB storage space extends across Drive, Gmail, and Google+ Photos. You can manage storage in several ways. For your own account, look at the bottom-left corner of the Drive page. If you pause your mouse pointer over the info posted there, a pop-up box displays how much each app is currently using. If you click the Manage link, you can view a page with more details, including which plan you're currently on.

If you run out of your allotted storage space, you can easily purchase additional storage. When you purchase a storage plan, it encompasses Drive, Gmail, and Picasa photo albums. As the Google Apps administrator, you can purchase Drive storage licenses and assign them to specific users. Single users can also purchase more storage space. Pricing plans vary, from $4.99 a month for 100GB to $99.00 a month for 1TB on up.

If you're administering your organization's account, you can use the Admin console page to make changes to billing; click the Billing option to check your account. You can look for assistance in adding storage using the Help Center. From the Billing page, click the Help icon and click Help Center. Type "add more storage" to find lots of information on how to add storage space and a run-down of all the available plans.

Sharing Files and Folders

You can collaborate with other users by sharing your files and folders. Sharing is useful in a variety of ways—you can share photo files with people outside your Google Apps organization, share a document file with a client, or share a folder of project-related files with everyone in your department. Google Drive's sharing features let you specify access levels, view edits with visibility options, and control exactly who sees your files. For example, you and your team are putting together a newsletter. Rather than have each member work on a separate file and then try to merge all the edits or pass around the document for everyone to add input, you can all work on the same file at the same time. This lets you see changes in real-time so everyone's working on the latest version. What a timesaver!

You can pick which files or folders you share and control the settings for each one. You might share some files with clients, for example, share others only with your team members, and keep others completely private. Visibility options include the following:

- **Private**—With the default setting, only you can access the file. The file remains private until you assign another visibility option.

- **Anyone with a link**—With this setting, you can share the link to anyone of your choosing. No one else can view the file without the exact URL.

- **Public on the Web**—Use this setting to make the file viewable by anyone on the Web.

- **Your domain only**—Use this setting to let your domain users find and access the document.

- **Your domain with the link**—Use this setting to keep the file out of the domain's search results; instead, domain users must know the link in order to access the file.

- **Specific people**—Use this setting to invite specific users to access the file, typically via an email invitation. All you need is their email address in order to allow them access to the file.

Visibility options control who sees your file

Visibility options control who sees your file

Editing options are available after you decide to share a file. These access levels only apply to files you create with Google Apps. You can grant other users three types of interaction with your file:

- **Can edit**—Allows full access to viewing, commenting, and viewing.

- **Can comment**—Allows viewing and comments, but not editing.

- **Can view**—Allows viewing only, no comments or editing.

- **Is owner**—Marks the owner of the file.

Access options control the
level of file interaction

When you share a file, you can notify others with an email message. This helps alert other users regarding the files they see on their own Drive.

>>>Go Further

When you share a file, you see the word "Shared" next to the file name in Drive's file list area.

UNDERSTANDING OWNERSHIP

When you create, sync, or upload a file to Drive, you're considered the owner of the file. As such, you have full control over the file, including the ability to invite others to access the file, control collaborator permissions, remove the file permanently, or transfer ownership to another user. Transferring ownership means you give up control over the file and you can no longer work with it as you once did. You can transfer ownership through a few steps. First you need to share the file with the person you want to transfer ownership to, and

>>>Go Further

it has to be someone in the same domain. When you've done that, open the Sharing Settings dialog box again (if it isn't already open). To do so, select the file on Drive and click the Share button to open the dialog box. Next, look for a drop-down arrow next to the person's name in the Who Has Access list. Click the drop-down arrow and click Is Owner. Click the Save Changes button, and the ownership transfer is complete. The file shows up in Drive as owned by the other user, and when that person logs onto Google Drive, they'll see they're the owner of the file now as well.

Share a File

Sharing files is just a matter of turning on a setting and specifying an access level. When you share a file, you need to enter the name or email address of the person you're sharing with and whether you want to notify them or not. If you opt not to notify them, they won't see what file you've shared until they log onto their own Google Drive.

1. Select the check box for the file you want to share.

2. Click the Share button.

3. Type the name or email address of the person you want to share with.

4. Click the drop-down and select an access level for the file.

5. Optionally, select the Notify People via Email check box (the box is selected by default unless you deselect it to opt out of sending an email notification).

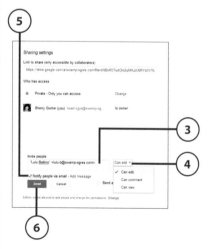

6. Click the Send button. (If you opt not to send an email notification, click the OK button that appears in place of the Send button.)

7. The user appears in the list of people who have access to the file. You can add more users, if needed.

8. Click the Done button.

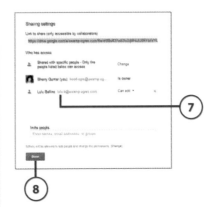

Lots of Opportunities to Share

The Share button on Drive isn't the only opportunity for sharing a file. You'll run into the Share option in lots of other places, including other Google Apps, the preview window, shortcut menus that appear when you right-click, and more. When you master how the Sharing Settings dialog box works, you can share items whenever you want.

Share a Folder

To share an entire folder, right-click the folder name and click Share or select the folder's check box in the list area and click the Share button. Both methods open the Share Settings dialog box. Now you can follow the same procedure as sharing a single file and specify who to share with.

It's Not All Good

Are You Sure About That?

You can certainly share with people outside of your organization's domain. In fact, the Share Settings dialog box seems to make it easy to do so. However, as soon as you do, Google quickly displays a prompt box asking if you're sure about sharing with outsiders, as if it's a big no-no. Although it seems a bit overly cautious—and somewhat annoying when you're trying to hook up a client with your latest advertising file for their approval—it's just trying to keep you and your data safe. Don't worry about the prompt box; just click Yes to continue. Think of it as a chance to verify you're sending the share status to the correct email address..

Edit User Access

To make changes to who you're sharing a file with, or change an access
level, you can revisit the Share settings dialog box.

1. Select the check box for the file
   you want to edit.

2. Click the Share button.

3. Make any changes to the settings;
   click the drop-down menu and
   change access levels.

4. Click the Save Changes button.

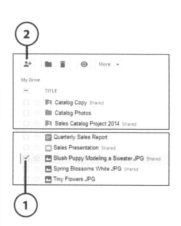

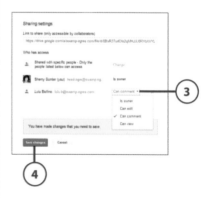

Remove Users and Make It Private

To unshare a file, click the Remove
button (x) next to the user's name
in the Share Settings dialog box
and click the Save Changes button. If you remove everyone from
the Who Has Access list (except
yourself), the visibility option
reverts to the Private setting.

Change the Visibility Option

By default, your file is private until you specify who to share it with or assign a visibility option. To control who sees your file, specify a visibility option.

1. Select the check box for the file you want to edit.

2. Click the Share button, and click the Change link.

3. Select a visibility option.

4. Click the Can View drop-down arrow and select an access level.

5. Click the Save button to return to the Sharing Settings dialog box.

6. Click the Done button.

Sharing Already?

If you're already sharing a file, Drive assigns the Specific People visibility option by default.

Make It Private Again

To return a file to private status, open the Sharing Settings dialog box and click the Change link to view Visibility options. Click the Specific People option and click the Save button. The Private setting appears in the list of who has access, other than yourself.

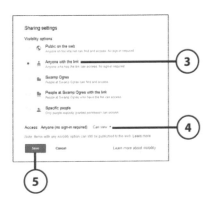

Share a Link

The link you see displayed at the top of the Sharing Settings dialog box is the link you can copy and paste in an email to share with others who, in turn, can follow the link to the file.

Syncing Files

Not only can you share your files with other users, but you can make sure they're shared successfully with your computer by syncing them with a Google Drive folder. There are times when you may want to work with the files on your computer rather than the cloud, for example. Perhaps you are going to be offline over the weekend but want to update an important document. You can download and install Google Drive for your computer (PC or Mac) and any files you place in its folder are automatically synced with your online files the next time you connect to the Internet.

When you have Google Drive installed on your computer, it places a special folder on your computer that looks like any other folder. Behind the scenes, though, this folder mirrors any changes to its contents to match your My Drive folder online. So anytime you delete, rename, or move a file, the changes occur online as well—and the same thing happens in reverse; any changes you make online are reflected in your computer's Google Drive folder. The Google Drive web app and your Google Drive folder are automatically synchronized as long as you have an Internet connection.

Install Google Drive on Your Computer

You can install Drive for your computer from Google Drive in your web browser. Once installed, a new Google Drive folder is added to your computer, along with a shortcut icon on the Taskbar (Windows) or in the upper-right corner of the desktop (Mac) for accessing commands, as well as shortcut icons for accessing Docs, Sheet, and Slides.

1. Click the Install Drive for Your Computer link at the bottom of your folder tree.

2. Click the Install Drive for PC or Install Drive for Mac button.

3. Click the downloaded file.

4. Click the Run button.

5. Click the Close button when the installation is complete.

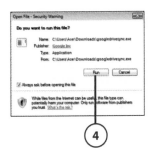

6. Click the Get Started button to find out how to get started with Google Drive for your computer.

7. Type in your user email and password to log onto your account.

8. Click the Sign In button, click the Next button, click the Next button, and click the Next button.

9. Click the Done button.

10. The Google Drive folder appears in your computer's folders list and populates itself with the files you are currently storing online.

Sync It

If you've been working offline and need to sync your files, you can click the Google Drive shortcut icon on the taskbar (Windows) or desktop (Mac) and click Sync.

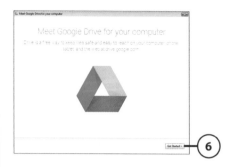

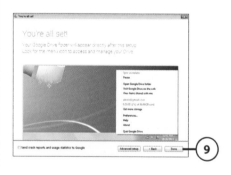

View Google Drive Folder Preferences

You can use the installed shortcut icon on the Taskbar (Windows) or in the upper-right corner of the desktop (Mac) for accessing commands related to the Google Drive folder, such as setting preferences.

1. Click the Google Drive icon on the Taskbar (Windows) or desktop (Mac).

2. Click Preferences.

3. View and make any changes to preference settings for your account, sync options, and startup settings.

4. Click the Apply Changes button.

What About Google Documents?

If you open a Google document in you Google Drive folder on your computer, such as a file you created in Doc, Sheets, or Slides, your default web browser launches to display the file and access the online app associated with the file.

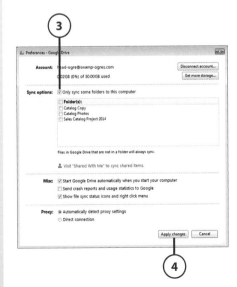

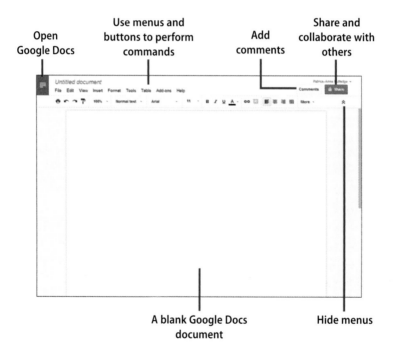

Open Google Docs

Use menus and buttons to perform commands

Add comments

Share and collaborate with others

A blank Google Docs document

Hide menus

In this chapter, you discover how to create, format, edit, print, and collaborate on documents using Google Docs:

→ Creating a document
→ Formatting documents
→ Inserting tables and other content
→ Managing your documents
→ Collaborating on documents
→ Using Google Docs tools
→ Printing and publishing documents

5

Creating Documents with Docs

Google Docs is the word processing application that's part of Google Apps. With Google Docs, you can create and save documents online; import documents from other applications; enhance your documents with images, links, drawings, and more; collaborate on documents with colleagues anywhere in the world; and export, print, and publish to the Web.

Opening Google Docs

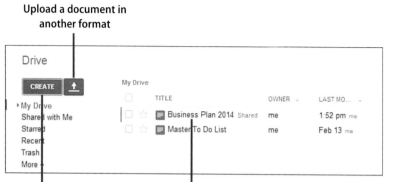

Upload a document in another format

Create a new document

Open an existing document

To get started with Google Docs, log into your Google account and navigate to Google Drive at https://drive.google.com.

From here, you can

- Click the Create button and select Document to create a new document.

- Click the Upload button and select Files to select a document in another format (such as Microsoft Word) you want to convert to Google Docs.

- Click the title of an existing document to open it.

Later sections in this chapter cover creating and opening documents in more detail.

Creating a Document

You can create a blank document from Google Drive or from within Google Docs itself. You can also create a document using a template.

Create a Document from Google Drive

1. While logged into your Google account, access Google Drive at https://drive.google.com.

2. Click the Create button.

3. Select Document from the menu.

4. Google Docs opens a new document window.

5. Click the document title. By default Google names all new documents "Untitled Document."

6. Enter a new document name.

7. Click the OK button.

Where Is the Save Button?

If you're used to working with Microsoft Word or another word processing application, you might wonder where the Save button is. Google Docs continuously saves your document without any action on your part so there is no need for a Save button.

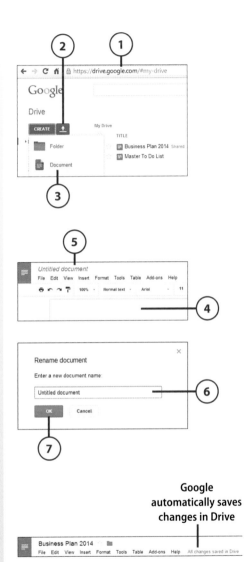

Google automatically saves changes in Drive

Create a Document from Google Docs

You can also create a new document from within Google Docs.

1. Click File.

2. Click New.

3. Click Document.

4. Google Docs opens a new document window.

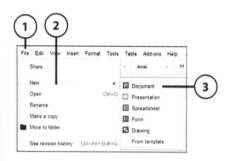

Click to rename the document

Create a Document from a Template

The Template Gallery enables you to create documents from pre-existing templates, which can save you time and effort. Sample templates include those for resumes, cover letters, invoices, recipes, proposals, press releases, meeting agendas, newsletters, and more.

1. Click File.

2. Click New.

3. Click From Template.

4. Optionally, click the Preview link if you want to view a template before creating a new document with it.

5. Click the Use This Template button next to template you want to use.

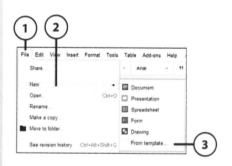

Search templates by keyword

Submit a template

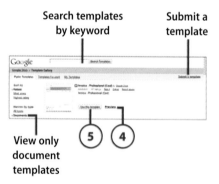

View only document templates

6. Google Docs creates a new document with the selected template.

Remember to rename
your document

>>>*Go Further*
SUBMITTING A TEMPLATE

If you have a document you'd like to share as a template with the Google Docs community, you can submit it. To do so, select the My Template tab in the Template Gallery and click the Submit a Template link. On the Submit a Template page, you can select an existing document from your Google Docs account and specify its category and description.

Upload a template
to submit

Read template policies
before submitting

It's Not All Good

Review Your Template Before Submitting It

Remember that any template you submit is available to public. Be sure to review it for any personal, confidential, or sensitive data before submitting to the Google Docs community.

Formatting Documents

You can format selected text in two ways:

- Using the buttons on the toolbar.

- Using the options available from the Format menu.

For example, you can use these formatting tools to apply a new font, font size, color, or style; bold, italicize, underline, or align text; create numbered and bulleted lists; and more.

Missing Toolbar Buttons

Depending on the resolution of your screen, not all toolbar buttons might fit on the toolbar. In this case, the More button displays, which you can click to view the remaining buttons. To hide this extra toolbar, click the More button again. If your screen has room for all buttons, the More button isn't available.

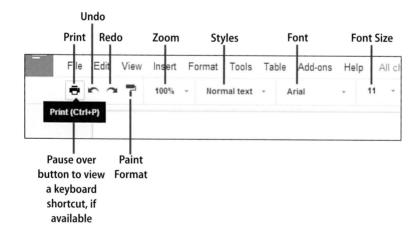

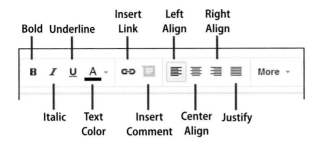

Bold Underline
Insert Link
Left Align
Right Align

Italic
Text Color
Insert Comment
Center Align
Justify

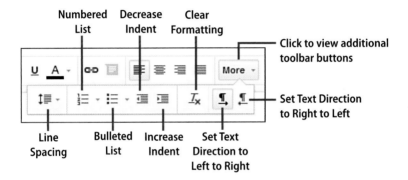

Numbered List
Decrease Indent
Clear Formatting

Click to view additional toolbar buttons

Set Text Direction to Right to Left

Line Spacing
Bulleted List
Increase Indent
Set Text Direction to Left to Right

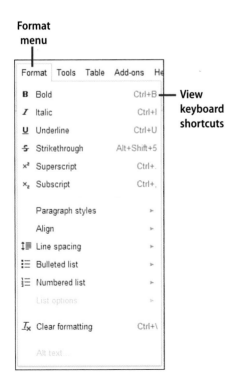

Format menu

View keyboard shortcuts

Google Docs Keyboard Shortcuts

If you don't want to use menus and buttons to perform commands, keyboard shortcuts are another option. To view a complete list of shortcuts, press Ctrl + /.

Select Text

To apply formatting and styles to text, you need to select it. You can

- Double-click a single word to select it.

- Triple-click in a paragraph to select it.

- Click and drag across other areas of text to select it.

- Press Ctrl + A to select the entire document.

Apply a New Font and Font Size

Although Google Docs includes styles with built-in fonts and font sizes, you can customize these if you prefer.

1. Select the text you want to format.

2. Click the Font button.

3. Select a font from the menu.

4. Click the down arrow to the right of the Font Size button and select a font size from the list or enter a specific size.

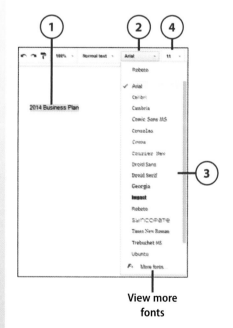

View more fonts

>>>Go Further
VIEWING MORE FONT OPTIONS

If you don't see your preferred font on the menu, click More Fonts. In the Fonts dialog box, you can view a larger selection of fonts, search for fonts by name, display fonts by type (such as serif, sans serif, handwriting, and so forth), as well as sort fonts by popularity or in alphabetical order.

Search fonts by name   Search fonts by type   Sort by popularity or other criteria

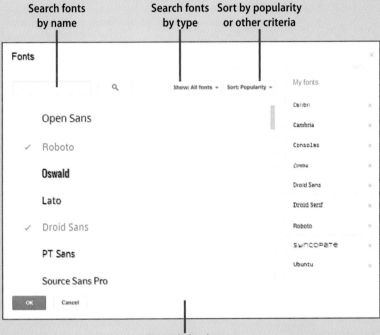

Fonts dialog box

Apply a Style

Google Docs comes with several default styles for normal text, titles, subtitles, and several headings. You can apply these styles to your document to organize its content as well as customize the styles with your favorite fonts and formats. By default, Google Docs applies the Normal Text style to your text.

1. Select the text you want to format.

2. Click the Style button. If your text is using the default style, this button is called Normal Text.

3. Select the style you want to apply.

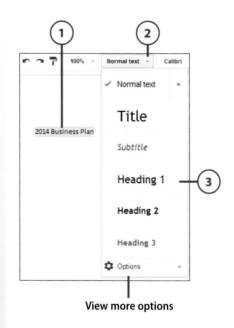

View more options

Customize and Save a Style

Google Docs enables you to apply a style you customize to other instances of that style in a document. For example, you might want to customize the Heading 1 style with a new font, font size, or other attributes (such as bold, underline, or italic).

1. Select the text whose style you customized.

2. Click the Styles button.

3. Click the arrow to the right of the style you customized.

4. Select Update [style] to Match. For example, if you want to update Heading 1, the menu option says Update "Heading 1" to Match.

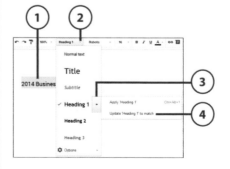

Save Customizations as Default Settings

If you customize styles, you can save these as the default settings for new documents by clicking Options on the Styles menu and clicking Save As My Default Styles.

Reset Customizations

If you decide you no longer want to keep your customizations, you can return to Docs defaults by clicking Options on the Styles menu and clicking Reset Styles.

Save as default styles

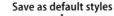

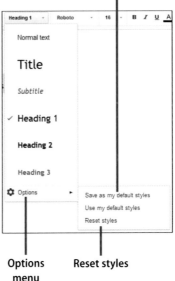

Options menu

Reset styles

Create Numbered and Bulleted Lists

Google Docs offers several styles of numbered and bulleted lists you can apply to a text series. For example, you can create an ordered list with sequential numbers or letters or an unordered list with bullets, circles, squares, or arrows.

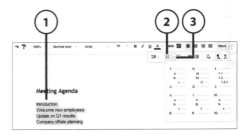

1. Select the text you want to format.

2. Click the Numbered List button to apply a numbered list style.

3. Click the down arrow to select another numbered list style.

4. Click the Bulleted List button to apply a bulleted list style.

5. Click the down arrow to select another bulleted list style.

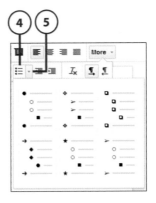

>>>Go Further

MORE OPTIONS FOR NUMBERED AND BULLETED LISTS

If the list styles on the toolbar don't suit your needs, you can further customize your lists by selecting Lists Options from the Format menu.

From here, you can

- Select a list style from the options.

- Restart list numbering at a number you specify. This option is only available for numbered lists.

- View more symbol options for your list. This option opens the Insert Special Characters dialog box, which enables you to use a special character as a bullet point. See "Insert a Special Character" later in this chapter for more information.

- Edit the prefix and suffix for your list. For example, you can replace the standard period suffix for a numbered list with a colon. This option is only available for numbered lists.

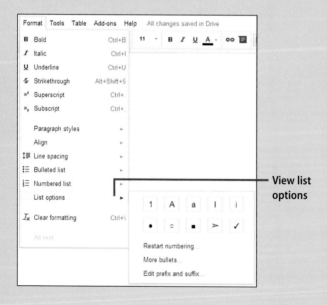

View list options

Use the Paint Format Tool

The Paint Format tool helps you save time by applying custom formatting to text in a single click.

1. Select the text with the formatting you want to copy.

2. Click the Paint Format button.

3. Select the text you want to format.

Apply Formatting to Multiple Text Selections

If you want to apply formatting to multiple text selections rather than just one, double-click the Paint Format button instead of single-clicking it. This enables you to apply to the format you copied more than once. When you finish, click the Paint Format button again to stop formatting.

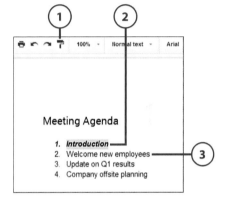

Inserting Content in a Document

Going beyond the basics enhances your documents and gives them a more professional look. From the Insert menu, you can insert any of the following:

- Images from your computer, Google Drive, or webcam

- Links to external sites

- Equations such as mathematical formulas and Greek letters

- Drawings such as rectangles, circles, and text boxes

- Tables to organize content

- Comments, which are useful for collaborating on documents

- Footnotes to provide reference information

- Special characters and symbols

- Horizontal lines, which can help break up sections of content

- Page numbers, counts, and breaks

- Headers and footers

- Bookmarks

- Tables of contents

Insert menu

Insert an Image

You can insert images less than 2 MB in size from a variety of sources including your computer, Google Drive, your Google albums, and more. Google Docs supports the following file formats: .gif (excluding animated gifs), .jpg, and .png.

1. Click Insert.

2. Click Image.

3. Click Upload to upload an image from your computer.

4. Click Take a Snapshot to take a picture with your webcam.

Google Might Request Webcam Permission

You might be prompted for access to your camera and microphone. If so, click the Allow option and click the Close button.

5. Click By URL to enter the URL of an image already posted on the Web.

6. Click Your Albums to insert an image from your Google album.

7. Click Google Drive to insert an image you uploaded to your drive.

8. Click Search to use Google Search to find an image on the Web.

9. Click the Select button to insert your specified image.

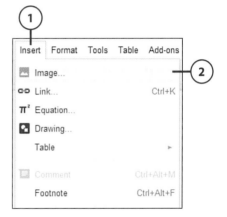

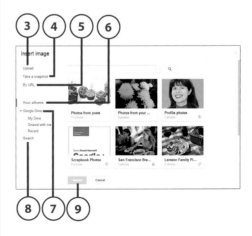

Insert a Link

You can insert a link to an external site in your document. Google Docs underlines your link to alert readers that they can click it to go to the link destination.

1. Select the location where you want to insert the link.

2. Click the Insert Link button.

3. Start typing the URL of the link you want to insert. As you type, Google Docs displays potential matches.

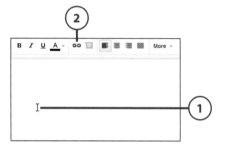

Copy and Paste a URL

Optionally, you can paste a copied URL in the Link text box, which is particularly useful for long links. Another option is searching for a specific page by entering keywords in this text box. Google displays a list of matches that you can select.

4. Enter the text to display for your link.

5. Click the Apply button.

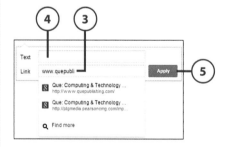

Insert a Drawing

Using the drawing tool, you can add visual appeal to your documents with lines, scribbles, circles, squares, rectangles, text boxes, and many other shapes.

1. Select the location where you want to insert the drawing.

2. Click Insert.

3. Click Drawing.

4. Select the down arrow to the right of the Line button to select the type of line you want to draw: a regular line, arrow, curve, poly-line, arc, or scribble.

5. Select the down arrow to the right of the Shape button to select the type of shape you want to draw (such as a square, circle, rectangle, arrow, callout, or equa-tion).

6. Click the Text Box button to insert a text box in your drawing.

7. Click the Image button to insert an image in your drawing. See "Insert an Image" earlier in this chapter for more information.

8. Click the Save & Close button to insert the drawing in your document.

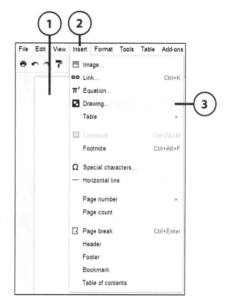

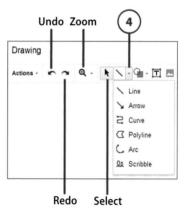

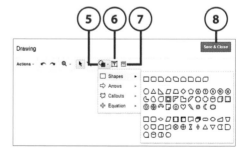

Additional Toolbar Buttons

Depending on the content you add to your drawing, additional toolbar buttons might appear. For example, if you add a shape, the Fill Color, Line Color, Line Weight, Line Dash, and More buttons appear. Click the More button to open another toolbar with options to change your font and font size, apply bold and italic, and more.

Edit or Delete a Drawing

To edit a drawing, select it and click the Edit link. To delete a drawing, select it and press the Delete key on your keyboard.

>>>Go Further

ADDITIONAL DRAWING OPTIONS

Click the Actions button for additional drawing options which enable you to

- View your drawing revision history.

- Download your drawing as a PDF, Scalable Vector Graphic image, PNG image, or JPEG image.

- Create WordArt on your drawing.

- Cut, copy, paste, or duplicate selected content.

- Copy your drawing to the Web clipboard for use in another application.

- Align, distribute, rotate, order, or group selected content.

Actions menu

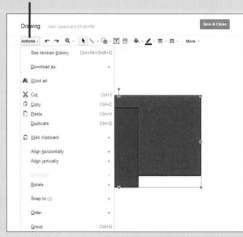

Insert a Footnote

A footnote contains additional content or reference material about a specific section of text in your document, particularly popular with academic papers.

1. Select the location where you want to insert the footnote.

2. Click Insert.

3. Click Footnote.

4. Enter your footnote text.

Delete a Footnote

To delete a footnote, position your cursor to its right and press the Backspace key. Be aware that you should do this in the text itself, not in the footnote at the bottom of the page.

Insert a Special Character

At times, you might need to insert special characters in your documents, including copyright, trademark, or currency symbols; em or en dashes; emoticons (such as a smiley face; or foreign language characters).

1. Select the location where you want to insert a character.

2. Click Insert.

3. Click Special Characters.

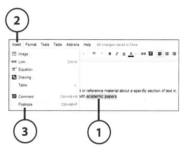

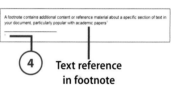

Text reference in footnote

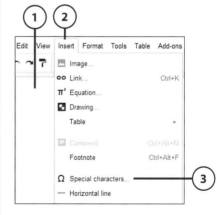

4. Select a category from the drop-down lists.

5. Select the character you want to insert.

6. Click the Insert button.

Insert a Bookmark

A bookmark is a shortcut to a specific location in your document. Bookmarks are most useful in large documents where you might want to quickly jump to specific content. For example, if you have a 40-page document, you can bookmark important sections and add links to these sections at the beginning of the document. Google Docs underlines any text you link to a bookmark just like an external link.

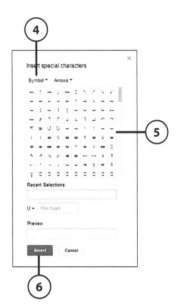

1. Select the document location where you want to insert the bookmark.

2. Click Insert.

3. Click Bookmark.

4. Select the text you want to link to the bookmark.

5. Click the Insert Link button.

6. Click the Bookmarks section.

7. Select the bookmark you want to link to.

8. Click the Apply button.

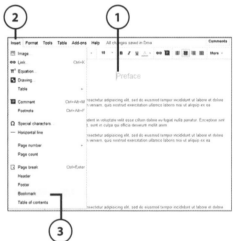

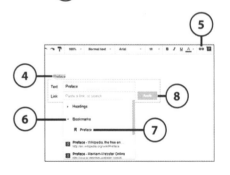

Change or Remove a Bookmark

If you want to change or remove a link to a bookmark, select it and click the Change or Remove link. If you want to remove the bookmark itself, select it and click the Remove link.

Insert a Table of Contents

A table of contents is another useful tool for longer documents. When you create a table of contents using Google Docs, it makes a clickable list of all your headings that you can click to jump to that section.

1. Select the document location where you want to insert the table of contents.

2. Click Insert.

3. Click Table of Contents.

4. Google Docs inserts the table of contents with clickable links.

Update or Delete a Table of Contents

If you change any of the headings in your table of contents, select it and click the Update Table of Contents to refresh this data. To delete a table of contents, right-click it and select Delete Table of Contents from the menu.

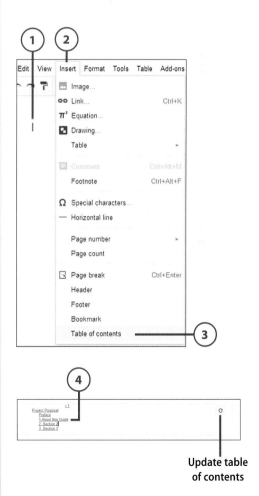

Update table of contents

Inserting a Table

A table enables you to organize and display document content in columns and rows. You can edit and format table data just like any other text in your document.

Insert a Table

1. Select the document location where you want to insert the table.

2. Click Table.

3. Click Insert Table.

4. Select the number of columns and rows you want to include.

5. The table displays in your document, where you can select cells to enter data.

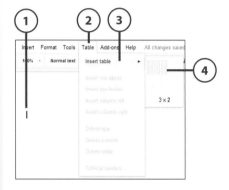

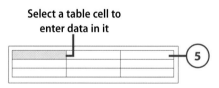

Select a table cell to enter data in it

>>>Go Further

TABLE EDITING AND FORMATTING OPTIONS

The Table menu offers numerous options for editing and formatting a table.

Table Formatting Shortcuts

You can also right-click in your table and select these options from a shortcut menu.

>>>Go Further

You can

- Insert rows above or below a selected row

- Insert columns to the right or left of a selected column

- Delete a selected row

- Delete a selected column

- Delete a selected table

- Specify table properties such as

  - Table border color and size

  - Cell background color

  - Cell vertical alignment: top (the default), center, or bottom

  - Column width and minimum row height in inches

  - Cell padding dimensions if you prefer something other than the default 0.069 inches

  - Table alignment: left (the default), center, or right

  - The number of inches you want to indent to the left (the default is zero)

Apply a Custom Color

Optionally, you can apply a custom color to your table border or cell background by clicking in the Custom section of the color palette and specifying an exact color in the dialog box that opens. For example, you could enter a color code (such as #006699).

Table menu

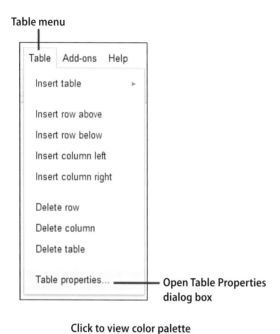

Open Table Properties
dialog box

Click to view color palette

Manage
your table
properties

Managing Your Documents

After you create a document, Google Docs makes it easy to open, rename, copy, download, and search it. You can perform any of these tasks from the File menu.

Open a Document

In addition to opening a document already stored on your Google Drive, you can also open a document shared with you or upload and convert a document from another application (such as Microsoft Word).

1. Click File.

2. Click Open.

3. Click Upload to upload a file from your computer and open it in Google Docs.

File Formats that Convert to Google Docs

You can upload and convert files from the following formats: .doc and .docx (Microsoft Word), .html, plain text (.txt), and .rtf.

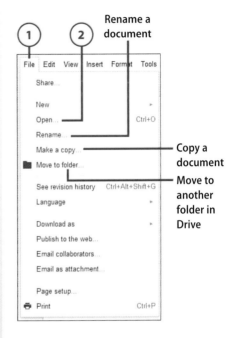

4. Click My Drive to view documents stored on your Google Drive.

5. Click Shared with Me to view documents someone else shared with you. See "Collaborating on Documents" later in this chapter to learn more about sharing documents.

6. Click Starred to view documents you starred in Google Drive.

7. Click Previously Selected to view documents you recently opened.

8. Click All Items to view all available documents.

9. Click the file you want to open.

10. Click the Open button.

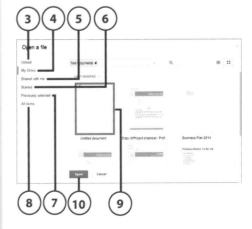

View Revisions History

If you make a mistake and save your document, don't worry. Using the Revision History pane, you can view prior versions and restore to one of them if you want. The Revision History pane displays all document versions by date and author.

1. Click File.

2. Click See Revision History.

3. Click a version to view it.

4. Click the Restore This Revision link to restore to a previous version.

5. Click the Close button (x) to close the pane.

Download a Document

You can download documents in Google Docs in any of the following formats:

- Microsoft Word (.docx)

- OpenDocument Format (.odt)

- Rich Text Format (.rtf)

- PDF Document (.pdf)

- Plain Text (.txt)

- Web Page (.html, zipped)

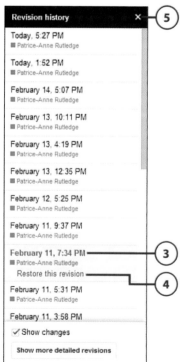

1. Click File.

2. Click Download As.

3. Select the file format you want.

Delete a Document

You can delete a document in Google Drive by selecting the check box to its left and clicking the Remove icon. Alternatively, you can right-click a document name and click Remove from the menu.

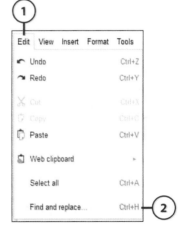

Find Text in a Document

You can quickly search for text in your documents. This is particularly useful for long documents.

1. Click Edit.

2. Click Find and Replace.

3. Enter the term you want to find.

4. Optionally, select the Match Case check box if you want to search only for the specific capitalization you entered.

5. Click the Next button to move to the next instance of this term.

6. Click the Prev button to go back to the previous instance of this term.

7. Click the Close button (x) to exit.

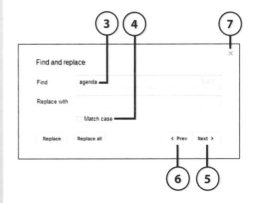

Replace Text in a Document

You can also search for and replace specific text in a document.

1. Click Edit.

2. Click Find and Replace.

3. Enter the term you want to replace.

4. Enter the replacement term.

5. Optionally, select the Match Case check box if you want to search only for the specific capitalization you entered.

6. Click the Replace button to replace the first instance of this term.

7. Click the Replace All button to replace all instances of this term.

8. Click the Close button (x) to exit.

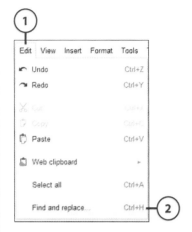

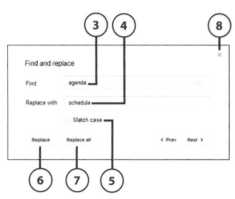

Viewing Documents

The View menu offers several options for viewing your documents. These include

- Print Layout

- Show Ruler

- Show Equation Toolbar

- Show Spelling Suggestions

- Compact Controls (hide menu and toolbar)

- Full Screen

By default, the Print Layout and Show Spelling Suggestions view options are selected and a check mark displays to their left.

A check mark displays next to a selected view option. Clicking an option without a check mark selects it. Clicking an option with a check mark removes it.

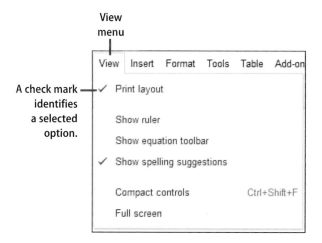

Collaborating on Documents

Google Docs offers several ways for you to collaborate on documents with colleagues anywhere in the world. For example, you can share documents, email collaborators, and email documents as attachments. See Chapter 4, "Storing and Sharing Files on Drive" for more information about these tasks.

You can also add comments to documents and share them with collaborators.

Add a Comment

Comments enable you to share feedback and commentary on documents with other people.

1. Select the text you want to comment on.

2. Click the Insert Comment button.

3. Enter your comment in the text box.

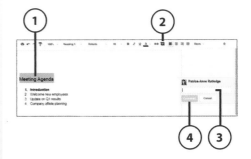

Send Comment Notifications by Email

To send someone an email about your comment, type the plus sign (+) and their email address in the text box, such as +patrice@ patricerutledge.com. If this person is in your Gmail address book, Google Docs displays a match as you type. If you haven't given this person permission to comment, you're prompted to do so.

---

4. Click the Comment button.

5. Google Docs displays your comment, name, date, and time.

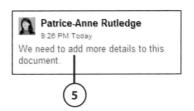

Work with Comments

You can click a comment to view it in more detail. From here, you can edit, delete, or reply to it. Click the Resolve button to close the comment and hide it from the discussion.

Optionally, you can review comments in one box by clicking the Comments button in the upper-right corner of the page.

Delete   Resolve

Edit   Reply

View and manage comments in one place

Using Google Docs Tools

The Tools menu includes several tools that help you enhance your documents. These include

- A spell checker. See "Perform a Spell Check" later in this section.

Tools menu

- The Research pane, which enables you to search the Web for information related to your document's content.

- A dictionary where you can search for definitions or synonyms.

- A word count tool that shows you the number of words and characters in your document.

- A translation tool that translates your document into another language.

- The Preferences dialog box, which enables you to specify automatic substitutions (such as (c) for the copyright symbol).

It's Not All Good

Translation Tool Limitations

Google Docs uses Google Translate (http://translate.google.com) to perform translations. Although this translation tool is useful for translating documents for casual use, you shouldn't rely on it for an accurate, professional translation.

Perform a Spell Check

1. Click Tools.

2. Click Spelling.

3. Click the Change button to change to the suggested spelling.

4. Click the Ignore button to ignore the suggested spelling.

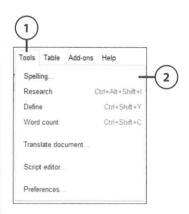

Tools	Table	Add-ons	Help
Spelling...			
Research		Ctrl+Alt+Shift+I	
Define		Ctrl+Shift+Y	
Word count		Ctrl+Shift+C	
Translate document...			
Script editor...			
Preferences...			

Spell Check Options

Click the down arrow to the right of the Change button and select Change All to change all instances of this word to the suggested spelling. Click the down arrow to the right of the Ignore button and select Ignore All to ignore all instances of this word. Alternatively, select Add to Dictionary to add the suspected misspelling to the dictionary so that the word doesn't get caught in future spell checks.

5. Click the Close button (x) to exit.

Show and Hide Spelling Suggestions

By default, Google Docs highlights suspected spelling errors with a red dotted underline. You can right-click this word to view suggested revisions. If you don't want to highlight suspected errors, click the View menu and click Show Spelling Suggestions to remove the check mark next to it.

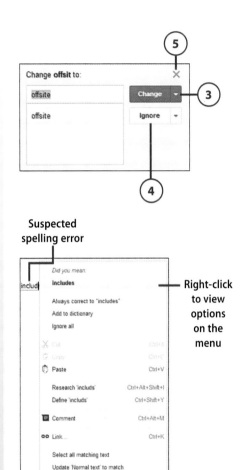

Suspected spelling error

Right-click to view options on the menu

Printing and Publishing Documents

After creating a document, you might want to print it or publish it to share with others.

Specify Page Setup Parameters

Before printing, you should specify the page setup parameters you want to use.

1. Click File.

2. Click Page Setup.

3. Specify a page orientation: portrait or landscape.

4. Select a paper size (such as letter, legal, or A4).

5. Select a page color. This is most useful for color printing.

6. Enter top, bottom, left, and right margins.

7. Optionally, click the Set As Default button if you want to use these settings as defaults for future pages.

8. Click the OK button.

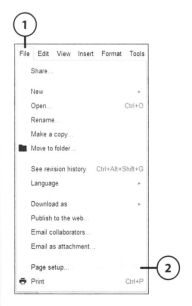

Print a Document

1. Click the Print button.

2. Click the Change button to select another printer if you don't want to print to the default printer.

3. Specify whether you want to print all pages, specific pages, or a range of pages.

4. Specify the number of copies you want to print.

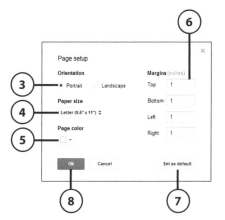

5. Specify print margins: the default, none, minimum, or custom margin settings you enter manually.

6. Select the Two-Sided check box if you want to print on both sides of the paper.

7. Select the Background Colors and Images check box if you want to print these images.

8. Click the Print button.

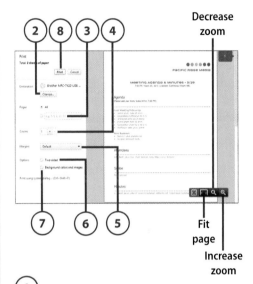

Publish a Document to the Web

Another way to share a document with others is to publish it to the Web. This option publishes a copy of your original document online.

1. Click File.

2. Click Publish to the Web.

Prevent Automatic Republication

By default, Google Docs automatically republishes your document when you make changes. If you don't want to do this, remove the check mark next to the Automatically Republish When Changes Are Made check box.

---

3. Click the Start Publishing button.

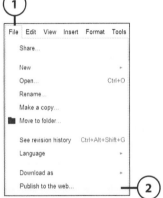

Automatically republish when changes are made

4. Click the OK button to confirm you want to publish this document.

5. Send the document link to anyone you want to share with.

6. Paste the embed code on an external website.

7. Share by clicking one of the following links: Google+, Gmail, Facebook, or Twitter.

8. Click the Close button.

Stop Publishing to the Web

If you decide you no longer want to publish a document to the Web you can reverse this action by selecting Publish to the Web from the File menu and clicking the Stop Publishing button.

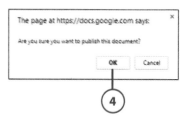

Stop publishing

It's Not All Good

Web Publishing Pitfalls

Remember that anyone who has your document URL can view it online, even if you don't provide it to this person directly. Think carefully before publishing a document to the Web and consider other options such as sharing with colleagues on Google Drive if you have privacy concerns. .

Working with Add-ons

Google Docs offers a collections of add-ons that you can install to enhance, improve, and streamline your documents. Popular add-ons include EasyBib Bibliography Creator, Template Gallery, Avery Label Merge, Track Changes, Hello Fax, Merge by MailChimp, and Consistency Checker.

Install an Add-on

1. Click Add-ons.

2. Click Get Add-ons.

3. Select the add-on you want to install.

4. Click the Free button.

5. Click the Accept button to add your add-on to the Add-ons menu.

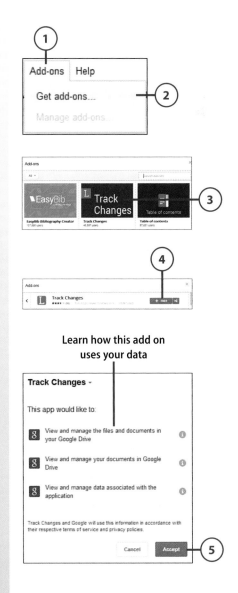

Return to Google Drive

Use menus and buttons to perform commands

Add comments

View your Google account

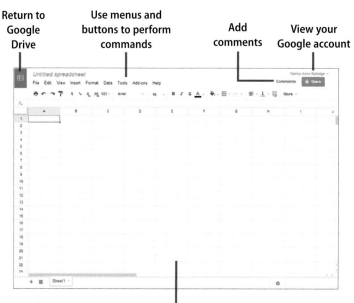

A blank Google Sheets spreadsheet

In this chapter, you discover how to create, format, enhance, print, deliver, and collaborate on spreadsheets using Google Sheets:

- → Creating a spreadsheet
- → Entering spreadsheet data
- → Formatting spreadsheets
- → Working with sheets, rows, and columns
- → Working with formulas and functions
- → Inserting charts, images, links, forms, and notes
- → Formatting spreadsheets
- → Managing spreadsheets
- → Collaborating on spreadsheets
- → Printing, publishing, and delivering spreadsheets

6

Tracking and Analyzing Data with Sheets

Google Sheets is the full-featured spreadsheet application that's part of Google Apps. With Sheets, you can perform calculations (from basic to complex), customize spreadsheets to suit your needs, and filter, sort, and analyze data. If you want to enhance a spreadsheet beyond basic numbers and text, Google Sheets also enables you to insert charts, images, links, forms, drawings, notes, and pivot table reports.

Getting Started with Google Sheets

Upload an existing
spreadsheet in
another format

Create a new
spreadsheet

Open an existing Spreadsheet
in Google Drive

To get started with Google Sheets, log into your Google account and navigate to Google Drive at https://drive.google.com.

From here, you can

- Click the Create button and click Spreadsheet to create a new spreadsheet.

- Click the Upload button and click Files to select a spreadsheet from another format (such as Microsoft Excel) you want to convert to Google Sheets.

- Click the title of an existing spreadsheet to open it.

Later sections in this chapter cover creating and opening spreadsheets in more detail.

A spreadsheet contains one or more sheets, whose tabs you can view at the bottom of the page. Each sheet contains multiple rows and columns. The intersection of each row and column forms a cell, in which you can enter data such as numbers, text, dates, and times as well as perform calculations.

Each cell has its own address that's comprised of its row heading and column heading, such as A1. Sheets uses this unique identifier when performing calculations.

Creating a Spreadsheet

You can create a blank spreadsheet from Google Drive or from within Google Sheets itself. You can also create a spreadsheet using a template.

Create a Spreadsheet from Google Drive

1. While logged into your Google account, access Google Drive at https://drive.google.com.

2. Click the Create button.

3. Click Spreadsheet. Google opens a blank spreadsheet.

4. Click the spreadsheet title. By default Google names all new spreadsheets "Untitled Spreadsheet."

5. Enter a new spreadsheet name.

6. Click the OK button. Google Sheets renames and saves your spreadsheet.

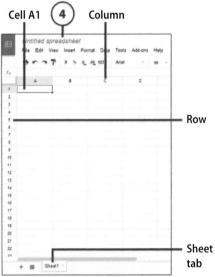

Where Is the Save Button?

If you're used to Microsoft Excel or another spreadsheet application, you may wonder where the Save button is. Google Sheets continuously saves your spreadsheet without any action on your part so there is no Save button.

Create a Spreadsheet from Google Sheets

If you're already using Google Sheets, you can easily create another spreadsheet. Simply click the File menu, click New, and click Spreadsheet. The process is identical to creating a new spreadsheet from Google Drive.

Create a Spreadsheet from a Template

The Template Gallery enables you to create spreadsheets from pre-existing templates, which can save you time and effort. Sample templates include those for timecards, project trackers, purchase orders, expense reports, budgets, and more.

1. Click File.

2. Click New.

3. Click From Template.

4. Optionally, click the Preview link if you want to view a template before creating a new spreadsheet with it.

5. Click the Use This Template button next to the template you want to open.

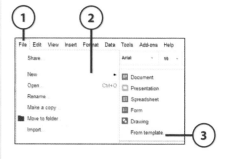

Search templates by keyword

View templates you've used

View templates you've submitted

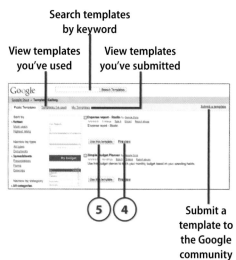

Submit a template to the Google community

Entering Spreadsheet Data

Entering basic data on a spreadsheet is straightforward. Type your data and press the Enter key to move to the next row in the same column. Optionally, you can also use the arrow keys on your keyboard to move to a cell in another direction.

Enter Sequential Data

If you want to save time when entering sequential data, Sheets offers several shortcuts. You can use this technique to enter a sequence of numbers or dates, such as 1, 2, 3 or June, July, and August. You can also use this technique for data that follows a pattern such as 10, 20, and 30.

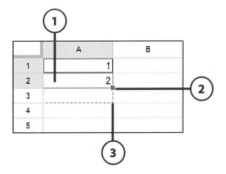

1. Make the first two entries in your sequence.

2. Select these entries with your mouse.

3. Drag the lower-right corner of your selection to the cell where you want to stop the sequence.

4. Google Sheets completes your sequence of data.

Editing Spreadsheet Data

If you want to edit existing cell data, double-click the cell and make your changes.

Formatting Spreadsheets

Google Sheets simplifies spreadsheet formatting with familiar options it shares with other Google applications such as Google Docs and Google Sheets. In addition, you can apply formatting specific to numerical data such as currency and percent.

Format Spreadsheet Content

You can format selected cells in two ways:

- Using the buttons on the toolbar.

- Using the options available from the Format menu.

For example, you can use these formatting tools to

- Format cell data as a currency, percentage, date, or time

- Apply a new font, font size, color, or style

- Bold, italicize, underline, or align text

- Apply borders

- Apply a fill color to a cell

- Merge cells

- Wrap cell text

Missing Toolbar Buttons

Depending on the resolution of your screen, not all toolbar buttons may fit on the toolbar. In this case, the More button displays, which you can click to view the remaining buttons. To hide this extra toolbar, click the More button again. If your screen has room for all buttons, the More button isn't available.

Google Sheets Keyboard Shortcuts

If you don't want to use menus and buttons to perform commands, keyboard shortcuts are another option. To view a complete list of shortcuts, press Ctrl + /.

Formatting toolbar   Additional formatting options

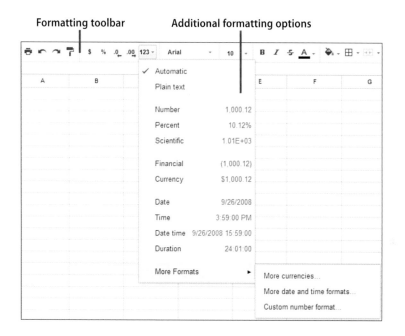

Print   Redo   Format as of Decimal
                             Currency   Places
                                         Decrease
                                         the Number

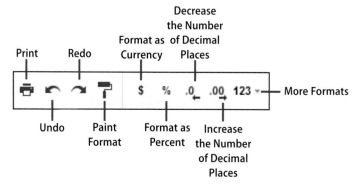

                                                    More Formats

Undo   Paint   Format as   Increase
              Format   Percent   the Number
                                          of Decimal
                                          Places

              Font   Text   Horizontal Wrap
Font   Size   Italic Color   Borders   Align   Text

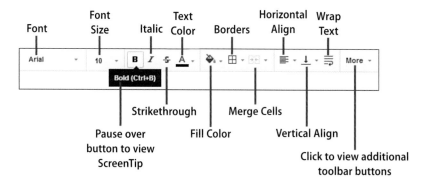

              Strikethrough   Merge Cells

Pause over   Fill Color   Vertical Align
button to view
ScreenTip   Click to view additional
                                           toolbar buttons

Wrap Text

If the text you enter in a cell is too long and overlaps into the next cell, you can resolve this problem by wrapping the text.

1. Select the text you want to wrap.

2. Click the Wrap Text button.

3. Google Sheets wraps the text to fit inside the cell.

Select entire sheet

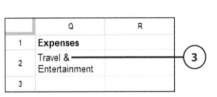

Wrap Text in All Cells

To wrap the text in all cells on a sheet, select the entire sheet and click the Wrap Text button.

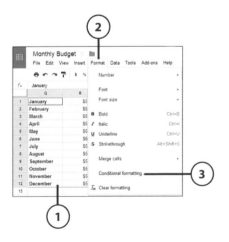

Apply Conditional Formatting

Conditional formatting enables you to format cells based on specific rules you define. For example, let's say you have a lengthy spreadsheet listing the number of units sold per quarter for each of your company's products. Using conditional formatting, you can highlight in red any numbers that fall below a certain criteria or highlight in green any numbers that exceed a certain criteria.

1. Select the data you want to format.

2. Click Format.

3. Click Conditional Formatting.

4. Specify the rule you want to apply.

5. Enter your criteria.

6. Specify formatting options such as applying a certain text or background color.

7. Verify that the data range you selected is correct.

8. Click the Save Rules button. Google Sheets applies the formatting rule to your spreadsheet.

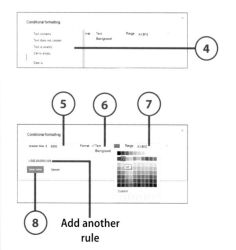

Add another rule

Working with Sheets, Rows, and Columns

Adding, deleting, and modifying sheets, rows, and columns are straightforward tasks in Google Sheets.

Insert a New Sheet

By default, Google Sheets opens a spreadsheet with one sheet named Sheet1. If you need to add another sheet, you can easily do so by clicking the Add Sheet button (+) in the lower-left corner of the page. For example, you may want to create additional sheets for each month, quarter, year, product, and so forth.

Google Sheets names each new sheet in sequence (Sheet2, Sheet3, and so forth) unless you rename them.

Click to add a new sheet

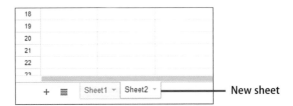

New sheet

Work with Sheets

When you right-click a sheet tab, Google Sheets opens a shortcut menu with the following options:

- **Delete**—Delete the selected sheet.

- **Duplicate**—Create a copy of the sheet in the same spreadsheet. Google Sheets names this copy "Copy of [Sheet Name]." For example, duplicating a sheet named Current Projects would be called Copy of Current Projects.

- **Copy to**—Copy the sheet to another spreadsheet.

- **Rename**—Change the name for the sheet other than Sheet1, Sheet2, and so forth.

- **Change Color**—Add a colored line to the bottom of a sheet tab. This is particularly useful if you want to highlight groups of tabs in a spreadsheet that contains numerous sheets.

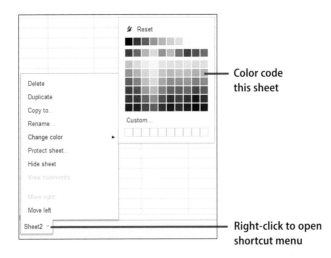

Color code this sheet

Right-click to open shortcut menu

Sheet highlighted
with a colored line

- **Protect Sheet**—Protect the sheet or range of data by specifying who has editing rights.

- **Hide Sheet**—Temporarily hide the sheet from view.

- **View Comments**—View any comments about this sheet, if available. See "Add a Comment" later in this chapter.

- **Move Right**—Move the sheet to the right.

- **Move Left**—Move the sheet to the left.

Unhide a Sheet

If you decide you no longer want to hide a sheet, you can unhide it. Simply click the View menu and click Hidden Sheets.

Work with Rows and Columns

Google Sheets makes it easy to insert, delete, hide, and resize rows and columns. You can also clear rows and columns of all data. Simply right-click a row or column and select the appropriate option from the shortcut menu.

Select Multiple Rows and Columns

If you want to select more than one row or column, select the first item, press the Shift key, and select the last item. The wording on the shortcut menu changes depending on the number of rows or columns you select. You can also select nonconsecutive rows and columns by pressing the Ctrl button while you click.

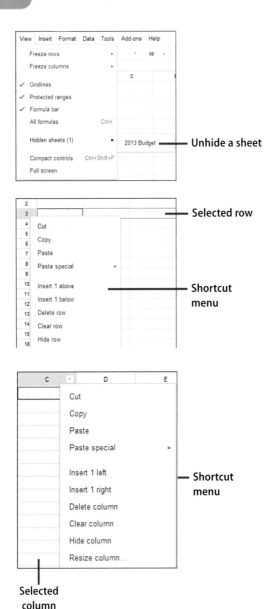

Unhide a sheet

Selected row

Shortcut menu

Shortcut menu

Selected column

Resize Rows and Columns

You can also resize rows and columns manually by dragging the edge or a row or column header. To resize automatically to fit the contents of a cell, double-click between header dividers.

Drag to resize manually

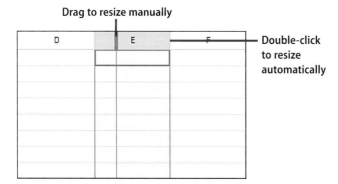

Double-click
to resize
automatically

Working with Formulas and Functions

You use formulas to perform calculations, such as adding two or more numbers. Google Sheets formulas are intelligent and efficient. If you include a cell in a formula and then update the data in that cell, the formula result updates automatically.

Although you can enter basic formulas manually, Sheets also includes numerous functions that help you create more advanced calculations, including complex financial and engineering calculations.

Enter a Formula Manually

One of the most common Sheets tasks is to create a basic formula that adds, subtracts, multiplies, or divides cell data. For example, if you want to add the contents of cells A1 and A2 and place this number in cell A3, you would enter =A1+A2 in cell A3.

1. Type the equal sign (=) in the cell where you want to place the formula result.

2. Type the cell address of the first cell of the formula.

Formula displays
here as well

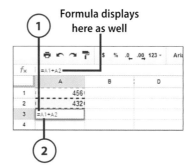

3. Type the corresponding operator, such as plus (+), minus (–), multiply (*), or divide (/).

4. Type the cell address of the second cell of the formula.

5. Press the Enter key to display your formula result.

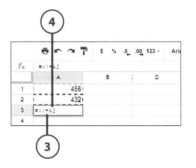

Add More Than Two Numbers

To add more than two sequential numbers in a formula, use the colon between the first and last of a series of cells. For example, to add cells A1 through A10, you enter the formula =A1:10. To add more than two non-sequential numbers, enter them individually such as =A1+B7+C10.

Using Numbers in Formulas

In addition to creating a formula based on cell content, you can also use an actual number in a formula. For example, to add 5 to the number in cell A10, you enter the formula =A10+5.

>>>Go Further

PERFORMING COMPLEX CALCULATIONS

If you need to perform complex calculations that include more than one operator, you need to use parentheses to indicate the order of your calculations. By default, Google Sheets performs multiplication and division calculations before addition and subtraction calculations unless you use parentheses to indicate an addition or subtraction should take place first.

For example, the formula =A1+B1*C1 would multiply B1 times C1 first and then add it A1. If you want to add A1 and B1 before multiplying by C1, your formula should read =(A1+B1)*C1.

Copy a Formula

Rather than entering a series of formulas for similar calculations, you can copy the pattern of a formula to adjacent cells. For example, let's say you have a spreadsheet that lists the number of sales for each of three products for every month of the year. You can summarize sales for one month and then copy the same formula for subsequent months, saving you time and effort.

1. Select the cell with the formula to copy.

2. Pause your mouse pointer in the lower-right corner of the cell until it becomes a crosshair.

3. Drag your mouse until you reach the last cell to fill with the copied formula.

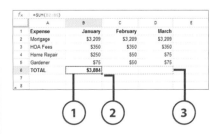

4. Google Sheets updates the spreadsheet with the copied calculations.

	A	B	C	D	E
1	Expense	January	February	March	
2	Mortgage	$3,209	$3,209	$3,209	
3	HOA Fees	$350	$350	$350	
4	Home Repair	$250	$50	$75	
5	Gardener	$75	$50	$75	
6	TOTAL	$3,884	$3,659	$3,709	
7					

④

How Google Sheets Copies Formulas

When Google Sheets copies a formula, it changes the cell references by row or column. For example, if the original formula were =A2-A1 and you copied it to the next cell to the right, the formula would read =B2-B1. If you don't want to change a cell reference by row or column, you can enter an absolute reference by placing a dollar sign before both the row and column reference. For example, entering =B2-A1 in a formula would prevent Sheets from changing the reference to cell A1 even when copied to other rows.

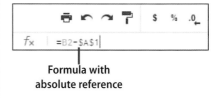

fx =B2-A1|

Formula with absolute reference

Use the SUM Function

Although a detailed discussion of working with functions is outside the scope of this book, it's useful to have a basic understanding of how they work. In this example, you use the SUM function to add a series of numbers.

1. Select the cells that contain the numbers you want to add.

2. Click the Functions button.

3. Click SUM.

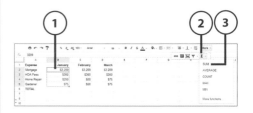

4. The formula displays in the adjacent cell.

5. Press Enter/Return to display the formula result.

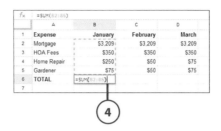

Performing Calculations Manually

Remember, you can also perform this calculation manually, as described in the previous section "Enter a Formula Manually." In general, it's best to use a function for formulas that go beyond basic calculations.

Inserting Content in a Spreadsheet

Although most spreadsheets contain just numbers and text, you can also enhance your spreadsheet with charts, images, links, forms, and drawings (see Chapter 5 for more information about inserting drawings).

You can access any of these options from the Insert menu. The toolbar also includes buttons for inserting a link or chart.

Insert a Chart

Charts offer a great option for displaying data in a visual way. Google Sheets enables you to create many different chart types including bar, pie, line, and column charts.

1. Select the cells you want to include in the chart.

2. Click the Insert Chart button.

3. Google Sheets displays a chart preview, using the optimal format for the data selected.

4. Optionally, select another chart type from the Recommended Charts section.

5. Click the Customize tab to modify the chart title text, color, and fonts.

6. Click the Insert button.

7. Google Sheets displays your chart on your spreadsheet.

View more chart types   Modify chart settings   **3**

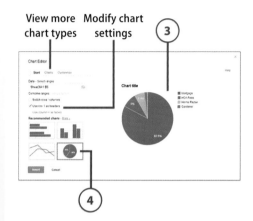

4

5

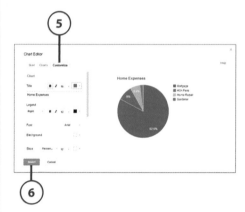

6

Quick edit mode   **7**   Delete chart

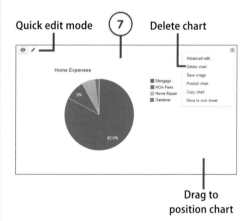

Drag to position chart

Insert an Image

You can insert images less than 2MB in size from a variety of sources including your computer, Google Drive, your Google albums, and more. Google Sheets supports the following file formats: .gif (excluding animated gifs), .jpg, and .png.

1. Click Insert.

2. Click Image.

3. Click Upload to upload an image from your computer.

4. Click Take a Snapshot to take a picture with your webcam.

5. Click By URL to enter the URL of an image already posted on the Web.

6. Click Your Albums to insert an image from your Google album.

7. Click Google Drive to insert an image you uploaded to your drive.

8. Click Search to use Google Search to find an image on the Web or find a suitable stock image.

9. Click the Select button to insert your specified image.

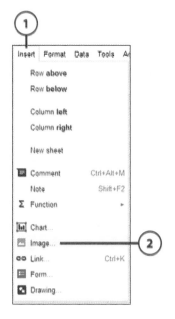

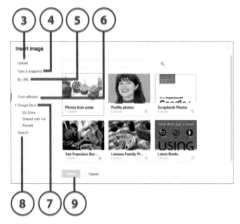

Drag-and-Drop Method

One easy way to insert an image is to drag it from your desktop and drop it on your sheet.

Insert a Link

The easiest way to insert a link in cell is to simply type it, such as www. quepublishing.com. Google Sheets underlines your link to alert readers that they can click it to go to the link destination.

You can also create a text-based link. For example, you could use the text "Que Publishing," which links to www.quepublishing.com.

1. Select the cell where you want to place the link.

2. Click the Insert Link button.

3. Enter the text to display in the cell.

4. Start typing the URL of the link you want to insert. As you type, Google Sheets displays potential matches.

Copy and Paste a URL

Optionally, you can paste a copied URL in the Link field, which is particularly useful for long links. Another option is searching for a specific page by entering keywords in this field. Google displays a list of matches that you can select.

5. Click the Apply button.

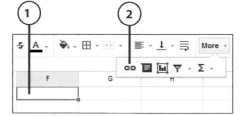

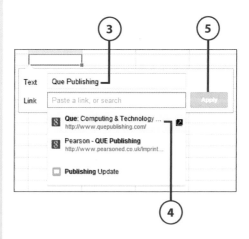

Insert a Note

A note is similar to a comment (see "Add a Comment" later in this chapter), but doesn't include the option for replies.

1. Select the cell where you want to add a note.

2. Click Insert.

3. Click Note.

4. Enter your note text and click in another cell.

5. Pause your mouse pointer over a cell that contains a note to view it.

Delete a Note

To delete a note, right-click its associated cell and click Clear Note from the menu.

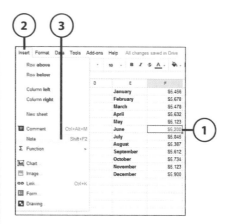

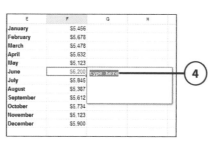

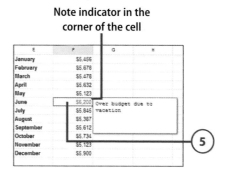

Note indicator in the corner of the cell

Managing Your Spreadsheets

After you create a spreadsheet, Google Sheets makes it easy to open, rename, copy, download, and search it. You can perform any of these tasks from the File menu.

Open a Spreadsheet

In addition to opening a spreadsheet already stored on your Google Drive, you can also open a spreadsheet shared with you, or you can upload and convert a spreadsheet from another application such as Microsoft Excel.

1. Click File.

2. Click Open.

3. Click Upload to upload a file from your computer and open it in Google Sheets.

File Formats That Convert to Google Sheets

You can upload and convert files from the following formats: .xls, .xlsx, .ods, .csv, .tsv, .txt, and .tsb.

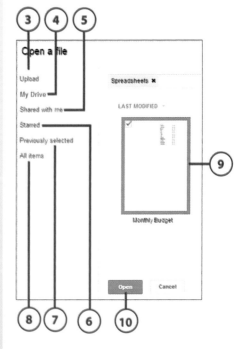

4. Click My Drive to view spreadsheets stored on your Google Drive.

5. Click Shared with Me to view spreadsheets someone else shared with you. See "Collaborating on Spreadsheets" later in this chapter to learn more about sharing spreadsheets.

6. Click Starred to view spreadsheets you starred in Google Drive.

7. Click Previously Selected to view spreadsheets you recently opened.

8. Click All Items to view all available spreadsheets.

9. Select the file you want to open.

10. Click the Open button.

Download a Spreadsheet

You can download a Google Sheets spreadsheet in a different file format.

1. Click File.

2. Click Download As.

3. Select the file format you want to use. Options include

- Microsoft Excel (.xlsx)

- OpenDocument format (.ods)

- PDF document (.pdf)

- Comma-separated values (.csv)

- Tab-separated values (.tsv)

- Web page (.html)

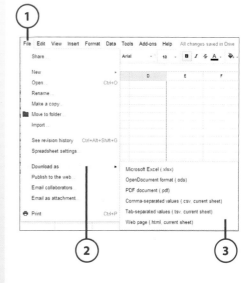

Downloading the Current Sheet Versus the Entire Spreadsheet

Be aware that .csv, .tsv, and .html files download only your current sheet, not your entire spreadsheet if it contains multiple sheets.

Edit a Spreadsheet

You can use the Edit menu to perform common editing tasks such as cutting, copying, and pasting; moving rows and columns; deleting rows, columns, and values as well as finding and replacing text.

Specify View Options

The View menu offers several options for viewing your spreadsheets. For example, you can

- Freeze specified rows and columns. Freezing enables you to view rows or columns that serve as headers even when you scroll through a long sheet.

- View or hide gridlines that separate cells, protected ranges, and the formula bar. By default, these options are all selected.

- View or unhide hidden sheets.

- Use compact spreadsheet controls, which hide the menu and toolbar.

- Display your spreadsheet in full screen.

View
menu

Delete a Spreadsheet

You can delete a spreadsheet in Google Drive by selecting the check box to its left and clicking the Remove icon.

Working with Spreadsheet Data

The Data menu offers several options for managing and organizing your spreadsheet data:

- Sort data by column using a variety of sort criteria

- Name a range of cells, which is useful for advanced formulas

- Protect a sheet or range by specifying who can edit this data

- Filter your data to display only what you want to see

- Create a pivot table report that analyzes complex data

- Set up data validation rules, which help ensure users enter only valid data in cells

Protect cell data

Add a description

Specify the data to protect

Specify who has access

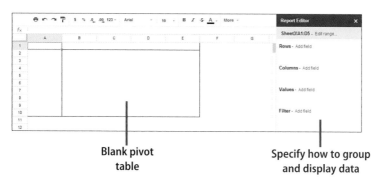

Blank pivot table

Specify how to group and display data

Data Validation
dialog box

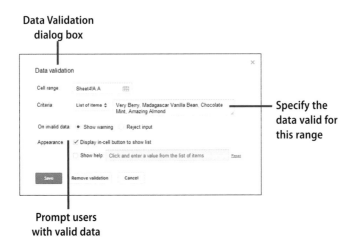

Specify the
data valid for
this range

Prompt users
with valid data

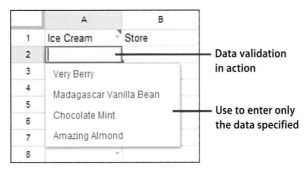

Data validation
in action

Use to enter only
the data specified

Sort Data by Column

By default, Sheets displays your
sheet data in the order you enter it.
At times, however, you may need to
view this data in a particular order.

1. Select a cell in the column on
   which you want to sort.

2. Click Data.

3. Click a sort order: A to Z or Z to A.

Sort by sheet
to keep related
columns together

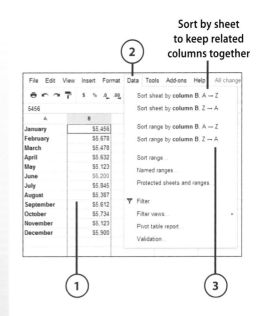

Perform an Advanced Sort

If the basic sort options don't suit your needs, Google Sheets offers advanced sorting options. For example, you can exclude a header row from a sort or sort by multiple criteria.

1. Select a range of data to sort; right-click and select Sort Range.

2. Select the Data Has Header Row check box if you don't want to sort your header row.

3. Select the sort column.

4. Specify the sort order.

5. Optionally, click the Add Another Sort Column link if you want to include additional sort criteria.

6. Click the Sort button.

Apply a Filter

Applying a filter enables you to control the data that displays on your sheets. Filters hide selected data temporarily so you can focus only on the data you need to see.

1. Select a range of data to filter.

2. Click the Filter button.

3. Click the filter arrow in the column you want to filter.

4. Deselect the check mark next to any data you don't want to display.

5. Click the OK button.

Click to select entire sheet

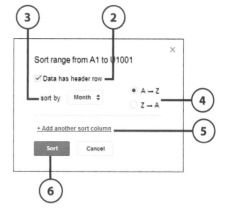

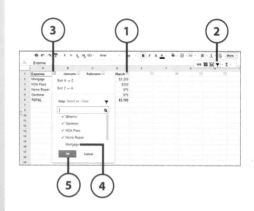

Turn Off a Filter

To turn off a filter, click the Data menu, and click Turn Off Filter.

Save a Filter View

Optionally, you can save a filter view for future use without having to create it again. This is particularly useful if you find yourself creating the same filters again and again. Click the Data menu, click Filter Views, and Save as Filter View to save a filter. You can also create a filter view from scratch. Simply click the Data menu, click Filter Views, and click Create New Filter View.

Collaborating on Spreadsheets

Google Sheets offers several ways for you to collaborate on spreadsheets with colleagues anywhere in the world. For example, you can share spreadsheets, email collaborators, and email spreadsheets as attachments. See Chapter 4, "Storing and Sharing Files on Drive" for more information about these tasks.

You can also add comments to spreadsheets and share them with collaborators.

Add a Comment

Comments enable you to share feedback and commentary on spreadsheets with other people.

1. Select the cell you want to comment on.

2. Click the Insert Comment button.

3. Enter a comment in the text box.

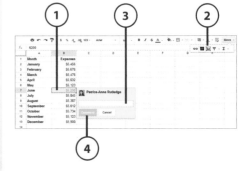

Send Comment Notifications by Email

To send someone an email about your comment, enter the plus sign (+) and their email address, such as +patrice@patricerutledge. com. If this person is in your Gmail address book, Google Sheets displays a match as you type. If you haven't given this person permission to comment, you're prompted to do so.

4. Click the Comment button.

5. Google Sheets displays your comment, name, date, and time.

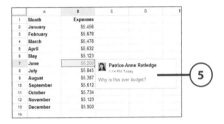

Work with Comments

You can click a comment to view it in more detail. From here, you can edit, delete, or reply to it. Click the Resolve button to close the comment and hide it from the discussion.

Optionally, you can review comments in one box by clicking the Comments button in the upper-right corner of the page.

Edit   Delete   Resolve

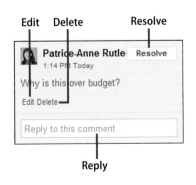

Reply

View and manage comments in one place

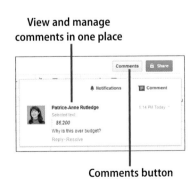

Comments button

Printing and Publishing Spreadsheets

After creating a spreadsheet, you may want to print it or publish it to share with others.

Print a Spreadsheet

Google Sheets provides several options for customizing a printed spreadsheet. For example, you can include row headers, a document title, sheet names, and page numbers or omit gridlines.

1. Click the Print button.

2. Specify what you want to print: the current sheet, all sheets, or data you've selected.

3. Specify the options you prefer.

4. Select a paper size.

5. Specify whether you want to fit your content to the width of the paper or print the actual size.

6. Select a page orientation: Portrait or Landscape.

7. Click the Print button.

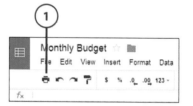

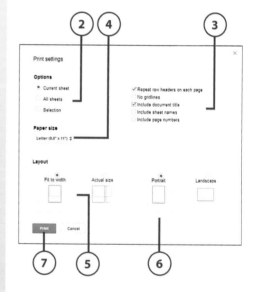

Publish a Spreadsheet to the Web

Another way to share a spreadsheet with others is to publish it to the Web. This option publishes a copy of your original spreadsheet online.

1. Click File.

2. Click Publish to the Web.

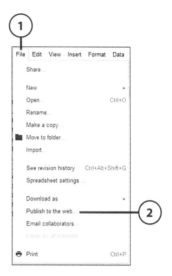

Prevent Automatic Republication

By default, Google Sheets automatically republishes your spreadsheet when you make changes. If you don't want to do this, deselect the Automatically Republish When Changes Are Made check box.

3. Click the Start Publishing button.

4. Click the OK button to confirm you want to publish this spreadsheet.

Stop Publishing to the Web

If you decide you no longer want to publish a spreadsheet to the Web, click the File menu, click Publish to the Web and click the Stop Publishing button to reverse this action.

Automatically Republish When Changes Are Made check box

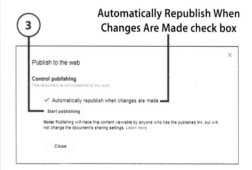

5. Send the spreadsheet link to anyone you want to share with.

6. Paste the embed code on an external website.

7. Share the link by clicking one of the following links: Google+, Gmail, Facebook, or Twitter.

8. Click the Close button to exit.

It's Not All Good

Understanding Web Publishing Pitfalls

Remember that anyone who has your spreadsheet URL can view it online, even if you don't provide it to this person directly. If you have privacy concerns, think carefully before publishing a spreadsheet to the Web and consider other options such as sharing with colleagues on Google Drive.

>>>*Go Further*

EXPLORING GOOGLE SHEETS ADD-ONS

Google Sheets offers a collection of add-ons that you can install to enhance, improve, and streamline your spreadsheet activity. Options include add-ons that enable you to install additional fonts and styles, automate spreadsheet workflow, analyze Google Analytics data, generate schedules, merge values, enhance find and replace functionality, and much more. Click the Add-ons menu and click Get Add-ons to open the Add-ons dialog box, which displays all available add-ons.

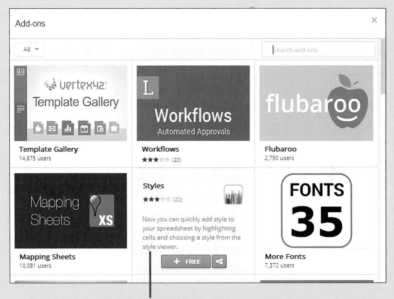

Pause over an add-on
to view details

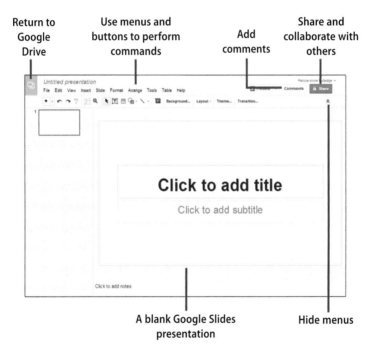

Return to Google Drive

Use menus and buttons to perform commands

Add comments

Share and collaborate with others

A blank Google Slides presentation

Hide menus

In this chapter, you discover how to create, format, enhance, print, deliver, and collaborate on presentations using Google Slides:

→ Creating a presentation
→ Applying slide layouts, backgrounds, and themes
→ Inserting tables and other content
→ Inserting text, images, links, videos, shapes, and tables
→ Formatting presentations
→ Managing presentations
→ Working with transitions and animation
→ Collaborating on presentations
→ Printing, publishing, and delivering presentations

Creating Presentations with Slides

Google Slides enables you to design a series of slides—enhanced with text, images, media, and transitions—that form a presentation you can deliver in person or on the Web. Google Slides includes easy-to-use tools and color-coordinated themes that simplify creating an attractive, well-designed presentation.

Getting Started with Google Slides

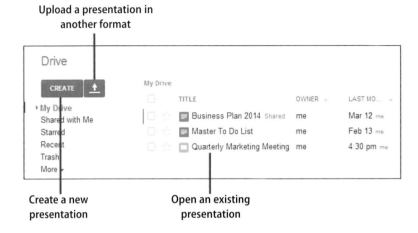

Upload a presentation in another format

Create a new presentation

Open an existing presentation

To get started with Google Slides, log into your Google account and navigate to Google Drive at https://drive.google.com.

From here, you can

- Click the Create button and click Presentation to create a new presentation.

- Click the Upload button and click Files to select a presentation from another format (such as Microsoft PowerPoint) you want to convert to Google Slides.

- Click the title of an existing presentation to open it.

Later sections in this chapter cover creating and opening presentations in more detail.

Creating a Presentation

You can create a blank presentation from Google Drive or from within Google Slides itself. You can also create a presentation using a template.

Create a Presentation from Google Drive

1. While logged into your Google account, access Google Drive at https://drive.google.com.

2. Click the Create button.

3. Click Presentation to open the Choose a Theme dialog box.

4. Select a theme.

5. Click the OK button.

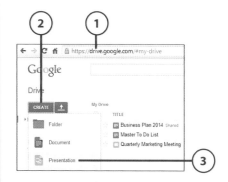

What's a Theme?

A theme is a standalone file with coordinated fonts, colors, and design effects that apply to a single presentation. If you've used another presentation application, such as Microsoft PowerPoint, you should already be familiar with this term. By default, Google Slides opens the Choose a Theme dialog box when you create a new presentation and selects the default theme, Simple Light. Optionally, you can choose another theme or import your own theme.

Import a theme

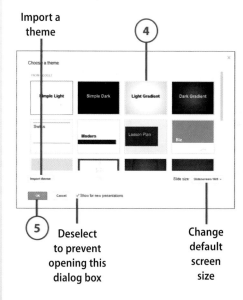

Deselect to prevent opening this dialog box

Change default screen size

6. Click the presentation title. By default Google names all new presentations "Untitled Presentation."

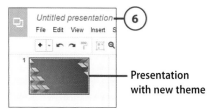

Presentation with new theme

7. Enter a new presentation name.

8. Click the OK button.

9. Click in a placeholder to add text.

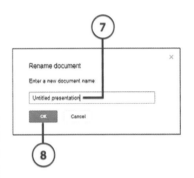

Where Is the Save Button?

If you're used to using Microsoft PowerPoint or another presentation application, you may wonder where the Save button is. Google Slides continuously saves your presentation, so there is no Save button.

New presentation name — **Google automatically saves changes in Drive**

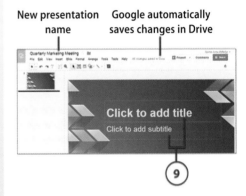

Create a Presentation from Google Slides

If you're already using Google Slides, you can easily create another presentation. Simply click the File menu, click New, and click Presentation. The process is identical to creating a new presentation from Google Drive.

Create a Presentation from a Template

The Template Gallery enables you to create presentations from pre-existing templates. You can find sample templates for resumes, cover letters, invoices, recipes, proposals, press releases, meeting agendas, newsletters, and more.

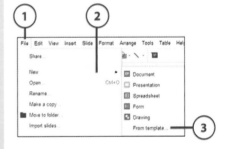

1. Click File.

2. Click New.

3. Click From Template.

4. Optionally, click the Preview link if you want to view a template before creating a new presentation with it.

5. Click the Use This Template button next to the template you want to open.

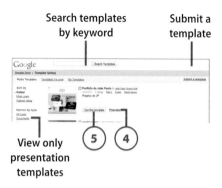

Search templates by keyword

Submit a template

View only presentation templates

Create a Presentation from Google Slides

If you're already using Google Slides, you can easily create another presentation. Simply click the File menu, click New, and click Presentation. The process is identical to creating a new presentation from Google Drive.

Working with Slides

Slides form the basis of all presentations. In this section, you learn how to use slide layouts and backgrounds to enhance your slides, add new slides, and apply new themes.

Apply a Slide Layout

A slide layout helps you add specific types of content to your slides. Slide layouts include placeholders for titles, body text, captions, and columns.

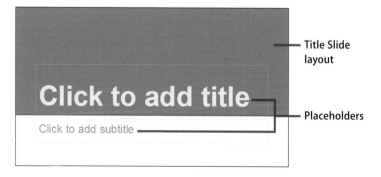

Title Slide layout

Placeholders

- **Title Slide**—Includes placeholders for a title and subtitle

- **Title and Body**—Includes placeholders for a title and body text

- **Title and Two Columns**—Includes placeholders for a title and two columns of body text

- **Title Only**—Includes a single placeholder for a title (useful if you want to add an image, table, or other shape to your slide)

- **Caption**—Includes a single placeholder for a caption at the bottom of the slide (useful for an image)

- **Blank**—Includes a slide with no content

By default, Slides applies the Title Slide layout to the first slide in your presentation and the Title and Body Layout to any subsequent slides you add.

To change the layout of a selected slide, click the Layout button and select layout you want to use.

Layout
button

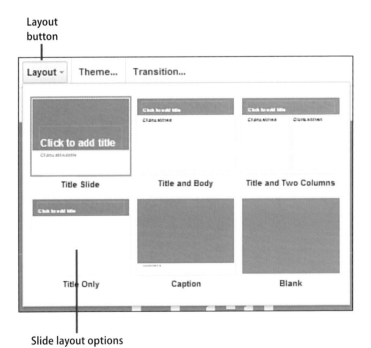

Slide layout options

Apply a Slide Background

Although many themes include color backgrounds, you may want to select your own. You can also use an image as a slide background.

1. Click the Background button.

2. Click the Color button.

3. Select a color from the color palette.

4. Click the Apply to All button if you want to apply this background to all slides in your presentation.

5. Click the Done button.

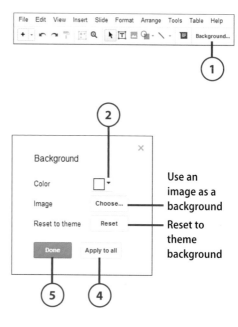

Use an Image as a Slide Background

Another option is to use an image as your slide background. For example, you may want to upload an image that contains a company logo or product. You can upload an image from your computer, Google Drive, or the Web. See "Insert an Image" later in this chapter for more information about working with images in Google Slides.

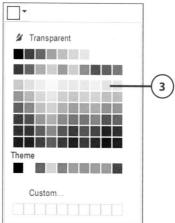

Apply a New Theme

Theme button

If you decide you don't like the theme you applied when you created your presentation, you can apply a new one by clicking the Theme button. See "Create a Presentation from Google Drive" earlier in this chapter for more information about themes.

Add a Slide to Your Presentation

New Slide Click to specify
button   layout

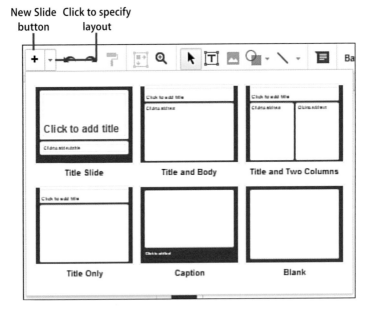

To add a slide to your presentation, click the New Slide button. Google Slides adds a new slide using the same layout as the previous slide. To specify a layout for a new slide, click the down arrow to the right of the New Slide button and select layout you want to use.

Import Slides from Another Presentation

If you want to reuse some slides from another presentation, you can import them. You can import from another Google presentation or from a Microsoft PowerPoint presentation in the .ppt or .pptx format.

1. Click Insert.

2. Click Import Slides.

3. Select a presentation in Google Drive.

4. Click the Select button.

5. Select the slides you want to import.

6. Click the Import Slides button.

Optionally, upload slides from your computer

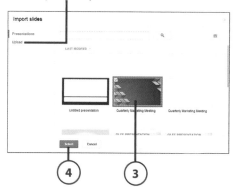

Click All Items to select all slides

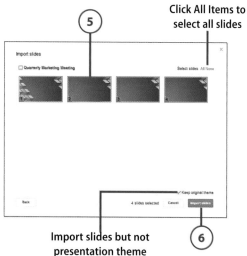

Import slides but not presentation theme

Organize Slides

To organize the slides in your presentation, you can drag and drop them on the left side of the page. You can also use the command on the Slide menu to move slides or their corresponding keyboard shortcuts.

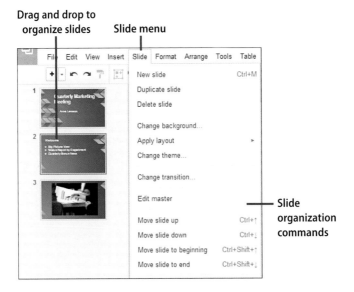

Duplicate Slides

To duplicate one or more slides, select the slides you want to duplicate and press Ctrl+D. This is particularly useful if you have only small changes to make.

Delete Slides

To delete one or more slides, select them and press the Del key.

Inserting Content in a Presentation

Entering basic text in your slide placeholders is just the beginning. An effective presentation requires much more than slides with text and bullet lists. Fortunately, Google Slides enables you to enhance your presentation with additional content, including the following:

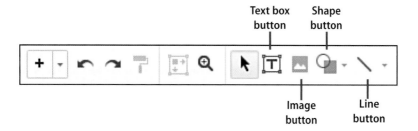

- Text boxes

- Placeholders (available only when you're editing the slide master)

- Images from your computer, Google Drive, or webcam

- Links to external sites

- Videos, including YouTube videos

- WordArt, which you can format using options on the toolbar

- Line and shapes such as circles

- Tables to organize content

- Animations to transition slides during a presentation

- Comments, which are useful for collaborating on presentations

You can access any of these options from the Insert menu. The toolbar also includes buttons for several of the most common types of content you may want to insert, such as text boxes, images, shapes, and lines.

Insert a Text Box

A text box is useful when you want to insert text outside of an existing placeholder.

1. Click the Text Box button.

2. Drag your cursor to create a box.

3. Type text in the box.

Insert an Image

You can insert images less than 5MB in size from a variety of sources including your computer, Google Drive, your Google albums, and more. Google Slides supports the following file formats: .gif (excluding animated gifs), .jpg, and .png.

Drag-and-Drop Method

One easy way to insert an image is to drag it from your desktop and drop it on your slide.

1. Click the Image button.

2. Click Upload to upload an image from your computer.

3. Click Take a Snapshot to take a picture with your webcam.

Google May Request Webcam Permission

Google Slides may prompt you for access to your web camera and microphone. If so, click the Allow option and click the Close button.

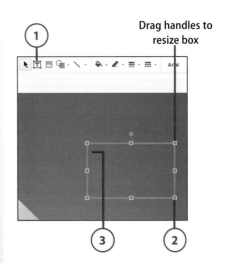

Drag handles to resize box

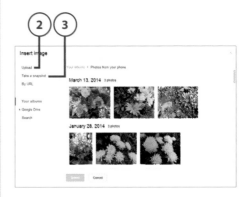

4. Click By URL to enter the URL of an image already posted on the Web.

5. Click Your Albums to insert an image from your Google album.

6. Click Google Drive to insert an image you uploaded to your drive.

7. Click Search to use Google Search to find an image on the Web or find a suitable stock image.

8. Click the Select button to insert your specified image.

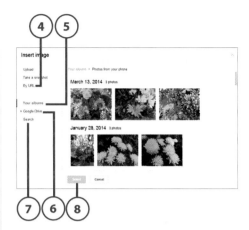

Insert a Link

You can insert a link to another slide in your presentation or to an external website. If you create a text-based link, Google Slides underlines your link to alert readers that they can click it to go to the link destination. You can also add links to shapes.

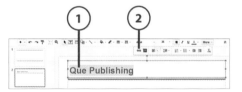

1. Select the text or shape to which you want to add a link.

2. Click the Insert Link button.

3. To insert a link to another slide, click Slides in This Presentation and select your slide.

4. To insert a link to an external website, start typing the URL of the link you want to insert. As you type, Google Slides displays potential matches.

5. Click the Apply button.

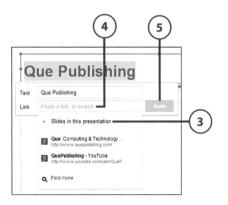

Copy and Paste a URL

Optionally, you can paste a copied URL in the Link field, which is particularly useful for long links. Another option is searching for a specific page by entering keywords in this field. Google displays a list of matches that you can select.

Insert a Video

Inserting online videos from YouTube offers a simple way to add multimedia to your presentations.

1. Click Insert.

2. Click Video.

3. To search for a video, enter the video topic or channel and click the Search button.

4. To enter the URL of a specific YouTube video, click the URL tab and enter the URL.

5. Select the video you want to insert.

6. Click the Select button.

7. The video displays on your slide.

Why Won't My Video Play?

You can play your video when you deliver your presentation. To verify that it plays properly, you should test it by clicking the Present button. See "Delivering Your Presentation" later in this chapter for more information.

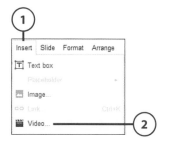

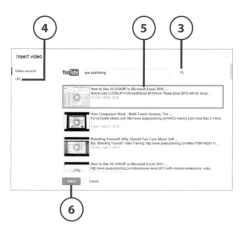

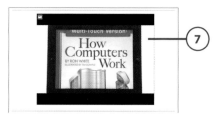

Insert a Line

You can add straight lines, arrows, curves, polylines, arcs, and scribbles. Using the toolbar buttons, you can format your line's color, weight, dash style, and arrowhead start and end.

1. Click the Line button down arrow.

2. Select a line type: Line, Arrow, Curve, Polyline, Arc, or Scribble.

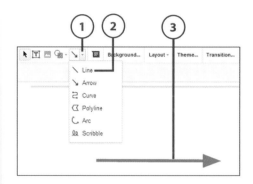

Default Line Options

Clicking the Line button directly creates a line in the format of the most recently created line. The button also changes based on the line type. The default style is Line.

3. Draw your line on your slide.

Insert a Shape

You can add visual appeal to your presentations with lines, scribbles, circles, squares, rectangles, text boxes, and many other shapes. You can use the toolbar buttons to format your shape, such as applying a fill color.

1. Click the Shape button.

2. Select a shape type: Shape, Arrows, Callouts, or Equations.

3. Select the shape type from the gallery.

4. Drag your cursor to create the shape.

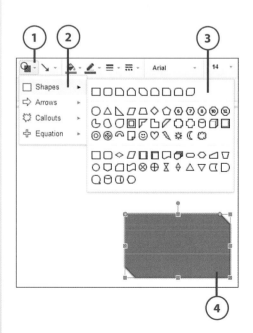

It's Not All Good

Arranging Objects

If your presentation includes multiple objects, you may need to order, group, align, or rotate them to achieve your desired effect. In Google Slides, an object refers to a text box, shape, image, line, and so forth. Using the tools available from the Arrange menu, you can maintain complete control over the position and appearance of your presentation objects.

Insert a Table

A table enables you to organize and display presentation content in columns and rows. You can edit and format table data just like any other text in your presentation.

1. Click Table.

2. Click Insert Table.

3. Select the number of columns and rows you want to include.

4. The table displays in your presentation.

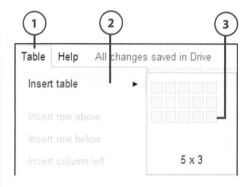

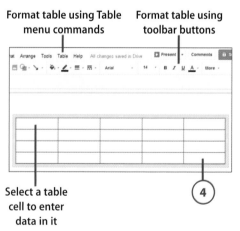

>>>*Go Further*

USING TABLE EDITING AND FORMATTING OPTIONS

The Table menu offers numerous options for editing and formatting a table.

Table Formatting Shortcuts

You can also right-click in your table and select these options from a shortcut menu.

You can

- Insert rows above or below a selected row

- Insert columns to the right or left of a selected column

- Delete and distribute rows and columns

- Merge or unmerge cells

You can also format tables by using the toolbar buttons such as Line Color and Fill Color.

Formatting Presentations

You can format your presentation slides in two ways:

- Using the buttons on the toolbar.

- Using the options available on the menu.

Although the Google Slides menu remains the same, the toolbar buttons change depending on your current action. For example, when you first create a presentation, the basic toolbar buttons appear.

If you select a placeholder, text, shape, table, or other object, the toolbar displays additional formatting options.

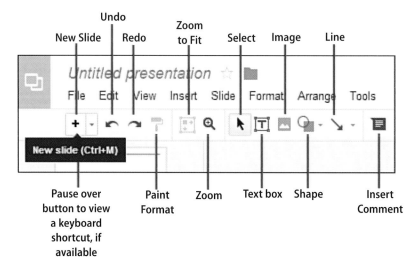

Undo
New Slide │ Redo │ Zoom to Fit │ Select │ Image │ Line

Pause over button to view a keyboard shortcut, if available │ Paint Format │ Zoom │ Text box │ Shape │ Insert Comment

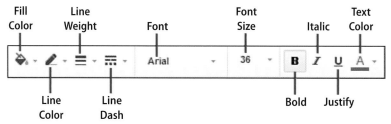

Fill Color │ Line Weight │ Font │ Font Size │ Italic │ Text Color

Line Color │ Line Dash │ Bold │ Justify

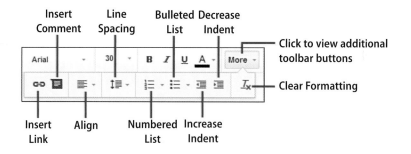

Insert Comment │ Line Spacing │ Bulleted List │ Decrease Indent │ Click to view additional toolbar buttons

Clear Formatting

Insert Link │ Align │ Numbered List │ Increase Indent

Missing Toolbar Buttons

Depending on the resolution of your screen, not all toolbar buttons may fit on the toolbar. In this case, the More button displays, which you can click to view the remaining buttons. To hide this extra toolbar, click the More button again. If your screen has room for all buttons, the More button isn't available.

Google Slides Keyboard Shortcuts

If you don't want to use menus and buttons to perform commands, keyboard shortcuts are another option. To view a complete list of shortcuts, press Ctrl + /.

Apply a New Font and Font Size

Although Google Slides includes themes with built-in fonts and font sizes, you can customize these if you prefer.

1. Select the text you want to format.

2. Click the Font button.

3. Select a font name.

4. Select a font size if you want to change the default size.

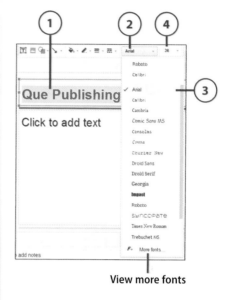

View more fonts

>>>Go Further

VIEWING MORE FONT OPTIONS

If you don't see the font you want on the menu, select More Fonts. In the Fonts dialog box, you can view a larger selection of fonts, search for fonts by name, display fonts by type (such as serif, sans serif, handwriting, and so forth), as well as sort fonts by popularity or in alphabetical order.

Create a Numbered List

Google Slides offers several styles of numbered lists you can apply to a text series such as an ordered list with sequential numbers or letters.

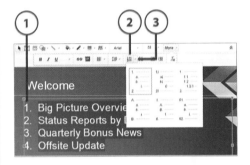

1. Select the text you want to format.

2. Click the Numbered List button to apply the default numbered list style.

3. Optionally, click the down arrow to select another numbered list style.

Create a Bulleted List

Another option is to create a bullet list. For example, you can create a list with bullets, circles, squares, or arrows.

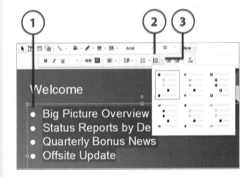

1. Select the text you want to format.

2. Click the Bulleted List button to apply the default bulleted list style.

3. Optionally, click the down arrow to select another bulleted list style.

>>>Go Further

USING MORE OPTIONS FOR NUMBERED AND BULLETED LISTS

If the list styles on the toolbar don't suit your needs, you can further customize your lists by clicking Lists Options from the Format menu.

From here, you can

- Select a list style from the options.

- Restart list numbering at a number you specify. This option is only available for numbered lists.

- View more symbol options for your list. This option opens the Insert Special Characters dialog box, which enables you to use a special character as a bullet point.

- Edit the prefix and suffix for your list. For example, you can replace the standard period suffix for a numbered list with a colon. This option is only available for numbered lists.

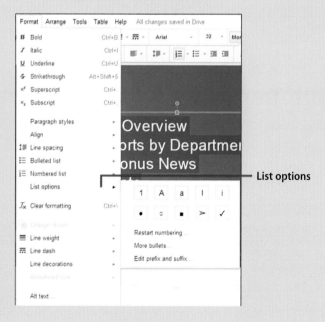

List options

Use the Paint Format Tool

The Paint Format tool helps you save time by applying formatting to text, shapes, or lines with a single click.

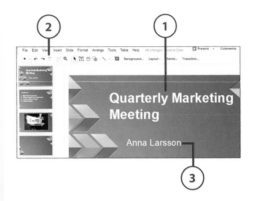

1. Select the text, shape, or line with the formatting you want to copy.

2. Click the Paint Format button.

3. Select the content you want to format.

Apply Formatting to Multiple Text Selections

If you want to apply formatting to multiple selections, double-click the Paint Format button instead of single-clicking it. This enables you to apply the format you copied more than once. When you finish, click the Paint Format button again to stop formatting.

Working with Transitions and Animations

Google Slides enables you to set transitions between slides as well as animate objects such as text, shapes, and more.

It's Not All Good

Understanding Transition and Animation Pitfalls

Although adding transition and animations can enliven your presentation, be careful not to overdo it. For the most professional results, select one transition effect to use for your entire presentation and use animation sparingly for emphasis. Be sure to test your effects before presenting to ensure that they enhance your presentation and don't detract from it.

Set Slide Transitions

You can apply a transition to a single slide or to the entire presentation. Transitions determine how to change from one slide to the next in your presentation. By default, when you move from one slide to another, the next slide appears immediately. When you use transitions, however, you can make the old slide fade away to reveal the new slide or make the new slide move from the right or left of the page to cover the old slide, for example.

1. Select the slide to which you want to apply a transition (or the first slide if you want to apply to the entire presentation).

2. Click the Transition button.

3. Select a transition effect.

4. Select a transition speed: Slow, Medium, or Fast.

5. Optionally, click the Apply to All Slides button if you want to apply this transition to all slides.

6. Click the Play button to preview your transition effects.

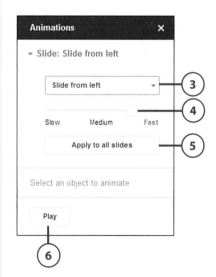

Animate Slide Objects

With animation, the motion applies to one or more slide objects, not the slide itself. You can apply animation to text boxes, images, shapes, and lines. For example, you can use animation to make text fly in or make a shape spin.

1. Select the object you want to animate.

2. Click Insert.

3. Click Animation.

4. Select an animation effect such as fade, fly, zoom, or spin.

5. Select an animation trigger: On Click, After Previous, or With Previous.

6. Select an animation speed: Slow, Medium, or Fast.

7. Click the Play button to preview your animation effects.

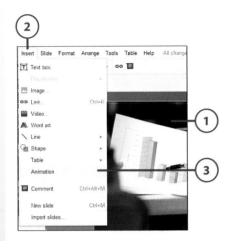

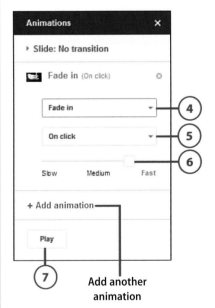

Add another animation

Managing Your Presentations

After you create a presentation, Google Slides makes it easy to open, rename, copy, download, and search it. You can perform any of these tasks from the File menu.

Open a Presentation

In addition to opening a presentation already stored on your Google Drive, you can also open a presentation shared with you or upload and convert a presentation from another application such as Microsoft PowerPoint.

1. Click File.

2. Click Open.

3. Click Upload to upload a file from your computer and open it in Google Slides.

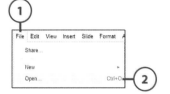

File Formats That Convert to Google Slides

You can upload and convert files from the following formats: .ppt, .pptx, and .pps.

4. Click My Drive to view presentations stored on your Google Drive.

5. Click Shared with Me to view presentations shared with you. See "Collaborating on Presentations" later in this chapter to learn more about sharing presentations.

6. Click Starred to view presentations you starred in Google Drive.

7. Click Previously Selected to view presentations you recently opened.

8. Click All Items to view all available presentations.

9. Select the file you want to open.

10. Click the Open button.

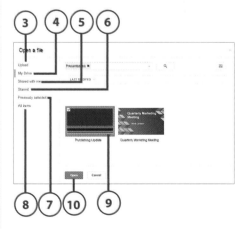

Download a Presentation

You can download a Google Slides presentation in any of the following formats:

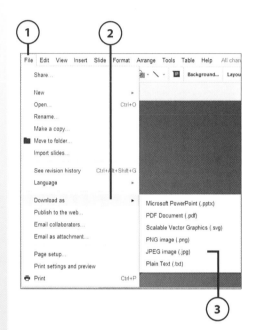

- Microsoft PowerPoint (.pptx)

- PDF Presentation (.pdf)

- Scalable Vector Graphics (.svg)

- PNG Image (.png)

- PEG Image (.jpg)

- Plain Text (.txt)

1. Click File.

2. Click Download As.

3. Select the file format you want to use.

Delete a Presentation

You can delete a presentation in Google Drive by selecting the check box to its left and clicking the Remove icon.

Editing Presentations

You can use the Edit menu to perform common editing tasks such as cutting, copying, and pasting; finding and replacing text; and selecting and deselecting objects.

**Edit
menu**

Specify View Options

**View
menu**

The View menu offers several options for viewing your presentations. For example, you can

- Display slide masters to view and customize.

- Change the slide view percentage on your screen. Fit is the default, but you can change this to 50%, 100%, or 200%.

- Show or hide spelling suggestions and speaker's notes.

- Use compact presentation controls, which hide the menu and toolbar.

- Display your presentation in full screen.

>>>Go Further

WORKING WITH SLIDE MASTERS

Slide masters help you achieve design consistency by storing data about a presentation's theme and slide layouts—such as colors, fonts, effects, background, placeholders, and positioning—and applying it consistently throughout your presentation. Each presentation contains at least one slide master.

In most cases, you won't need to do anything to the slide master but you can customize it if you choose and have a good knowledge of presentation design. For example, you can change the default fonts, placeholders, background design, color scheme, or bullets; reposition placeholders; and add a logo. You can also create additional slide masters.

Edit master   Close master

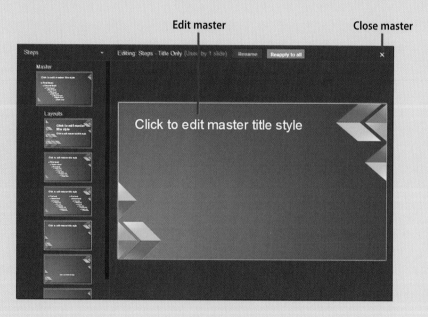

Collaborating on Presentations

Google Slides offers several ways for you to collaborate on presentations with colleagues anywhere in the world. For example, you can share presentations, email collaborators, and email presentations as attachments. See Chapter 4, "Storing and Sharing Files on Drive" for more information about these tasks.

You can also add comments to presentations and share them with collaborators.

The File menu offers options for collaborating

Specify sharing options

Add a Comment

Comments enable you to share feedback and commentary on presentations with other people.

1. Select the text or object you want to comment on.

2. Click the Insert Comment button.

3. Enter a comment in the text box.

Send Comment Notifications by Email

To send someone an email about your comment, enter the plus sign (+) and their email address, such as +patrice@patricerutledge. com. If this person is in your Gmail address book, Google Slides displays a match as you type. If you haven't given this person permission to comment, you're prompted to do so.

---

4. Click the Comment button.

5. Google Slides displays your comment, name, date, and time.

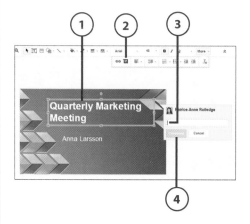

Work with Comments

You can click a comment to view it in more detail. From here, you can edit, delete, or reply to it. Click the Resolve button to close the comment and hide it from the discussion.

Optionally, you can review comments in one box by clicking the Comments button in the upper-right corner of the page.

Using Google Slides Tools

The Tools menu includes several tools that help you enhance your presentations. These include

- A spell checker. See "Perform a Spell Check" later in this section.

- The Research pane, which enables you to search the Web for information related to your presentation's content.

- A dictionary where you can search for definitions or synonyms.

- The Preferences dialog box, which enables you to specify automatic substitutions such as (c) for the copyright symbol.

Perform a Spell Check

1. Click Tools.

2. Click Spelling.

3. Click the Change button to change to the suggested spelling.

4. Click the Ignore button to ignore the suggested spelling.

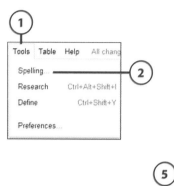

Spell Check Options

Click the Change button down arrow and click Change All to change all instances of this word to the suggested spelling. Click the Ignore button down arrow and click Ignore All to ignore all instances of this word or click Add to Dictionary to add the suspected misspelling to the dictionary.

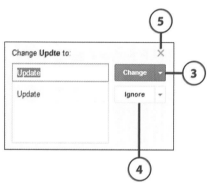

5. Click the Close button (x) to exit.

Show and Hide Spelling Suggestions

By default, Google Slides highlights suspected spelling errors with a red dotted underline. You can right-click this word to view suggested revisions. If you don't want to highlight suspected errors, click the View menu and click Show Spelling Suggestions to remove the check mark next to it.

Suspected spelling error   Right-click to view options on the menu

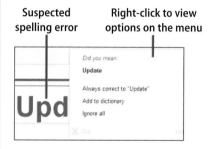

Printing and Publishing Presentations

After creating a presentation, you may want to print it or publish it to share with others.

Specify Print Settings and Preview Your Presentation

Before printing, you should specify the page setup parameters you want to use.

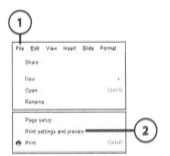

1. Click File.

2. Click Print Settings and Preview.

3. Specify a handout style: 1 Slide With Notes, 1 Slide Without Notes, or a handout with options for 1, 2, 3, 4, 6, or 9 slides per page.

4. Specify a page orientation: Portrait or Landscape.

5. Click the Print button.

6. Click the Change button to select another printer if you don't want to print to the default printer.

7. Specify whether you want to print all pages, specific pages, or a range of pages.

8. Specify the number of copies you want to print.

9. Click the Print button.

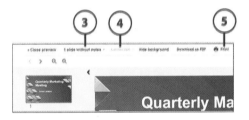

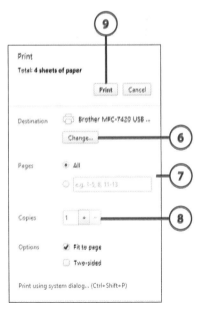

Print Without Previewing

To print your presentation with the default settings, press Ctrl+P.

Publish a Presentation to the Web

Another way to share a presentation with others is to publish it to the Web. This option publishes a copy of your original presentation online.

1. Click File.

2. Click Publish to the Web.

Prevent Automatic Republication

By default, Google Slides automatically republishes your presentation when you make changes. If you don't want to do this, deselect the Automatically Republish When Changes Are Made check box.

3. Click the Start Publishing button.

4. Click the OK button to confirm you want to publish this presentation.

5. Send the presentation link to anyone you want to share with.

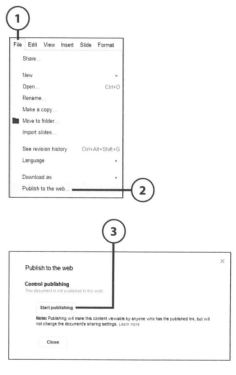

6. Paste the embed code on an external website.

7. Share the link by clicking one of the following links: Google+, Gmail, Facebook, or Twitter.

8. Specify a presentation size: Small, Medium, Large, or Custom.

9. Specify when to advance to the next slide (three seconds is the default).

10. Click the Close button.

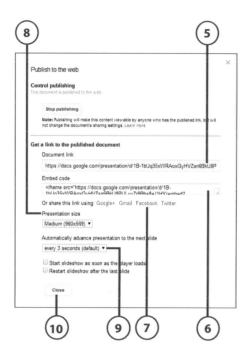

Stop Publishing to the Web

If you decide you no longer want to publish a presentation to the Web, click the File menu, click Publish to the Web and click the Stop Publishing button to reverse this action.

It's Not All Good

Understanding Web Publishing Pitfalls

Remember that anyone who has your presentation URL can view it online, even if you don't provide it to this person directly. Think carefully before publishing a presentation to the Web and consider other options such as sharing with colleagues on Google Drive if you have privacy concerns.

Delivering Your Presentation

After you create, polish, and review you presentation, it's time to deliver it.

Create Speaker Notes

Speaker notes are a useful tool for many presenters. You can add speaker notes at the bottom of any slide. These notes are for your reference and don't display on your actual slides.

Add speaker
notes

If you don't see this section at the bottom of your slides, click the View menu and click Show Speaker Notes.

Deliver Your Presentation

To deliver your presentation using default settings, click the Present button. Optionally, you can click the Present button down arrow to choose one of the following options: Present from Beginning, Present with Speaker Notes, or Present in New Window.

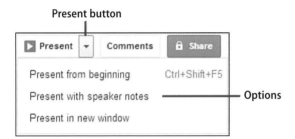

Google opens your presentation in full screen. You can navigate your presentation using the keyboard, mouse, or toolbar buttons (move your cursor if this is hidden).

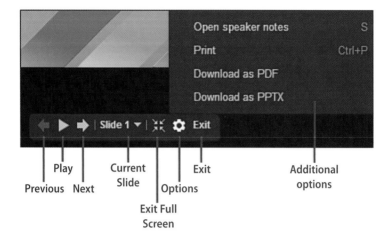

Play

Previous   Next

Current
Slide

Options

Exit Full
Screen

Exit

Additional
options

Presentation Options

For more choices, click the Options button on the toolbar. This opens a menu enabling you to open speaker notes, print, download as a PDF, or download as a PPTX (PowerPoint format).

Add Google Hangouts for
video conferencing

In this chapter, you learn how make use of Google's Hangouts app to communicate in real time via chat, video conferencing, and phone calls:

→ Exploring what you can do with the Hangouts app and what you need to get started

→ Learning how to enable or install the Hangouts app for your scenario

→ Discovering instant messaging via the Hangouts chat window

→ Finding out how to connect with others online using video calls

→ Seeing how easy it is to make a phone call from your computer

Communicating with Hangouts

The Google Hangouts app is a unified messaging service that brings you and the people you connect with together at the same time. You can use the app to hold video conference calls, voice calls, and instant-message friends, family, coworkers, clients, and the rest of the world. The Hangouts app is available for every type of platform and device—computers (PC and Mac), tablets, smartphones. Time to find out what it is and how you can use it!

Exploring Hangouts

Google Hangouts allows you to communicate via messaging or video conferencing, or even make voice calls. Similar to apps like Skype and FaceTime, Hangouts offers both one-on-one interaction as well as group interaction regardless of where in the world you are located—as long as you have an Internet connection, of course. Hangouts is built into Google+ (Google's social layer) and Gmail (users must enable it in Gmail to use it). Hangouts replaces previous chat capabilities both services offered, as well as the stand-alone Google Talk app. You can also install Hangouts as a browser plug-in or an app on your tablet or mobile device, as well as a desktop app on your computer.

You can use Hangouts for a variety of functions:

- Webinars
- Staff meetings
- Interviews
- Presentations and product demos
- Customer service support
- Lectures
- Business meetings
- Family get-togethers

Enable It, First!

Attention, Google Apps for Business/Education/Government administrators: if you want everyone in your organization to use Hangouts, you need to enable Google+ premium features for them. . You can set some parameters for how they use the app, including whether they can create live feeds, invite people outside of your domain, or restrict messaging. Visit the Other Google Services page via your Admin console to locate Google+ premium features.

Google Hangouts app

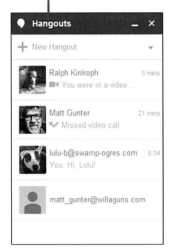

When you start the Hangouts app, it looks a lot like a pop-up box, which is usually in the lower-right corner of your screen. It lists people you can communicate with, and it's ready to start a new session whenever you are.

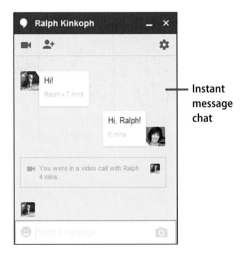

Instant message chat

A text-based chat, or instant messaging, happens in a separate Hangouts window, whether you chat one-on-one or with a group. The Hangouts windows can be minimized to move them out of the way, undocked and dragged around the screen, or closed entirely when you finish using them.

— Video chat

A video chat opens in a larger window, showing all the participants and, if applicable, tools you can access during the session.

Get Started with Hangouts

Before you use Hangouts, make sure you know what you need to get started and you're up-to-date with the necessary system requirements.

- You need a web camera and a microphone in order to utilize the video conferencing part of the app. If you don't have either of these items, you can always just chat the text-based way.

- Computer users can download Hangouts as a desktop app and instantly chat without having to open your browser. (You need at least a 2GHz dual core processor or greater.)

- Browser users can install a plug-in for Hangouts. (You'll need the latest browser versions of each in order to use app.)

- Smartphone users need a Google+ account and the Hangouts for Android app. iOS (iPad or iPhone) users can download the app as well.

It's Not All Good

It Doesn't Always Work!

Although Hangouts is supposed to work with every browser, most Android and iOS devices, and computer platforms, it doesn't always work like it's supposed to. You may run into trouble trying to install the app. If you do, visit the Google site for help. You may find some other routes for downloading and installing the app for your situation.

For example, when I tried to download the app from the official Hangouts page on Google, it didn't want to install on my Internet Explorer browser (version 11). I found a workaround on another Google download page.

You might also consider using to a Google+ account or asking your administrator to enable Google premium services because Hangouts is an standard feature offered with Google+.

Adding the Hangouts App

You won't find the Hangouts app listed with the rest of your Google Apps for Business icons. Instead, you need to download it, enable it, or install it, depending on your situation. Once you get the app, you can start it with the Hangouts icon, which appears in different places based on your computer or device. Here are a few routes you can use to add Hangouts:

- If you're already a Google+ user, Hangouts is already available; look for it on the right side of the page.

- If you use Gmail, you can add Hangouts from your Gmail page.

- If you use a mobile device or computer, you can add Hangouts from Google's Hangout web page (www.google.com/hangouts.

- If you run into any problems adding the plug-in to your browser, you can try downloading the plug-in from another Google page.

When you're ready to use Hangouts, you can look for the app's icon. A click on the icon starts the app.

If you installed the desktop app on your computer, look for the Hangouts icon on the taskbar, for example.

Hangouts
icon on
Windows

If you installed a browser app, look for the Hangouts icon in your browser shortcuts or tools.

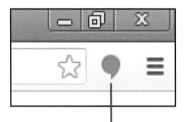

Hangouts icon in your browser

If you enabled Hangouts in Gmail, look for the Hangouts icon at the bottom of the left pane.

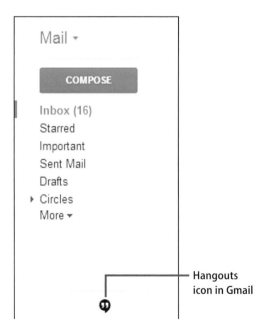

Hangouts
icon in Gmail

Install the Hangouts App as a Plug-in

If the Hangouts app isn't already installed as a plug-in for your browser, smartphone, or tablet, it's easy to add it. Your steps may vary slightly depending on what device you're installing to.

1. In your browser's address box, type www.google.com/hangouts and press Enter/Return.

2. Click the Get Hangouts button.

3. Click your device of choice.

4. Click the Add button to complete the install.

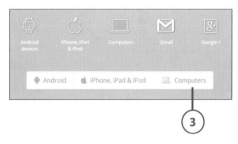

Install the Desktop Hangouts App

You can choose to add Hangouts to your computer's desktop so you can access it with a click.

1. In your browser's address box, type www.google.com/tools/dlpage/hangoutplugin and press Enter/Return.

2. Click the Download Plugin button to download the plug-in.

3. Click the plug-in to install it.

4. Click the Run button to install the file.

5. Click the Close button to exit.

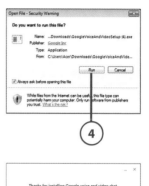

Enable the Hangouts App in Gmail

Another way to get the Hangouts app is through your Gmail page. Gmail displays an invite to try the new Hangouts app in the left pane in the Chat list.

1. Click your profile photo at the top of the Chat list on the Gmail page.

2. Click Try the New Hangouts to add it to Gmail

3. In the overview wizard, click the Next button to continue, and click the Next button to continue. Click the Okay, Got It button to enable the app.

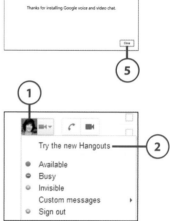

Enable Google+ Premium Features

If you're the domain administrator, you can enable all the Google+ features for your organization, which includes allowing access to the Hangouts app. This lets other users on your team use the app.

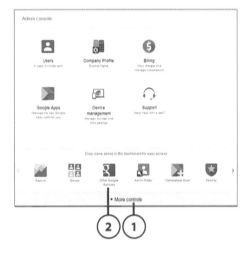

1. Click More Controls on the Admin console.

2. Click Other Google Services.

3. Scroll down to find the Google+ service and click Configure Premium Features.

4. Click the Enable Google+ Premium Features button. It may take up to 24 hours to turn on these features for all of the users in your organization.

>>>*Go Further*

USING ADMINISTRATOR CONTROLS FOR YOUR TEAM

To control exactly what your domain users can do with Hangouts, you need to visit the Settings for Talk/Hangouts page. From the Admin console page, click the Google Apps icon. This opens a listing of services; click the Talk/Hangouts service.

From the Talk/Hangouts page, you can click the Share Settings link to set policies for chatting with people outside of your domain, or click the General Settings link to uninstall the service.

You can control settings such as enabling users to chat outside of your domain, allowing both voice and video calls, and automatically accepting invitations between users. You can also use the Talks/Hangouts page to turn the Hangouts app on or off for everyone; click the drop-down arrow under the app icon and select an option.

Working with Chat Hangouts

Instant messaging, also referred to as live chat or text chat, is incredibly easy; you just type your conversation. You can chat with someone one-on-one or chat with a group of people. The conversation scrolls upward in the Hangouts window with each user's input appearing as a text balloon. The most recent comment appears at the bottom of the window. You can scroll up and down to view different parts of your conversation.

Start a Chat in Gmail

One of the easiest ways to access Hangouts and start a conversation is through Gmail.

1. Click the Hangouts icon on the Gmail page if the Chat list isn't already displayed.

2. Click the name of the person you want to contact.

3. In the Hangouts mini window, type your message text and press Enter/Return.

4. If the other person is available, they can respond directly to you.

5. Click the Close button (x) to exit.

What Are Emoji?

Emoji are the ideograms or smiley icons used in messaging to convey a range of emotions, feelings, and actions otherwise difficult to display in text messaging. Originating in Japan, hence the name, emoji icons are appearing in all manner of Gmail and chat messages. To add emoji or smiley characters to your chat, click the icon in the bottom-left corner of the Hangouts window, click a category, and click an icon to insert.

Click to insert emoji

Show Yourself As Unavailable

If you know you're going to be busy, you can click the drop-down arrow at the top-right corner of the Hangouts window, click Snooze Notifications and select a time span to turn off notifications.

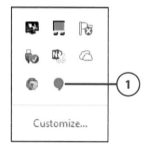

Start a Chat in Hangouts

Another way to start a chat is using the Hangouts icon to open the Hangouts window. The Hangouts window keeps a list, appropriately called the Hangouts list, of people in your network.

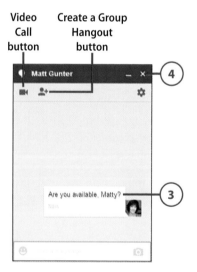

1. Click the Hangouts icon.

2. Click the person you want to chat with in the Hangouts window.

3. Type your message text and press Enter/Return. If the other person is available, they can respond directly to you.

4. Click the Close button (x) to exit.

Turn It into a Video Chat

To turn any message chat into a video chat, click the Video call button located in the upper-left corner of the Hangouts window.

Video Call button   Create a Group Hangout button

Add More People to Your Current Chat

To add more people to your chat, click the Create a Group Hangout button at the top of the Hangouts window. The Add People window lets you choose other people to invite into your conversation. Click a person and click Add People to create a new chat window.

It's Not All Good

Blocking a User

To prevent someone from messaging you, you can block them. In the chat window, click the Settings button (looks like a gear or cog) and click Block username (where username is the name of the person you want to block) and click the Save button. Hangouts adds the user to your blocked list. To view the list, click the drop-down arrow in the main Hangouts window and click Blocked People. You can unblock a user from this window.

Invite a New Contact

You can easily invite users that do not appear on your contacts list. When you do, they receive an invitation to join you in a chat.

1. Click New Hangout in the Hangouts window.

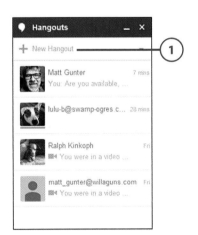

2. Enter the name or email address of the person you want to invite. If the user isn't found in your contacts, click the entry to send an invitation.

3. Hangouts sends an invitation.

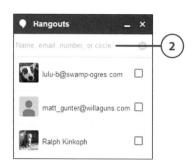

Insert a Picture into Your Chat

You can insert a picture to share with the person or person's you're chatting with and Hangouts adds it to the conversation.

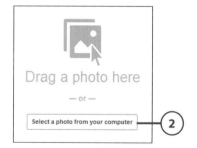

1. To add a picture to your conversation, click the camera icon.

2. Click Select a Photo from Your Computer button. Navigate to the picture file you want to insert and select it and click the Open button.

3. Click the Select button. Hangouts inserts the image.

Archive Your Chat

You can keep a copy of your chat, which is helpful if you need to make notes later or recall what was said.

1. Click the Settings button in the Hangouts window.

2. Click the Archive button to close the conversation window and archive the file.

3. To view the archive, click the drop-down arrow.

4. Click the Archived Hangouts button.

5. Click the conversation you want to open.

Clear Your Window

You can clear a chat window's previous conversation. Click the Settings button to display the Options window and click Delete. Click the Save button and Hangouts removes the previous chat text. To forego keeping a chat log entirely, select the Hangout History check box in the Options window.

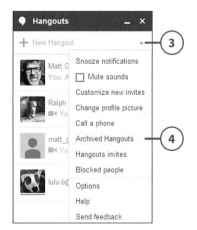

Video Conferencing with Hangouts

With a web camera and microphone, you can have face-to-face conversations using Hangouts. Called video calling or video conferencing, this feature is a great way to bring people together for a variety of purposes, such a meetings or interviews. Video calls in Hangouts open a separate window showing video feed from each person in the group. The window also offers tools you can utilize during your video call.

Hangouts On Air

Google's Hangouts On Air page can help you get started with broadcasting your video calls on a YouTube channel and sharing your video conferencing with the public. To learn more about it, visit the Hangouts On Air page at plus.google.com/hangouts.

Start a Video Call

You can start a video call from the Hangouts window using the video call icon.

1. Click the name of the person you want to video chat with in the Hangouts window.

2. Click the Video Call button.

3. The Google+ Hangouts window opens and sends a call to the person. If the other person is available and answers, you can begin your video chat.

Change the View

You can click the pictures at the bottom-right corner of the video chat window to switch between viewing yourself or viewing the other person or persons.

4. Pause your mouse pointer over the top center area of the window to view controls.

5. Click the Invite People button to invite another user.

6. Pause your mouse pointer over the left side of the window to view the Google Apps tools.

7. Click the End Call button to end the call.

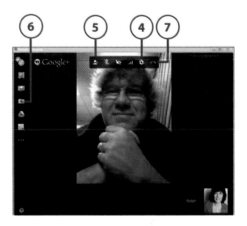

Mute the Sound or Stop the Camera

You can use the Microphone and Video Camera buttons on the top toolbar (top center of your video call window) to mute the sound or turn off your camera. The buttons toggle on or off; click a button to turn the feature on or off. If you mute your mic, no one can hear you during the video conference. If you turn your camera off, the other users see your profile picture instead of the video feed.

>>>Go Further
USING APPS ON A VIDEO CALL

You can view a toolbar of apps along the left side of the video chat window. The default apps listed can help you during your conference. The toolbar include apps for sharing a Google Drive folder or adding a comment pane to the window (which is useful for people who can't use the microphone to interact). You can add more apps designed for Hangout video chats by clicking the More apps button.

Answer a Video Call Invite

Responding to a video chat invitation is fast and easy. Invites pop up in a Hangouts window, When you respond, a video call window opens.

1. Click the Answer button in the Hangouts window.

2. The video call window immediately opens and you can start your video chat.

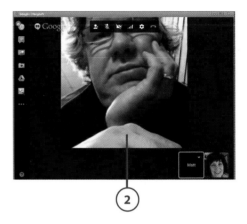

Invite Someone to Your Video Chat

You can invite other users to a video call in progress.

1. Click the Invite People button in the video call window.

2. Enter the person's name or email in the box.

3. Click the Invite button to send an invitation.

Invite Multiple Users at Once

You can invite as many users as you like before opening a video chat window. Starting with the Hangouts window, click the New Hangout box, and select the check box for each user you want to include or enter in their email addresses. Click the Video Call button when you're ready to start the chat and notify each user.

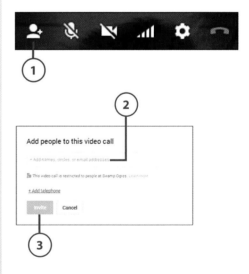

Video Calls Outside Your Group

You can invite people outside of your organization to video chat with you, but Hangouts prompts you with a warning. Depending on your situation, you may need to use caution about what you discuss outside of your company, for example. The same is true if you elect to make a Public video call.

Share Your Screen

Using the Screenshare app, you can share your computer screen with everyone during a video conference. For example, if you have a photo you want to share, you can open it onscreen and activate the Screenshare app so everyone else can see it.

1. Click the Screenshare button in the video call window.

2. Select the window you want to share.

3. Click the Start Screenshare button. Click the Screenshare button again to close the app.

Try Fullscreen View

If you activate Fullscreen, users can see everything you do onscreen, including mouse movements, opening and closing program windows, and so on.

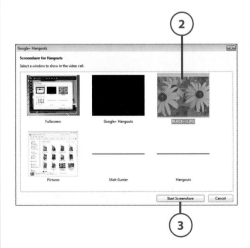

Open a Chat Pane

You can open a group chat pane that allows everyone to chime in via text. You might use this app to let everyone input notes or allow users without audio to comment.

1. Click the Chat button in the video call window to open a chat pane.

2. Enter your comment text and press Enter/Return.

3. Click the Close button (x) in the chat pane or click the Chat button again to close the app.

Open a Google Drive File

You can use the Google Drive app to upload a file from Drive to the video call window, and if you share the file, others can interact with it. You can also create a notes or sketch file to save and jot down notes or sketches as you work together. Notes are automatically saved on your Drive account as Hangouts Notes:[date] [time], listing a proper date and time of course.

1. Click the Google Drive button in the video call window.

2. Navigate to the file you want to open, select it, and click the Select button to open the file in the video call window.

3. Click the Expand button.

4. Click the Add button.

5. Click the Create Shared Notes or Create Shared Sketchpad button.

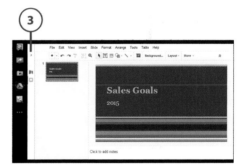

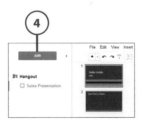

6. Click the Open button to confirm you're sharing the document and email address.

7. The app displays a new notes or sketches file. You can now add notes about your video call.

8. Click the Google Drive button again to close the app.

Viewing Different Files

You can switch back and forth between open files; expand the display, and click the file you want to view.

Save a File

You can convert the document from the video call window into another format. At the end of the call, click the File menu, click Download As, and specify a file type.

Play with Google Effects

For something fun, you can turn on Google Effects. This app features several galleries of graphic art items you can add to your video picture, such as hats or eyewear. You might use this app in conjunction with the Capture app to take photos of your video call participants and save them as a photo album.

1. Click the Google Effects button in the video call window to open a panel of effects.

2. Use the navigation buttons to scroll through the galleries to see the different effects.

3. Click the one you want to try. The effect is immediately applied to your video picture.

4. Click the Close button (x) in the pane or click the Google Effects button again to close the app.

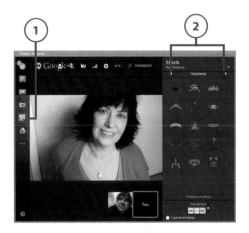

Take a Photo

Capture your favorite video chat moments with a picture using the Capture app. When you activate this feature, Hangouts alerts the other users that you are about to take a picture. You can take a picture of the video call window and everyone in it and save the images in a photo album on Google+. The album is shared with everyone who attended the video call.

1. Click the Capture button in the video call window.

2. Click the Camera button to take a picture. You and everyone else in the video call will hear a shutter sound and see a photo flash when the photo is taken.

3. The picture is saved and added to the corner of the window. You can continue taking more pictures. When you're ready to view them click the photo stack to view all of the photos taken during your online session.

4. Click the Capture button again to close the app.

Phone Calling with Hangouts

You can place a landline or mobile phone call from Hangouts. Hangouts opens the video call window where you can carry on your conversation while managing the time. The window also includes a keypage you can use if you're required to dial an extension before reaching someone.

Calls made to the U.S. and Canada are free. Other rates apply to international calls. You can check rates by clicking the drop-down arrow in the Hangouts window and clicking Rates. A Google page opens detailing phone calling rates that might apply.

Place a Phone Call

Use the Hangouts window to start a call, and then use the video call window to do all the talking.

1. Click the drop-down arrow in the Hangouts window.

2. Click Call a Phone.

3. Enter the full phone number, including the area code needed.

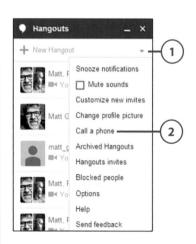

4. Click the call entry to start your call in the video call window.

5. When the call is answered, you can begin your conversation.

6. Click the End Call button to end the call.

7. Click the Close button to exit.

First Time Users Must Authorize It

The first time you use the phone call feature, you must agree to Google's terms of service. Just click the I Accept button when it appears and click the Proceed button to continue.

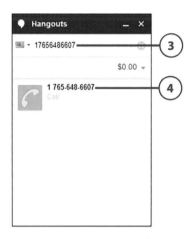

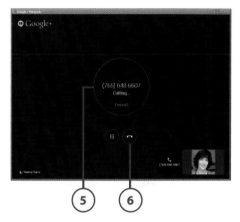

Use Google Sites to create
all kinds of web pages

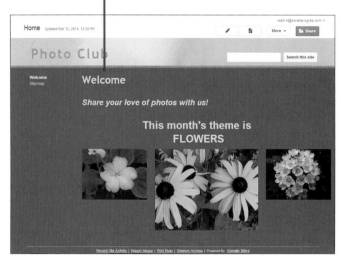

In this chapter, you learn how to build your own website using the Google Sites app:

- → Exploring the types of sites you can create
- → Learning how to build your own website
- → Discovering how to customize a web page, add images, change layout, and insert gadgets
- → Adding more pages to your site
- → Learning how to share your site with others

Creating Websites with Sites

Google Sites is an app designed especially for building and sharing websites and wiki pages. As part of the Google Apps suite, you can use Sites to create a team-oriented site where everyone can come together to collaborate, exchange information, files, and communicate. You can create professional-looking sites for your business or organization based on a wide range of templates and themes.

Exploring Sites

A website is a great way to convey an idea, message, or establish your online presence. It's also a great way to bring people together. Google Sites offers a quick way to build a website, and it really shines when you need to create a central spot for collaborating. Whether you want to reach a large audience or a targeted group, like your classroom students or office project team, you can create an attractive, easy-to-use website with Google Sites that meets your goals.

There are a lot of great web design programs available today, and although Sites does not offer the same amount of customizing and design options, you might be surprised to see all that you can do with the app. You can use it in a variety of ways, and here are just a few ideas:

- Create a central page for your club members to meet, exchange ideas, and advertise activities.

- Create a site focused on a project and help each team member accomplish goals and tasks.

- Make an intranet site for disseminating information throughout your corporation.

- Design a website for your wide-flung family to come together and share pictures and news.

- Create a site for mobile devices, such as advertising your latest product or event.

- Build an employee profile page that helps your department personnel get to know each other.

- Make a classroom learning module that acts as an instructional guide as well as resource material for a course.

- Design your own blog site for sharing regular blogging entries.

What's a Wiki Page?

A wiki page is a web app or page that allows users to add and modify its content. You can build pages with Sites that allow everyone who uses the page to add and edit content, interact dynamically, and see changes in real time.

Benefits to Using Sites

Sites is an excellent tool for creating simple websites, but if you're looking to build a full-featured e-commerce or business site, you probably need to check into some of the more sophisticated web design programs. However, if you want to group your site with all of your other Google activities—such as emailing messages, scheduling calendar events, creating documents, and storing files—Sites is a convenient tool to use and it's handy to have your website tied directly with your Google account.

Here are a few benefits of using Sites:

- You don't need to be a certified web designer to use Sites. In fact, you don't need to know anything about HTML (HyperText Markup Language). Creating a web page is as easy as editing a document.

- You can tap into a huge array of templates for all kinds of page types, everything from a basic web page to user-submitted templates from other Sites page authors.

- With permission settings, you can control who has access to your site, limiting it to just a few or opening it up to the entire Internet.

- You can embed multimedia items in your pages, share calendars, add forms, and more, all of which accesses other Google apps.

- Your Sites pages utilize the same powerful search technology as the Google.com site, allowing you to search across pages and content.

- You don't have to outlay costs for web programming and upkeep.

- Google Sites is free with any Google account, including Google Apps for Business/Education/Government.

There is a downside to Google Sites. It isn't as intuitive to use as other Google Apps, and Google doesn't offer much in the way of guidance. Hopefully, this chapter can help you a bit and show you where to find what you need, even though it can't possibly cover every nuance you'll run into with designing your own website.

Tour Sites

Google Sites isn't as feature-loaded on its home page as some of the other apps, but when you start editing your web page, you'll quickly find lots of tools you can use. The first time you open Sites, the home page looks a little empty.

Google Sites home page

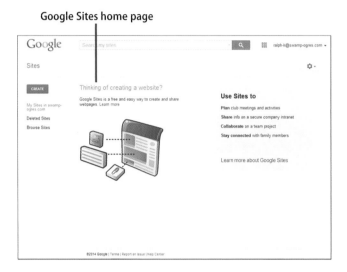

As you create sites, you can use the Google Sites home page to view a list of all your sites. The list, located in the middle of the page, also includes sites others have shared with you. To view a site, just click its name.

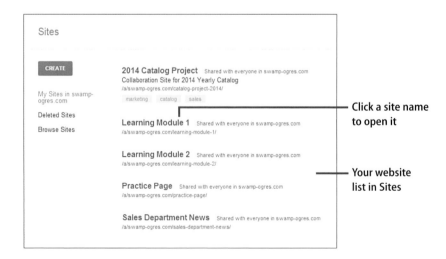

Click a site name to open it

Your website list in Sites

When you open your website, the initial page you created awaits you. Typically, if you chose a template from the library, the page you open contains some placeholder items and/or text. If you created a blank page, you might see theme elements or a mostly empty page. Anytime you want to add or edit content, you must switch to editing mode.

Click to return to the Sites home page

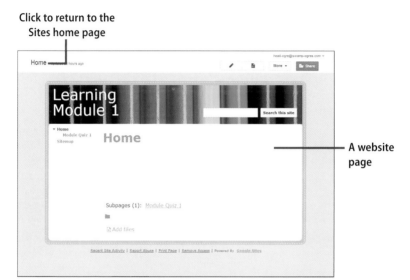

A website page

When you finish working with a site, you can return to the Sites home page. Click the Home button in the top-left corner of the window.

Building Sites

There are several routes you can take to building a website. You can adapt a template or you can build your own page from scratch. There are dozens of templates you can chose from, but to really learn your way around Google Sites, I strongly suggest you first create a practice site, something you can use to acclimate yourself to how the app works.

Technically, all sites you create are based on a template of some sort, but starting with a blank template allows you to see how page elements come together to make a website. If you're looking for some preset design elements, you can add a theme to control colors, fonts, and background design for the page, and then insert additional elements as needed.

Build a Basic Website

These steps show you how to build a basic site based on a blank template. You can use the subsequent sections in this chapter to build on your basic site.

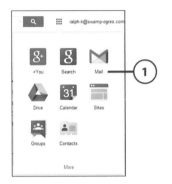

1. Click the Apps icon and click Sites, or click the Sites link on the Navigation bar. You can also navigate to sites.google.com in your browser's address bar.

2. Click the Create button.

3. Click Blank Template (it's usually selected by default).

4. Enter a name for the site.

5. Google checks to see if the site name is in use and fills in the URL automatically.

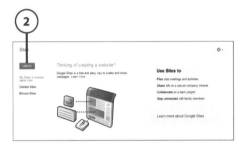

It's Taken!

The Site Location box automatically fills in the site's full URL, and Google Sites checks to see if the location is available. If the website name is already used by someone else, try another name, such as a variation on your first choice.

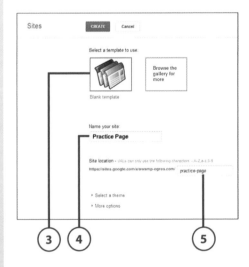

6. Optionally, click the Select a Theme link and select a theme for your site.

7. Click the Create button.

8. Sites opens your newly created page. When you finish working with the page, click the Back to My Sites button to return to the Sites home page.

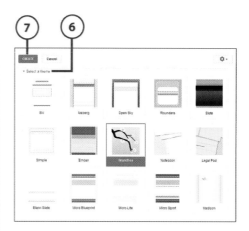

Using Pre-built Templates

If you'd rather not build a site from the ground up, you can find numerous templates in the gallery. Templates offer you pre-built pages that feature a design and layout geared toward a purpose, such as project work sites or classroom sites. Some templates are for an entire site and offer you lots of pages for a bigger website; other templates are just page templates, giving you a single page to build on. You can revise any template you find to suit your own needs. To peruse templates, click the Browse the Gallery for More box on the Create page.

Removing Sites

To remove a site you no longer want, like a practice site you set up to learn all the tools and features, you can remove the website. To do so, open the site, click the More button and click Manage Site. From the General tab, look for a Delete This Site button to start the process.

Customizing Your Page

Now that you've created a web page, it's time to customize it to make it your own. You can change the layout, add text, images, videos, links, and more. To edit a page, you need to switch to editing mode. When you do, Sites displays tools you can use to add and edit items on your page. In editing mode, a toolbar of formatting tools appears at the top of the page, along with a menu bar with more commands.

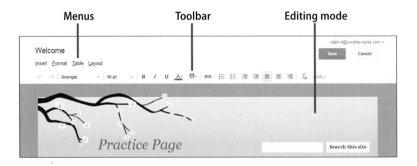

Your web page is composed of different parts, such as a header at the top featuring the site name, a Navigation bar or site map to link to other pages you add later, a search box that allows users to search the site, and content boxes to hold information. Even a blank template isn't exactly blank. It provides some default content areas (the text boxes where you type in your text, a header, sitemap, and search box). You can use the formatting tools to make changes to your content. You can change the layout to change the site structure for the content area in the middle of the page. The layout organizes content into boxes, so you have areas to place text, images, and other items to design a page.

The other page elements, such as the site header, are edited through the Manage Site page. You can also turn page elements on or off, or add new ones using the Edit Site Layout page.

You can add different types of content to your site in editing mode using the Insert menu. The Insert menu has options for adding three types of items: common items, gadgets, and Google items.

Common types of content include things like images and links. You might, for example, insert a horizontal line on the page to separate content boxes, or add a table of contents.

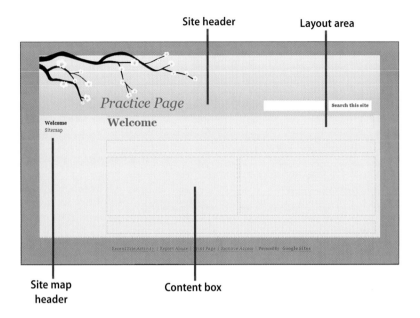

Site header

Layout area

Site map header

Content box

Gadgets are mini-apps, either HTML-based or JavaScript (a popular programming language built into browsers), that you embed into a page. Gadgets can add a dynamic element to your page, such as a news element that streams live new stories or mortgage calculator visitors can use to figure out a payment, even interactive games. There are thousands of gadgets you can plug into your pages.

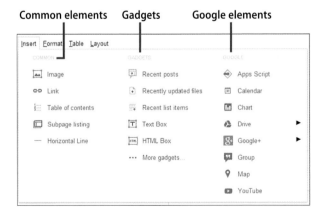

Common elements   Gadgets   Google elements

Lastly, Google items include things like embedding your calendar, YouTube video, or map, for example. As you can see there's a lot you can add to customize your website.

Add Your Text

You can add text or replace place-holder text with your own content. As you fill a content box with text, the box expands to fit whatever you put in it.

1. Click the Edit button.

2. Select the text you want to replace.

3. Enter your text.

4. Click the Save button to save your work and exit editing mode.

It Won't Let Me Edit the Text!

Depending on the template and theme you select, not all text boxes let you change the text or its formatting. For example, the header text displaying the page name cannot be changed from editing mode. Instead, you must open the Manage Site page and use the Themes, Colors, and Fonts link to edit the site header.

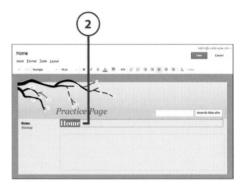

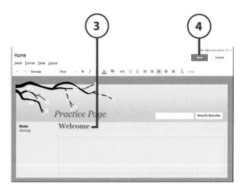

>>>*Go Further*
EDITING OTHER PAGE ELEMENTS

Need to edit other page elements, such as the site header font or the page background color? Unfortunately, you can't use Site's editing mode to make changes to these elements. Instead, you use the Manage Site tools. Click the More button in the upper-right corner of the Sites page, and click Manage Sites. The Manage Sites page opens with links to different settings and options.

To change the default fonts of your template or theme, click the Themes, Colors, and Fonts link on the left side of the window. This displays a mockup of your page along with the various controls for the page elements. You can click which page element to modify. For example, if you want to change the site header's font, click the Site header option, click Title, click the Font drop-down menu and choose something else.

You can use the settings displayed on this window to change page background color, assign another theme, insert background images, and much more. When you finish making changes, click the Save button at the top of the window.

Format Text

You can use the formatting tools in editing mode to change the appearance of selected text. For example, you can change the font and size, change the alignment, or change the text color.

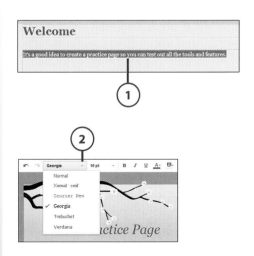

1. Click and drag to select the text you want to format.

2. Click a formatting tool from the toolbar; for example, to change the font, click the Font drop-down arrow and select a font.

3. You can continue changing formatting as needed, such as adjusting the font size or color.

4. Click the Save button to exit and save your changes.

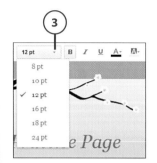

Oops!

If you make a mistake with any of the editing changes you apply, click the Undo button on the toolbar to immediately undo your action.

>>>Go Further
SO MANY EDITS, SO MANY VERSIONS!

Google Sites keeps track of the revisions you make to your website. If you find you've made one modification too many, you can return to an earlier version of the page to start again. The Revision History list keeps saved copies of your work automatically. To view the list, click the More button (in the upper-right corner of the Sites page) and click Revision History.

The Manage Site page displays the Pages settings and lists all of your saved versions of the page. Click a version to view it. A copy of the page appears. If you decide this is the version you want to return to, click the Revert to This Version link. If it's not the right version, click the Back button in your browser to return to the version history listing and try another.

It's not uncommon for page editing actions to result in buggy content, so returning to an earlier version can help you remove an unwanted gadget, for example, that you can't seem to remove on your own.

Change the Layout

You can change your page's layout in editing mode and select from a gallery of preset layouts. The layout applies to the area within the page, not the site map or header area.

1. With the page displayed in editing mode, click Layout.

2. Select a layout option.

3. In the layout, click inside a content box to add text or other items.

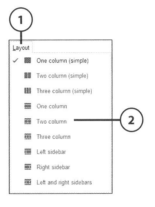

Expanding Content Boxes

The layout's content boxes expand to fit whatever you insert into them, such as text or images. The more you add, the bigger the box grows vertically.

Save and Exit

You don't have to click the Save button after each change unless you're done editing your page. You can continue editing as much as you like. If you do save and exit, just click the Edit button to return to editing mode again.

Insert an Image

Inserting pictures is easy and you can choose from three size settings to resize them. You can insert images from the web if you know the URL, or you can upload an image from your computer.

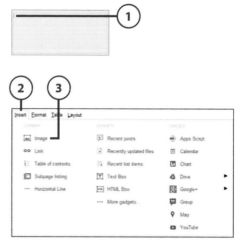

1. With the page displayed in editing mode, click the content box where you want to insert the image. (A cursor always marks your location in a content box.)

2. Click Insert.

3. Click Image.

4. To upload an image, click the Upload Images button. (If you've previously uploaded an image, it is listed in the box for you to reuse.)

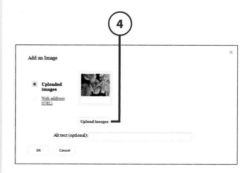

5. Navigate to the image file you want to upload and select it.

6. Click the Open button.

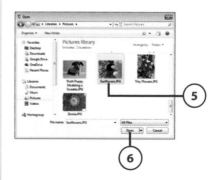

7. Select the added image in the list, if necessary.

8. Click the OK button.

9. The image is inserted along with a toolbar (the toolbar appears only when the image is selected); to resize the image, click S for small, M for medium, or L for large.

10. The image resizes. Optionally, you can use the mini toolbar to control the placement and properties of the image.

Are You Using a Web Image?

To use a web image, click the Web Address option and type in the URL for the image (or copy and paste it). Be mindful of copyright issues when using images from the Web. If you don't have permission to use the image, it's considered copyright infringement.

Use a Google Drive or Google+ Image

If you already have a photo you want to use stored on Google Drive, you can easily insert it. Click the Insert menu, click Drive, and click Image. Select your image file and click Select to add it. The same thing applies to Google+ photos; click the Insert menu, click Google+ , and click Photo.

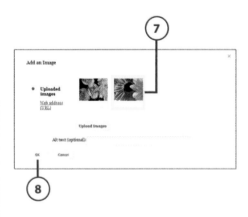

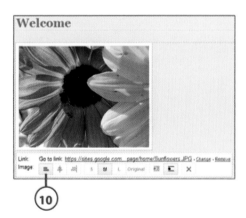

Add a Link to Another Website

You can add a link to a content box that takes the user to another website or another page on your own site.

1. With the page displayed in editing mode, click the content box where you want to insert the link.

2. Click the Link button.

3. Click Web Address.

4. Enter in the URL or paste it into the Link to This URL box.

5. Sites automatically fills in the Text to Display box with the same information. Optionally, you can type in different text.

6. Select the Open This Link in a New Window check box to have the link open in a new window, which also keeps your site open for the user.

7. Click the OK button.

8. The link is inserted along with a toolbar to check out the link, change it, or remove it.

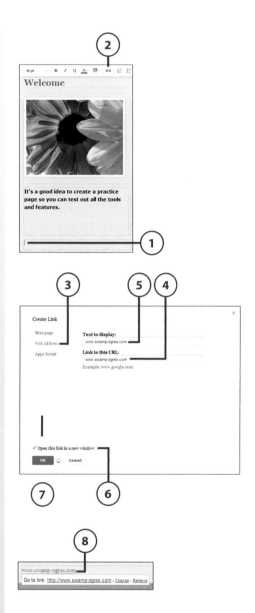

Add Videos

You can insert videos from your Google Drive or YouTube. Open the page in editing mode and click where you want the video to appear. To insert a video, click the Insert menu, click Drive, and click Video or YouTube (you'll need to know the URL of the video). After you've selected the video, you can modify the display size and title. Save your changes and the clip is embedded. To play it, exit editing mode and click the clip's Play button.

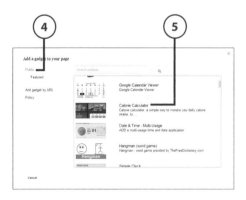

Add a Gadget

You can add dynamic content to your page that allows users to interact, running mini-app scripts for a variety of purposes. You can choose from a vast library of scripts written by other Google users as well as gadgets designed by Google.

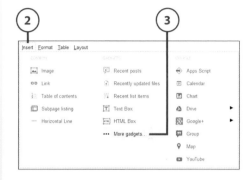

1. With the page displayed in editing mode, click the content box where you want to insert the gadget.

2. Click Insert.

3. Click a gadget or click More Gadgets to view a gallery of scripts.

4. Unless you see the gadget you want listed, click the Public link to view a much larger list of available gadgets.

5. Click a gadget to learn more about it.

6. Click the Select button to use the gadget.

7. Set the configuration controls for the gadget, such as display size or title.

8. Optionally, click the Preview Gadget button to see what it will look like on your page.

9. Click the OK button.

10. The gadget is inserted as a placeholder. Click or select the gadget to display a toolbar of positioning and properties controls.

11. Click the Save button.

12. You can now interact with the gadget or see it in action.

Reconfigure It

If your gadget doesn't quite look right on the page, you can reconfigure its size or placement. Return to editing mode, click the gadget, and click the Properties button on the mini toolbar. This reopens the configuration box so you can make adjustments to the gadget's size.

Remove an Item

If you insert an item you no longer want, such as a gadget or an image, you can remove it from the content box. First, click the item to select it and display its associated mini toolbar. Next, click the toolbar's Remove button (it looks like an X), or in the case of links, it actually says Remove. You can also press Delete on your keyboard.

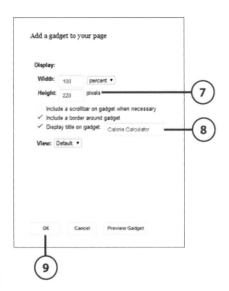

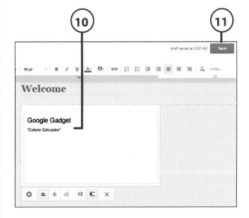

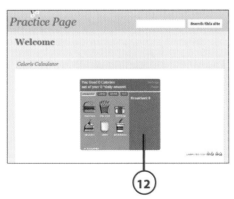

Adding Pages

The first page created when you build a new website is called the landing page or home page. It's your main website page. You can add more pages to the hierarchy of your site to add more content and branch off of the landing page. Site hierarchy can make pages all one level or pages that are subordinate to other pages.

Page Types

Google Sites offers several different types of pages you can add:

- **Web page**—This is a regular web page, just like the one you started with; you can use it to add content and modify the layout and formatting to suit your needs. It looks just like the original page you started the site with, but with a comments section added to the bottom.

- **Announcements**—Similar to a blog page, this page type lists posts chronologically with the most recent at the top of the page. It's great for press releases, reviews, or weekly meeting notes. The Announcements page type includes a New Post button. Users can click the button to add a new posting to the page.

- **File cabinet**—Use this page type to store and organize files and share them with others. The page includes buttons for adding files, moving files, deleting files, inserting files from Google Drive, and links. Users can also subscribe to changes, which means they receive a notification when changes are made to the files listed here.

Web page type

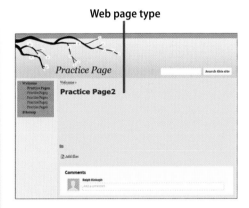

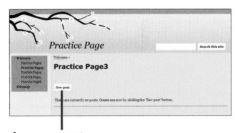

Announcements page

File Cabinet page

- **List page**—Just like its name, this page type is handy for making lists of information.

- **Start page**—A customizable page, it lets users add their own gadgets for personalizing, such as a weather gadget to get the latest info on their area. Start pages look differently for every user, depending on what gadgets they add.

Already Have Pages?

If you built your website using a site template, then it most likely already includes additional pages. You just have to add your own content to each of the template pages.

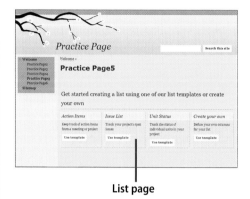

List page

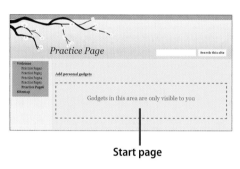

Start page

>>>Go Further
REORDERING PAGES

You can specify page location or order for your site. Hierarchy helps you construct a site in a logical manner and direct users to different content. Site map menus help guide users to main pages that stem from your home page, whereas subpages offer expanded content to any main or top-level page. Top-level pages exist at the same level as your home page and work well for main topics or categories in your site. For example, you might add a page dedicated to feedback or another for resources and users go from page to page in a sequence. Subpages exist below a page in the hierarchy and are good for expanding on the information found on the page above it in the structure.

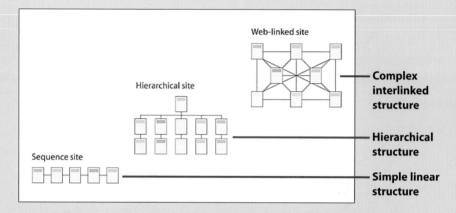

For example, if your main page is growing too long, you can help make content more readable by placing some of it on a subpage. Let's say your page presents the topic of flowers. Subpages off of the main page might expand the topic coverage to growing perennials, growing annuals, and transplanting flowers.

If you have a complex website in mind, you might need to interconnect each page so users can link in every direction to view more content. You can add links to your subpages on the main page, making it easy for users to locate content. You can click a page on the home page to view it.

Add a Page

Websites are collections of individual pages. You can add more pages to build your site and include more content.

1. Open your site and click the New Page button.

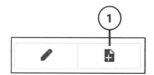

2. Enter a name for your page; Google Sites checks to see if the URL is available.

3. Click the Page Template drop-down arrow.

4. Select the type of page you want to add.

5. Select a location for the page.

6. Click the Create button.Google Sites adds the new page and opens it in editing mode; you can now start customizing it with your own content.

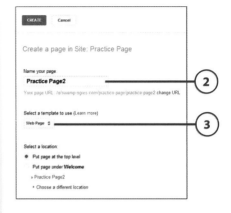

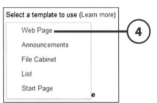

Remove a Page

To delete a page you no longer want, open the page, click the More button, click Delete Page, and click Delete to confirm the deletion. Just remember, any sub-pages to the page and file attachments for the page are deleted, too.

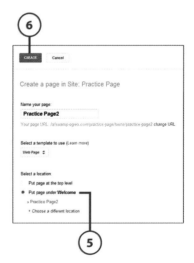

Add Links to Subpages

You can create a list of links to sub-pages in the left sidebar of your main page or another page of your choosing. Users can click a link to navigate to the subpage. If you added a subpage to your home page, page links might already appear in the navigation sidebar by default.

1. Open the page where you want to add links to subpages and click the More button.

2. Click Page Settings.

3. Select the Show Links to Sub-pages check box.

4. Click the Save button.

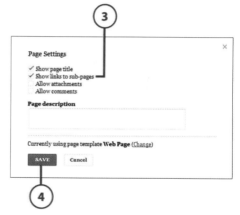

Turn Off Comments

Depending on the template, some pages you add automatically have the comments turned on. Open the new subpage, click the More button and choose Page Settings to open the Page Settings dialog box. To turn comments off, deselect the Allow Comments check box. Click Save and the comment section is removed.

Reorganize Pages

If you need to move pages around in your website structure, you can visit the Pages page. Here you can view your hierarchy listed in an outline format and drag pages around to rearrange their order. Page and sub-page hierarchies can be expanded and collapsed much like a folder tree.

1. Click the More button.

2. Click Manage Site.

3. Click Pages.

4. Click the Hierarchy button, if it's not already selected.

5. Click the Expand icon to expand the hierarchy tree. (Conversely, clicking the collapse icon collapses the tree.)

6. Click and drag a page to a new location in the hierarchy.

7. The page is moved.

8. Click the page name to return to the site page.

Two Views

The Pages options toggle between two views of your pages. You can view the site structure as a tree, or you can view a list detailing each page. The details view lets you see who authored the page, how many revisions it has, and when it was last updated.

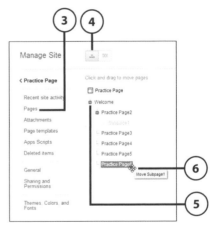

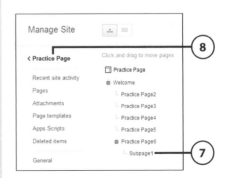

Sharing Your Site

You can share your website with other people, like coworkers or team members, and allow them editing privileges to help you create and maintain the site. By default, everyone on your domain has viewing and editing privileges unless you specify otherwise. You can also invite users outside your group to view or edit the pages, as long as they have a Google account or a Google Apps account.

Permission settings come in two flavors: site-level and page-level. With site-level permissions, authorized users can access and edit all the pages in your website. With page-level permissions, users can only access and edit the designated page.

When it comes to access, you can set it to "can view" only, which lets others view the pages but not edit them, or you can set it to "can edit," which lets users make changes to your pages. With "can edit" access, users can add and delete pages, change content, add comments, and subscribe to changes.

If you assign someone else ownership of the site, they have all the same abilities as you do as the site creator. Owners can do everything as those who "can edit," as well as set access levels, change the site name, and delete the site.

After you enable sharing and editing privileges, other users can work on your website at the same time as you. You can see their changes as they happen.

Share Your Site

You can share your site with other users by inviting them to access it and specifying what level of access they're allowed.

1. Open your home page and click the Share button.

2. Click in the Invite People box and enter the email address of the person you want to share with.

3. Click the drop-down arrow to specify an access level: Can View or Can Edit.

4. Click the Send button to notify the person via email.

5. Sites add the user to the list. Click the page name to return to the web page.

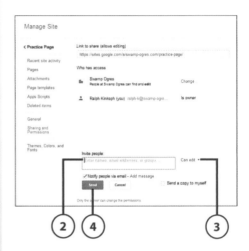

Change Visibility Settings

By default, everyone on your Google account domain can find and edit these web pages. To change this setting, click the Change link and select another option. You can make the site public to the Internet, only to those with a link to it, or to specific people. You can also limit the site to just viewing and no editing.

**Vault is an
archiving tool**

In this chapter, you learn all about the basic tools the Vault app offers for archiving and searching through your organization's communication data:

→ Finding out what you can do with Vault
→ Signing up for Vault and assign licenses
→ Learning how to create retention rules, matters, and holds
→ Seeing how easy it is to search for data
→ Finding out how to export a search list and run an audit report

Archiving with Vault

Vault is a data retention and retrieval service offered by Google. As an e-discovery (electronic discovery) tool, it utilizes the security and safety features of Google's servers to capture account data for archiving and searching. If your company is required to adhere to strict compliance standards, Vault can help you safeguard all the data records for your organization.

Exploring Vault

You and your organization can use Vault to archive, manage, and preserve email data and chat messages for information governance. Litigation costs and hassles can knock a company for a loop these days, running up thousands of dollars and precious time. E-discovery is often a big part of litigation costs, because it can be very time consuming to search and find relevant data in a mountain of information. That's where Vault steps in—the app helps you manage critical information and backup important data. You can use Vault to proactively archive data and find the information when you need it.

- **Email and Chat Archiving**—Control how often emails and on-the-record chats are retained and expunged from all Google systems.

- **Full Search Functions**—Search your entire organization's email and chat records for keywords, date, or by user account.

- **Setup Legal Holds**—Set up message holds to back up data in Vault to meet legal or compliance obligations.

- **Export Data**—Review email and chat data in standard formats by exporting data.

- **Create Audit Reports**—Track user actions within Vault during a specified time period and export audits in CSV format for reviewing in a spreadsheet viewer.

Search for archived data messages in Vault

Vault works by creating a single archive to manage all of your organization's email and chat message data in one place, eliminating the need to duplicate data in separate systems. All of your communication data, incoming and outgoing, is routed through the Vault servers, capturing everything a user communicates and shares in their account. Administrators are able to search the entire domain for specific keywords or messages. In addition to meeting compliance requirements, Vault is also a great way to securely backup your data. No software is required, just add the service to your Google Apps suite.

Adding the Vault App

You can try out Vault for 30 days, free, before deciding to purchase it. You can buy Vault for $5 per month per user. Once you add it, you can assign licenses to specific people in your organization to use Vault. You can add the Vault app to your current array of Google Apps by way of the Admin console

Getting Vault for Education, Nonprofit, or Government Users

If you currently use Google Apps for Education/Nonprofit/Government edition, you need to contact your Google account manager or sales representative to purchase Vault.

Add the Vault App

To add the Vault app to your Google Apps account, simply sign-up for the service.

1. Click the Get More Apps and Services link on the Admin console page.

2. Click the Add It Now button under the Vault service.

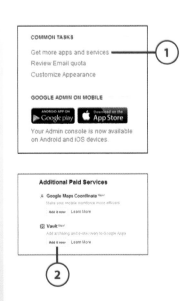

3. Click the Continue button to purchase Vault or sign-up for the 30-day free trial.

4. Select a plan option.

5. Click the Continue button.

6. Select the Google Apps for Business agreement check box.

7. Click the Continue button.

8. Click the Continue Using Hangouts or Disable Hangouts button.

③

Using Vault with Hangouts

During the sign-up process, you must accept a Vault-Hangouts amendment if you opt to continue to use Hangouts in your organization. This is because of partial compatibility between Vault and Hangouts. Any chat messages recorded in Hangouts are searchable for e-discovery purposes, placed on hold, and exportable. Hangouts, for example, keeps a history of text chats unless deleted. These are called "on-the-record" messages. However, Vault's retention and archiving policies are not applied to on-the-record messages that expire beyond the specified retention period. They're still part of the user's Hangouts histories, but expunged by Vault.

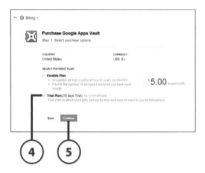

④   ⑤

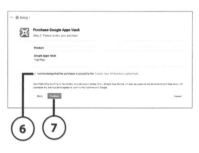

⑥   ⑦

⑧

9. If you opt to continue using Hangouts, you must agree to the amendment; click the I Accept button.

10. The Billing page appears listing your billing details to complete the sign-up process.

Adding Vault Takes Time

After you complete the sign-up process, it might take a few hours for the Google to add Vault to your list of apps. If you try to log onto Vault before approval goes through or before licenses are assigned, you might receive an error message.

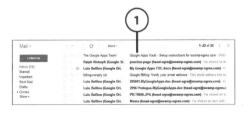

Assign Licenses

Google sends you an email welcoming you to Vault. You can use the links in the email to assign licenses and get started setting up Vault. When you assign users a license to access the Vault app, you're granting them privileges to create and work with matters (specific cases and investigations), view and work with account holds (preserving a user's communications), manage searches, exports, audits, and retention rules.

1. Click the Google Apps Vault message with setup instruction in Gmail to open it.

2. Click the License Manager link to specify users.

3. Select the check box next to the user you want to authorize.

Each User Needs a Vault License

Keep in mind that each user whose data you want to retain, search, hold, or export must have a Vault license.

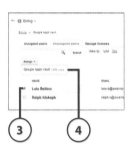

4. Click the Assign drop-down arrow and click Google Apps Vault.

5. Click the Assign License button.

6. The license is assigned and the user is added to the Assigned Users tab.

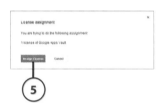

Changing Admin Roles

Just because you assign a Vault license doesn't mean the user has Vault privileges. You need to give users privileges first. To grant a user administrative rights to use Vault, you can change the user's system role through the Admin console. Adding administrative rights gives users privileges to various apps in your domain.

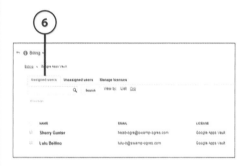

Understanding Privileges

Make sure users who have access to Vault understand the sensitive nature of the data Vault backs up and the legal issues of its importance.

Changing Licenses

To make license changes for Vault users, click the Billing icon in the Google Apps Admin console page, look for the Google Apps Vault row and click the Manage Licenses icon at the far right. This opens the licenses page where you can make changes to users in the list or add new users.

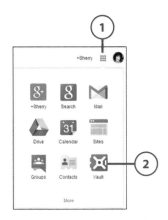

Sign In to Vault

If you are the administrator or you've been granted access to the service, you can sign in to Vault using the app icon or the Vault sign-on page (https://ediscovery.google.com) in your browser window).

1. Click the Apps icon.

2. Click the Vault icon.

3. Enter your password.

4. Click the Sign In button.

5. The Google Vault page opens.

Finding Help

To get help with any aspect of Vault, consult the Google Help Center. From the Vault page, click the Settings button (looks like a gear or cog icon), and click Help.

Setting Retention Rules

Vault allows you set retention rules to determine what content is retained or not, and what criteria it meets before it's no longer available to anyone on the system. You can apply multiple rules to your domain, but some precedences take place. For example, if a user is on hold—that is their message data is preserved in order to meet legal or compliance obligations—then any retention rule does not apply to their data until the hold is lifted.

You can create two types of retention rules, a customized rule or a default rule. A customized rule lets you choose the criteria, such as a certain date, whereas a default rule applies to the entire domain.

Set a Custom Retention Rule

When setting up a custom retention rule, you can choose to base the parameter on an organizational unit (if you have different levels in your domain), a sent date, and terms (keywords that appear in the messages).

1. Click the Retention category.

2. Click the Add Rule button.

3. Set the parameters for the rule.

4. Specify a retention period.

5. Click the Save button to create the rule.

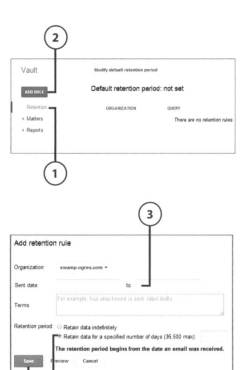

Set a Default Retention Rule

You can select from three options when setting a default rule. You can choose not to set a retention period, set a specified number of days, or retain data indefinitely. If you choose not to set a period of time, users control how long they keep their message data. If you do specify a time period, all the data is expunged after the time is reached. The last option, keeping the data indefinitely, means the data is always in the Vault.

1. Click the Retention category.

2. Click the Modify Default Retention Period button.

3. Select an option.

4. Click the Submit button.

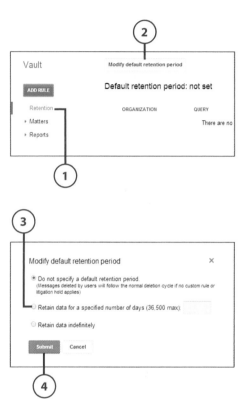

Working with Matters

When working with data retention and retrieval services, like Vault, a different lingo applies to the tasks you perform. The term "matter" is such an example. A matter is defined as a container for message data pertaining to a specific issue, such as a legal case or customer complaint for example.

Matters are viewable in the Vault page under the Matters category. From this main list you can open a matter, sort the list, share matters, close matters, or move them to the Trash folder for deletion. Each of the main categories listed under the Matters heading act a as a folder; you can move matters from one category to another, such as moving a finished case to the Closed category.

Create a New Matter

When you create a new matter, you're making a new "folder" to hold tasks and actions associated with the topic, including searches, account users, and export files.

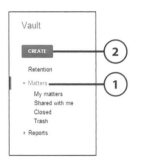

1. Click the Matters category.

2. Click the Create button.

3. Enter a name and description for the matter

4. Click the Create New Matter button.

5. The matter is added where you can start adding components to it, such as hold or query search.

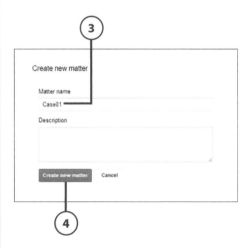

Understand What Matters

You can think of a matter much like a case folder with all the associated actions and tasks pertaining to the data grouped within it. Those actions include things like search queries run on the data, a list of accounts allowed to access the matter, a list of accounts with litigation holds, any exported sets of data, and an audit trail for the matter.

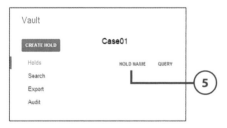

Add a Collaborator

If you have other users in your organization working with you on a case, you can add them as collaborators to the matter.

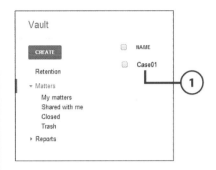

1. Click the matter you want to open.

2. Click the Share button.

3. Enter the mail address of the user you want to add.

4. Optionally, select check boxes to notify users by email and copy yourself as well.

5. Click the Save and Close button.

Remove a Collaborator

To remove a collaborator from the case, open the matter and click the Share button. In the Permissions box, click the Remove button next to the collaborator's name. Click the Save and Close button to exit.

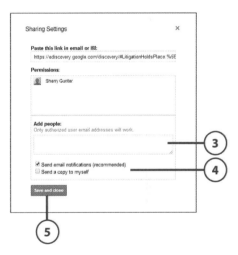

Creating Holds

The term "hold" is another part of the data retention and retrieval language. A hold is preserving messages in the Vault indefinitely while a case is going on. You can place a hold on a user's account and any message data they remove is only removed from their view. The data itself is still in the Vault, which means you can search it and audit it. When a hold is in place, Vault preserves email messages, file attachments, and even content from the user's Sent Mail, Drafts, Trash, and Spam folders. Chat history is also included. As long as a user has a hold on their account, Vault administrators can view and search the user's messaging data. When a hold is removed, retention rules still apply.

Create a Hold

Any holds pertaining to a matter are listed on the Holds list page when you open the matter to view all of it's components. Any user whose content is on hold must have a Vault license. If not, you'll need to add one.

1. Click the matter you want to edit in the Matters list.

2. Click Holds, if it's not selected already.

3. Create the Create Hold button.

4. Enter a name for the hold.

5. Set any parameters you want to include.

6. Click the Save button.

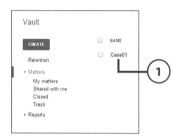

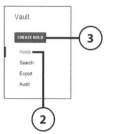

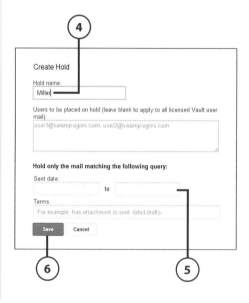

Searching Message Data

After you create a matter, you can run a search for information related to the case. When you start a search, you can use fields to fill in what information you're looking for, such as account names (email addresses of the users you're searching), sent dates, and keywords.

Search for Data

You can add a new search to any matter. Search results appear in their own page for you to view, export, or audit.

1. Click the matter you want to open.

2 Click Search to display search fields.

3. Click the source.

4. Enter your search criteria in the appropriate fields.

5. Click the Search button to display the search results list . To view an item, click a message.

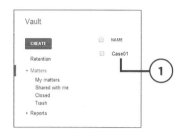

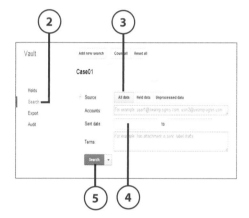

Specify What You're Searching

You can designate whether you're searching all the data in your domain, held data, or unpro-cessed data. If you opt to search only held data, Vault searches all the data found in any hold assigned to the matter. If you select to search for unprocessed data, Vault looks through all the metadata tags of attachments.

Exporting and Auditing Data

You can use Vault's Reports feature to export search results from any account. You can then download the information as a file. Exported files are available for 15 days, after which they are automatically deleted. If you don't download the file before the 15 days are up, you have to run the search and export procedure again.

You can also use Reports to create an audit report. Audits create a detailed report about a user's actions within Vault over a specified amount of time.

Export Search Results

Before you export a search you first need to create a search. When you've done that, you can utilize the Export command from the search results list.

1. Open your search results list.

2. Click the Export Results button.

3. Enter a name for the export.

4. Click the Begin Export button.

5. The results appear on the Export page.

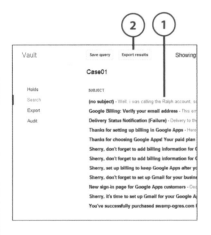

Viewing the Exported Data

The message data you export is saved in the MBOX file format, an industry-standard for email messages. You can use a text editor application, such as Microsoft Notepad or Wordpad, to open and read the data (but not the file attachments), or a different email program.

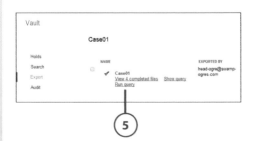

Run an Audit Report

You can run an audit report on Vault actions and create a CSV file that immediately downloads to your computer or mobile device.

1. Click Reports.

2. Click Audit.

3. Specify a date range.

4. Enter the users on whom you want to run the report.

5. Select the check boxes for the actions you want to include.

6. Click the Download CSV button to create and download a report file.

Viewing Audit Report Data

You can view the audit report CSV files in most spreadsheet programs, including Google Sheets.

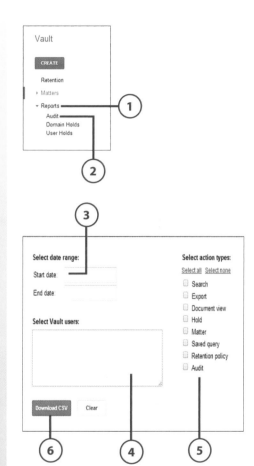

Chrome web browser is an excellent companion to Google Apps

In this chapter, you explore the Google Web browser and some other Google Apps to help you with your organization:

→ Discovering how to download Chrome and surf the Web
→ Pinning your Admin console page as a tab
→ Creating your own Google groups
→ Building a Google+ for Business page

Exploring Other Google Tools

You're not just limited to the apps included with your Google Apps for Business/Education/Government account. There are plenty more apps and features you can tap into to help you manage, grow, and advertise your organization. This final chapter gives you a look at a few more, starting with the Google web browser, Chrome.

Browsing the Web with Google Chrome

There are a variety of web browsers on the market today—Internet Explorer, Opera, Firefox, and Safari to name a few—and you probably already have a favorite that you use. Google's Chrome Web browser is one of the newer kids on the block. Offering a minimalist interface, Chrome's streamlining makes it faster and more efficient, and certainly worth a try. If you aren't already using Chrome, you might want to check it out.

The Google Chrome interface is simplified, clean, and neat. The address bar, also called the omnibox, is where you type in the address of a website, just like any other browser. The address box also doubles as a search box, so you can look up information on the Web.

Off to the far right side of the bar is the Chrome menu button. Rather than clutter the browser window with controls and features, you can click the Chrome menu button to reveal features and customization options.

Chrome menu button

New tab	Ctrl+T
New window	Ctrl+N
New incognito window	Ctrl+Shift+N
Bookmarks	▸
Recent Tabs	▸
Edit	Cut | Copy | Paste
Zoom	– | 100% | + | ⌞ ⌝
Save page as...	Ctrl+S
Find...	Ctrl+F
Print...	Ctrl+P
Tools	▸
History	Ctrl+H
Downloads	Ctrl+J
Signed in as head-ogre@swamp-ogres.com...	
Settings	
About Google Chrome	
Help	
Exit	Ctrl+Shift+Q

Chrome also features behind-the-scenes malware and phishing protection to help you stay secure online, and automatic updates so you're always using the latest features and security fixes.

Download the Browser

If you haven't downloaded the browser yet, start by visiting the Google Chrome website at www.google.com/chrome. You can download an executable file and run it to open the installer. After you do, the complete Chrome installation package downloads and installs itself. Just follow the onscreen instructions as they appear. At the end of the process, the Chrome icon appears on your desktop (Windows) or in your Applications folder (Mac). Click the icon to launch the browser.

Surf the Web

You can use the same techniques for viewing web pages in Chrome as you do with other browsers.

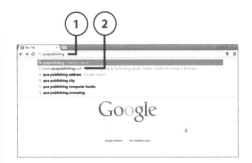

1. Open the Chrome browser window and type the URL for the site or page you want to visit in the address box.

2. As you type, Chrome displays a list of possible matches. You can click one or keep typing. Press Enter/Return to open the page.

Using the Address Box to Search

Remember, the address box doubles as a Google search tool, so you can use it to search for keywords or phrases rather than typing in a URL.

3. Click links to open additional pages. If you need to reload the page, click the Reload This Page button.

4. Click the New Tab button to open a new tab.

5. Click a tab to switch between tabs and view it.

6. Right-click a tab to view a menu of tab commands.

7. Click a tab's Close button (x) to close it.

Open a Link in a New Tab

You can open a link in a new tab rather than lose your place in the current page. Simply right-click the link and click Open Link in New Tab.

Open Windows Instead of Tabs

If you want to open a new browser window instead of just adding a tab, you can click the Chrome menu button and click New Window.

>>>*Go Further*
GOOGLE ACCOUNT SIGN IN

You don't have to, but you may prefer to keep your browser settings synchronized across devices. You can sign in to Chrome using your Google account and utilize your bookmarks, saved passwords, history, and other browser settings. With your account, you can sign in from any computer, tablet, or mobile device.

To sign in, click the Chrome menu button and click Sign In to Chrome. The same Sign in page you use to access your Google Apps appears and you can enter your name and password to sign in. After you've signed in, you can access all of your favorite bookmarks and browser settings.

If you're using a public computer, however, you might not want to utilize your private Google account. Even if you sign out before leaving the computer, you may still be signed in to Chrome, which could allow access to your personal information.

If you need to allow other people to access the Internet with your computer and Chrome, you can add more users, each accessing their own personal settings. To add a user, click the Chrome menu button and click Settings. On the Settings page, click the Add New User button under the Users heading. This opens a new Sign in page; enter the username and password and click Sign In. The new account is added to the user list along with a special user icon (which can be changed by clicking the Edit button and clicking another icon). To switch users, click the user icon in the top-left corner of the Chrome browser window and select another user.

Add a Bookmark

You can add bookmarks to your favorite pages. Chrome keeps a list of bookmarks available through the Chrome menu under the Bookmarks category, or you can turn on the Bookmark bar.

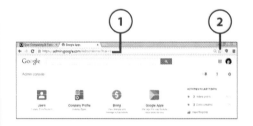

1. Navigate to the page you want to bookmark.

2. Click the Star icon in the address bar.

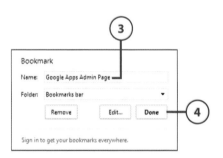

3. Enter a name for the page, if needed.

4. Click the Done button.

5. Click the Chrome menu button.

6. Click Bookmarks to view the bookmarks.

7. Click a bookmark to display the page.

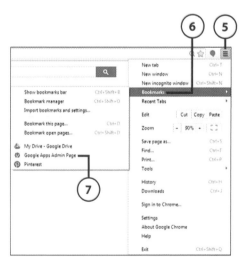

Turn on the Bookmark Bar

The Bookmark bar contains all the bookmarks you create. The Bookmarks bar is not displayed by default. To display it, click the Chrome menu button, click Bookmarks, and click Show Bookmarks Bar. You can also choose to keep it on every time you open the browser; click the Chrome menu, click Settings, and select the Always Show the Bookmarks Bar check box under the Appearance heading, and click the Settings tab's Close button (x) to exit.

Pin a Tab

If you find yourself using the same pages time and again, you can pin them as tabs in the browser window so they're always ready to go with a click. For example, you might pin your Google Calendar or Drive app page.

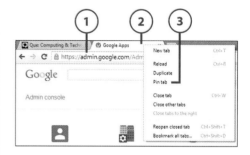

1. Navigate to the page you want to pin.

2. Right-click the tab.

3. Click Pin Tab.

4. Chrome places the tab as a smaller icon in the top-left corner of the browser window. Click the tab whenever you want to view the page.

Unpin a Tab

To unpin a tab, right-click it and click Unpin tab from the menu.

Working with Google Groups

Google Apps for Business/Education/Government comes with a Google Groups for Business app. You can use it to create groups as mailing lists or forums, collaborate with colleagues, and more. For example, you might use a Google Groups to hold an online discussion about a project you and your team are tackling.

Each group you create starts with a simplified home page and a forum view so users can easily scan and navigate multiple topics. You can assign roles to different members to control how they participate in the group, such as starting new posts or managing email lists.

- **Email List**—Acting like a mailing list, you can use this type of group to email everyone at once, share content, and invite users to meetings. The group uses its own dedicated email address, unlike the groups you create in Gmail's Contacts manager.

- **Collaborative Inboxes**—Use this type of group to manage questions from colleagues or customers much like a support team. Different group members can volunteer or be assigned to follow through and resolve issues as they appear as topics.

- **Web and Q&A Forums**—This group is most similar to Internet discussion forums. Use this group type to dedicate to related topics, or as a Q&A forum for users to answer other user's questions.

As users post topics and comments to a group, the group page lists the latest entries.

Click My Groups to view your groups list

Groups Home page

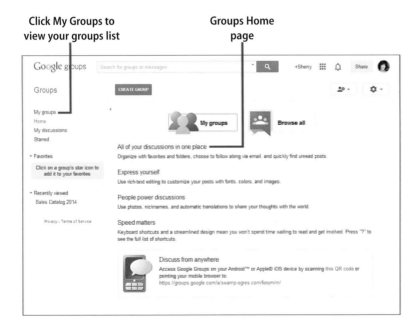

Free Google Groups

Google Groups is also a free service that lets users connect and interact all in one place. Discussion groups on the Internet, also called message boards or forums, have been around for quite some time. Google Groups takes the idea and makes it easier to create, join, and participate in groups. Anyone can subscribe to a group, providing it's open to new members, and interact with group discussions, even sharing Google calendars and docs. Google Groups for Business differs in that it's available for your organization only unless you open it to the public or invite people outside of your organization to join.

Enable Google Groups for Business

Before you can use Google Groups for Business, it first has to be enabled for your organization. If you're the administrator, you can use the Admin console page to enable the app.

1. Click the Get More Apps and Services link on the Admin console page.

2. Click the Add It Now button under Groups for Business to enable the app for all the users in your organization.

Not the Administrator?

If you're not the account administrator, you'll need to ask yours to enable Groups.

Create a Group

To create a group, fill out the group's details using a form. You can name the group, assign its unique email address, and specify the group type.

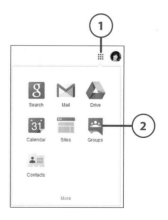

1. Click the Apps button.

2. Click the Groups icon.

3. Click the Create Group button.

4. Enter a name for the group.

5. Enter an email address; the address is automatically part of your Google account, which uses your domain.

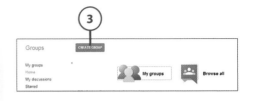

6. Enter a description for the group.

7. Click the Select a Group type drop-down arrow and select a group type.

8. Optionally, assign permissions now, or wait and assign them later.

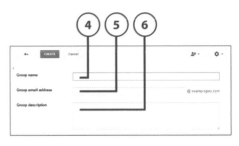

9. By default, anyone in your organization can join the group. To limit who joins, click the Select Who Can Join button and select who you want.

10. Click the Create button.

11. Click the Okay button.

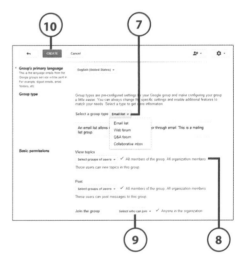

The empty group page opens and you can add a welcome message, start inviting others, and more.

Invite People to a Group

You can send out email invitations to people you want to invite to the group.

1. Click the Settings button.

2. Click Group Settings.

3. Click Invite Members.

4. Enter the email addresses of the users you want to invite.

5. Enter an invitation message.

6. Click the Send Invites button.

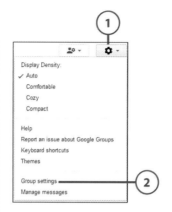

Tracking Invites

As part of your group management, you can check on outstanding invitations to see who hasn't responded yet. Click the Manage link and click the Outstanding Invitations link in the left pane.

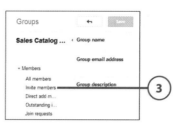

Start a Topic

To create a new topic, you fill out a form much like an email message. You can also include formatting, attach files, and more. After a topic has been started, other users can post comments to continue the discussion.

1. Click the New Topic button on the Groups page.

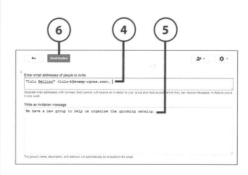

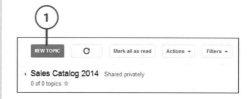

2. Enter a subject for the topic.

3. Enter the discussion text.

4. Click the Post button.

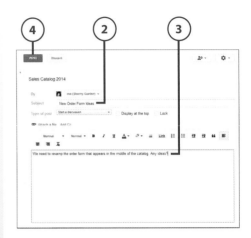

Delete a Post

To remove a post you no longer want on the group page, select the post, click the Actions button, and click Delete.

Find Basic Permissions Settings

You can control permissions settings through the group Manage feature. You can specify who views topics, who is allowed to post, who can join, and whether external people can join the group.

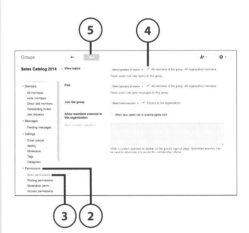

1. Click the Manage link on the Groups page.

2. Click Permissions.

3. Click Basic Permissions.

4. Select the permission settings you want.

5. Click the Save button.

More Managing

The Manage link opens more than just permissions. The left side of the page reveals a variety of settings and options you can assign. The categories listed there can expand or collapse to view various controls.

Understanding Google+ for Business

Google+ Pages allow businesses, institutions, and organizations to create a public identity online within the Google+ framework. You can use a business page, for example, to promote a product or brand. Much like a Google+ profile page let users socialize online, Google+ Pages let your business interact with customers, clients, and the Google+ social scene at large. A Google+ Business Page is also a great way to gain greater search visibility on Google.com.

A Google+ Page is free. You can create a page using one of five categories:

- Product or brand

- Company, institution, or organization

- Local business or place

- Arts, entertainment, or sports

- Other (use this option if your organization doesn't fit in the other categories)

After you create a page, you can start filling in profile information, adding photos, and managing your page.

>>>Go Further
WHAT IS GOOGLE+?

Google+ is a social network that adds a social layer to the already popular Google content. Free to Google users, you can use Google+ to create profile pages, post status updates and photos, and locate people you know. With the purpose of bringing people together across apps and sharing web content, Google+ lets you network with circles of friends, family, and coworkers. By defining groups as circles, you can interact with them differently. With a Google+ account, you view updates from other people in your circles, called Stream, and participate in video conferencing calls and instant messaging with Hangouts, to name just a few features.

Enable Google+

Before you can set up a Google+ page for your organization, you must first enable Google+ for your account. You can enable Google+ for everyone on your team through the Admin console page.

1. Click More Controls on the Admin console page.

2. Click the Other Google Services icon.

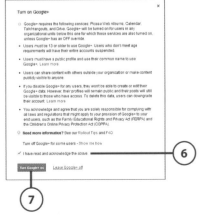

3. Scroll down the page and click Google+.

4. Click the drop-down arrow and click On for Everyone.

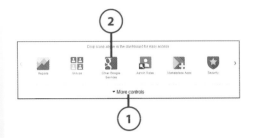

5. Click the Turn ON for everyone button in the message box.

6. Read the terms of service and select the I Have Read And Acknowledge the Above check box.

7. Click the Turn Google+ On button to enable it.

Create a Google+ for Business Page

Google walks you through the steps for creating a page. Your steps might vary slightly based on the type of category you select. At the end of the procedure, you can go directly to your page, or view a tutorial about setting up your page.

1. In the address box, type www.google.com/+/business/ and press Enter/Return.

2. Click the Get Your Page button.

3. Click the category that best matches your type of organization. Depending on what you select, you may have to narrow down the type.

4. Enter the business name.

5. Optionally, add a website and specify content appropriateness if applicable.

6. Select the agreement check box.

7. Click the Continue button.

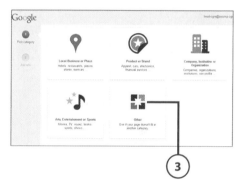

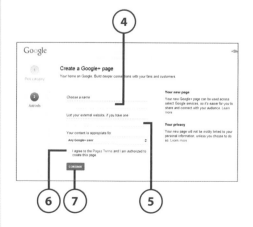

8. Click the Open Your Page button to go directly there or click the Get Started button to run through a tutorial.

9. Your new page opens.

Learn More About Google+ Page

To learn more about building and using a Google+ Page, open the Help Center. Click your profile picture in the upper-right corner and click Dashboard. Click the Dashboard drop-down arrow and click the Help link at the bottom of the menu.

Other Google Apps to Try

There are many more apps you can use to help you and your organization. The Google Marketplace is full of them, and more are added daily. Some apps are free, others are available for a fee.

Here are a few of our choices for helpful apps:

- **Google Maps Coordinate**—You can use this management tool app to coordinate and dispatch mobile workers in the field. Using real-time visibility, you can see where your employees are and help schedule their activities, assigning jobs to the nearest people, get updates about tasks, and coordinate projects. Click the Get More Apps and Services link from the Admin Console to find this app.

- **Google Maps Engine Pro**—A professional mapping tool, you can use this app to visual data on a map, importing addresses and other locations and mapping out location databases. By importing data such as sales leads and office locations, businesses can analyze and share the information to better plan operations. Click the Get More Apps and Services link from the Admin Console to find this app.

- **Freshbooks**—]If you're in need of billing tools, this app offers features for tracking time, sending invoices, and collecting online payments.

- **Expensify**—Make your expense reporting tasks a breeze with this app. You can import receipts from bank accounts, credit cards to create tracking reports, and more.

- **SurveyMonkey**—Use this app to collect all kinds of data on all kinds of topics. Perfect for creating polls and questionnaires, SurveyMonkey can save you time and help you analyze the results.

- **TripIt**—Help keep your employees trips organized and coordinated with travel itineraries, confirmation emails, maps, and more.

- **Aviary**—Looking for a capable image editor for your photos? Aviary offers design tools for retouching photos, creating logos, and more.

You can find these apps through the Google Marketplace; visit google.com/appsmarketplace.

Index

A

about
    Calendar, 7, 15, 71
    Docs, 7, 16, 129
    Drive, about, 7, 15-16, 99
    Gmail, 7, 14, 41
    Google Apps, 3, 7, 11
    Hangouts, 18, 241
    other Google tools, 311
    Sheets, 7, 17, 167
    Sites, 7-8, 19, 267
    Slides, 7, 17-18, 201
    Vault, 19-20, 295

access
    levels, specifying, 117-119
    options, 120

account
    customizing, 11
    personalizing, 31
    signing up for, 11
    tools, 31

Actions menu, 146

activate services, 31

activity
    logs, viewing, 31
    stats, 30

add
    apps, 34
    comments, 157-158, 230
    contacts, 59-60
    coworker's calendar, 79
    events, 83-84
    Hangouts app, 245
    more storage, 117
    new calendar, 78
    numbers in cells, 180
    sheets, 175
    signature, 65
    subfolders, 110
    users
        Chrome, 315
        to account, 32
    Vault app, 297-299

Add a Reminder link, 88

Add Task button, 90

Add Users link, 28

add-ons
    install, 165
    Sheets, 199
    working with, 165

additional
    storage, purchasing, 117
    toolbar buttons, 146

address box, Chrome, 312

Admin console
    about, 11
    add Vault via, 297
    adding users, 28
    billing, 117
    bookmarking, 29-30

Domains tool, 23
enable Google+, 324
exploring, 29-31
page, upgrading from, 25
sample page, 10
tour of, 28

Admin Roles and Privileges
link, 33

administration
tasks, spot for, 29
tools, taking tour of, 28

administrator enabling
Groups, 319

advanced sort, performing,
193

advertising-supported Gmail
accounts, 42

AdWords, 6

Agenda view, 75

alarm clock icon, 87

all-day events
displaying, 74
scheduling, 81

Allow comments check box,
289

Analytics, 6

animating objects, Slides,
224

animation
pitfalls, 222
working with, 222

announcements page, 285

answer a video call, 258

Anyone with a link setting,
118

app
adding, 34
available in each edition,
21
browsing, 20
customizing settings for,
31
enable and disable, 31
to fit your business, 6
using on video call, 257

Apple Mail, using with Gmail,
14

apply
email label, 54
filter, Sheets, 193
new font and font size,
219
style, 138

appointments
adding block, 85-86
color coding, 87
keep track of, 15
tracking, 7

apps
Calendar, 7, 15, 70-96
Capture, 262, 263
Docs, 7, 16, 128-165
Drive, 7, 15-16, 98-127
Effects, 262
Forms, 108
Gmail, 7, 14, 40-69
Groups for Business, 317-
322
Hangouts, 18, 240-265
others to try, 327
Screenshare, 259
Sheets, 7, 17, 166-199
Sites, 7-8, 19, 266-292
Slides, 7, 17-18, 200-238
Talk, 242
Vault, 19-20, 294-309

Apps icon, 73

archive
chat, 255, 296
message, 56, 296
with Vault, 19

Archived Hangouts button,
255

assign
licenses, Vault, 299-300
labels to messages, 52

attach a file to email, 49

attachments, viruses in, 50

audit
data, Vault, 308-309
report data, viewing, 309
reports, create, 296

trail for matter, 304

auditing industry standards,
12

automatic
email reply, 66
republication, preventing,
234

Automatically Republish
check box, 163

automatically resize columns,
179

automating calculations, 17

Avery Label Merge, 165

Aviary, 327

B

Back to Inbox button, 48

background, apply to slide,
207

backup
data, 12
securely, 297
system, Drive as, 15
with Google Drive, 7

BCC (blind carbon copy), 47

benefits of
Google Apps, 7, 11
using Sites, 269

billing, 31
changes to, 117

blank Docs document, 128

blocking a user, 253

blog site, 268

Blogger, 6

bookmark
Admin Console, 29-30
deleting, 149
inserting, 142, 148
sign in page, 38

Bookmark bar, Chrome, 316

broadcast video calls on
YouTube, 256

Browse Interesting Calendars, 79

browser
  choosing, 25
  pin and unpin tabs, 317
  updating, 25

browsing
  other apps, 20
  web with Chrome, 312-315

build
  basic website, 272-273
  Google+ page, 326

bulleted lists, creating, 139, 140

business
  cost per user, 21
  Google+ for, 323
  information, filling in, 26
  meetings, 242
  page, create on Google+, 325-326
  web-based apps for, 11

button displays, 172

C

calculations, perform manually, 183

Calendar
  about, 15, 71
  access from mobile phone, 96
  add
    appointment, 85-86
    events, 80-82
    new, 78
    others, 79
  adjust density, 75
  Agenda view, 75
  app, 6, 7, 70-96
  assign a due date with, 62
  change view, 73-75
  color coding, 87
  create
    event, 86
    tasks, 89, 90
  edit items, 86

exploring, 72-75
list, 76-77
manage displays, 72
navigation arrow buttons, 76
Navigation bar, 72
permissions settings, 93
Quick Add feature, 83-84
sample page, 70
scheduling capabilities, 72
shared system calendar, 6
synchronizing with Gmail, 43
view
  other users, 73
  your schedule, 15

calendars
  deleting, 77
  export, 95
  import, 94
  keep private, 93
  sharing, 92-93
  in Groups, 318

camera, stop in video call, 257

Can comment, 118, 120

Can edit, 118, 120

Can view, 118, 120

Capture button, 263

categories, Google+ pages, 323

CC (carbon copy), 47

cell
  adding numbers in, 180
  moving to another, 171

change
  calendar view, 73-75
  color, Sheets, 176
  difficulty of, 13
  layout, 279
  licenses, Vault, 301
  profile picture, 36
  view in video call, 257
  visibility option, 123
  your reply, 68

chart
  create, 17

insert in spreadsheet, 183-184

chat
  add people to, 253
  archiving, 255, 296
  Hangouts, working with, 250
  insert picture into, 254
  pane, opening, 260
  start
    in Gmail, 251
    in Hangouts, 252
  turn message into video, 252
  window, clearing, 255

Check Availability button, 27

Choose File button, 51

Chrome
  add bookmark, 316
  add users, 315
  browser page, 310
  browsing web with, 312-315
  installation, 313
  menu button, 312
  new tab or window, 315
  omnibox, 312
  pin and unpin tabs, 317
  sign in, 315
  surf the web, 314
  web browser, 3, 24

Chrome menu button, 316

Circles, Google+, 61

classroom learning module, 268

cloud
  computing
    fewer costs with, 13
    understanding, 3, 4
  storage
    about, 99
    free with Google, 7
    organizing, 110
    other services, 100
    with Drive, 15
  technology, freedom of, 11

cloud-based
Calendar, 71

club members, central page for, 268

collaborating on
documents, 157
spreadsheets, 194-195

collaboration
setup, 4
tools, 12

collaborative inboxes, Groups, 318

collaborator, add or remove, 305

collapse inbox list, 45

colleges, Google Apps free for, 5

colon, adding cells, 180

color coding appointments, 87

columns
sort data by, 192
working with, 177, 178

comment
notifications, 230
pane, add to video call, 257

comments
adding, 157-158, 194
button, 159, 195
inserting, 142
turn off, 289
working with, 159, 195, 230-231

Compact Controls, 156

company
logo, uploading, 35
profile, 25, 31, 35

complex calculations, 181

compliance requirements, 297

computer, adding Hangouts, 245

conditional formatting, 174-175

configure features, 31

Consistency Checker, 165

Contact Manager tool, 59

contacts
adding new, 59-60
create Gmail index of, 43
details, filling in, 59
editing, 60
importing, 69
invite new, 253-254
managing with Gmail, 41
using existing, 46

Contacts Manager, Circles, 61

content
boxes, expanding, 279
create new from Drive, 101
insert in spreadsheet, 183
inserting, 141-142
search Drive, 115

conversations, saving, 18

convert file formats, 153, 188-189

copy a formula, 181-182

copy and paste a URL, 144

copyright
issues, 281
symbols, inserting, 147

cost of
Business and Government accounts, 5
software, 4

coworker's calendar, adding, 79

create
document, 130-131
email label, 53
files, 107-108
folder, 110
Google+ business page, 325-326
Group, 61, 319-320
holds, Vault, 305-306
matter, 304
numbered and bulleted lists, 139, 140

presentations, 201, 202-205
spreadsheet, 168, 169
task in Gmail, 62-63

Create a Group Hangout button, 253

Create button
new file, 108
on Drive, 102
preset apps, 107

Create Calendar button, 78

Create New Folder link, 111

Create Shared
Notes button, 261
Sketchpad button, 261

criteria for
search, 114
sorting files, 116

crunching numbers with Sheets, 17

CSV file
create, 309
exporting as, 69
upload, 32

custom
colors for tables, 151
email address, 6, 21

customer support, 12, 21
Hangouts, 242

customize
style, 138, 139
the 4 days view, 74

customized retention rule, 302

customizing
Gmail, 64
lists, 221
web page, 274
your account, 11

D

dashboard
Admin console page, 29
Google Apps, 2

open Help Center from, 326

data
export and audit, 308-309
keeping secure and private, 12
loss of, 12
organizing spreadsheets, 191
retaining, 303
safety of, 13
storage of, 7
  in Gmail, 14

default retention rule, 302, 303

delete
calendar, 77
contact, 60
document, 155
drawing, 146
event, 81, 82, 86
files, 113
footnote, 147
message, 55
note, 187
post, 322
presentation, 226
slides, 210
spreadsheet, 190
web page, 288

Delete Forever, 114

delivering your presentation, 236-238

desktop
computing solutions, 11
install Hangouts app on, 247-248

Details and Activity button, 103

details, adding to events, 82

device
Calendar working with, 15
edit web pages from, 8
management, 31
synchronize browser settings, 315

dictionary, 160, 231

discovering benefits of Google Apps, 3

discussion
boards, 12
groups on Internet, 318

displaying
day, week or month, 76
email tabs, 53
files in Drive, 127

DNS (Domain Name System), 22

managing settings, 23

Docs
about, 6, 16, 129
Actions menu, 146
app, 128-165
blank document, 128
bookmarks, 148
collaborating, 157
comments, 158, 159
continuous saving, 131
copy and paste a URL, 144
create documents, 129, 103-131, 132
delete a document, 155
download documents, 154-155
drawing, 146
find text in document, 155
fonts, 136-137
footnotes, 147
get started, 130
insert a drawing, 145
insert menu, 142-143
integrated with Drive, 101
keyboard shortcuts, 134, 135
list options, 140
managing documents, 152
new document from Drive, 107
open a document, 153
opening, 130
printing and publishing, 161-164
replace text, 156
revisions history, 154

special characters, 147-148
spelling, 160-161
storage, 117
styles, 138, 139
table of contents, 149
tables, 150-151
templates, 132-134
text, 136
toolbar buttons, 134, 135
tools, 159, 160
using, 7
view options, 157
viewing documents, 156-157
working with add-ons, 165

documents
collaborating, 157
create
  from Docs, 16, 129, 132
  from Drive, 131, 132
  in cloud, 7
  new, 130-131
deleting, 155
downloading, 154-155
editing, 21
find text in, 155
formatting, 134
printing, 162-163
replace text in, 156
republishing, 163
sharing, 18
viewing, 156-157

docx format, 154

domain
check availability, 27
custom email addresses for, 21
primary or secondary, 23
registration package, 23
verifying, 27

domain host, account with, 22

domain names
about, 5, 22
purchasing new, 26
using existing, 26
verifying, 22

web page for, 23

Domains
tool, 23

download
attachment, 50
document, 154-155
file, 116
files from Drive, 109
presentation, 226
spreadsheet, 189

Download CSV button, 309

Download Plugin button, 247

downsides of using Google
Apps, 13

draft emails, 48

drag and drop
file, 106
messages, 56
method, 185, 212

drawing
create from Drive, 108
inserting, 141, 145
options, additional, 146

Drive storage, 21

Drive
about, 6, 7, 15-16, 99
access options, 120
Activity pane, 103
app, 98-127
cloud storage with, 7
create
document from, 131, 132
new content from, 101
new file, 102, 107-108
new folder in, 110
presentation from, 203-204
spreadsheet from, 169
drag and drop files, 106
exploring, 100-104
files, searching, 114, 115
first time access, 101
folder tree, 109
Grid view, 104
help topics, 104
how to use, 99
installing, 110, 125-126

List view, 104
navigating, 101-103
onscreen elements, 101-102
open docs, 130
preset filters, 108, 109
Restore button, 114
sample page, 98
Search box, 103
setting preferences, 127
Share button, 121
storage, 117
Trash feature, 113
upload
file to video, 261-262
files, 105
folders, 106-107
using photo from, 281

DropBox, 100

due dates, managing with
Gmail, 43

duplicating slides, 210

E

e-disc, expense, 296

e-discovery (electronic discovery), 295
with Vault, 19-20

EasyBib Bibliography Creator,
165

edit
presentations, 226
site header, 276
spreadsheet data, 171, 190
user access, 122

Edit Event form, 83

Edit Site Layout page, 274

editions of Google Apps, 21

edits, out-of-sync, 12

Effects for video picture,
262-263

em or en dashes, inserting,
147

email
account, managing, 7
archiving, 296
comment notifications,
158, 230
invitation to view file, 118
label
applying, 54
creating new, 53
list, Google Groups,
317-318
managing with Gmail, 41
moving from another
account, 67-68
programs, 4
reminder, 88
searching messages, 14
send notifications by, 195
tabs, displaying, 53
task list, 64
using multiple labels, 54

embedding calendar on web
page, 275

emoji, 251

emoticons, 147

employees
only one, 21
profile page, 268
travel, reducing, 8
working on documents, 4

Empty Trash button on Drive,
113

enable
Google Groups for
Business, 319
Google+ premium fea-
tures, 249
Google+, 324
Hangouts app in Gmail,
248
mobile notifications, 95

Enable Folder Upload option,
107

engineering calculations,
Sheets, 179

enter
sequential data, 171
spreadsheet data, 171

errors, spelling, 161

events
add to calendar, 80
adding, 83-84
details, 82
attaching files to, 15
edit and delete, 86
invite others to, 83
pop-up reminder for, 87-88
remembering, 15

exact phrase, finding, 115

Excel, 17, 169
viewing, 112

expand inbox list, 45

exploring
Calendar, 72-75
Drive, 100-104
Google tools, 310-327
Hangouts, 242-244
Sites, 268-270
Vault, 296-297

export
calendar, 95
contacts, 69
data, Vault, 296, 308

F

FaceTime, 242

family
get-togethers on Hangouts, 242
website, 268

features in Gmail, 45

file
attach to email, 49
attachment, download, 50
cabinet, page, 285
create new from Drive, 107-108
delete, 113
display in Drive, 127
download, 116
drag and drop, 106
filtering view on Drive, 102
formats, 153, 185, 188-189

inserting, 51
move between folders, 111
open, 113
preview, 112
rename, 112
search, 114, 115
share, 117-119, 120-121
sort, 116
storing and sharing on Drive, 99
syncing, 124
type, save video as, 262
types of, Drive, 101
unsharing, 122
uploading, 105

filter
applying, 193
email messages, 14
turn off, 194
view of files, 109

Find a Time tab, 83

find
and replace, 156
archived messages, 56
text in document, 155

Firefox, 24, 312

folder tree, screenshot, 109

folders
and files, managing, 108
create new, 111
renaming, 112
sharing, 121
upload to Drive, 106-107

fonts
applying, 136, 219
dialog box, 136-137
view more, 219

footnotes, inserting, 142, 147

formats
image, 212
Slides, 225, 226

formatting
cells, 174
documents, 134
email signature, 65
presentations, 217
spreadsheets, 172

text, 136, 141

Forms, create in Drive, 108

formula
copying, 181-182
enter manually, 179-180

formulas and functions
working with, 179
writing, 17

forums, 12
Google Groups, 317
tab, Gmail, 52

forward a message, 48-49

free
data storage in Gmail, 14
Google Groups, 318
trial of Google Apps, 8, 22

Freshbooks, 327

friend's calendar, adding, 79

Full Screen, 156
view, 259

G

gadget
add to web page, 274, 275, 283-284
reconfiguring, 284
removing from web page, 278

Get Hangouts button, 247

Get More Apps and Services link, 34

get started
Docs, 130
Google Apps, 11
Hangouts, 244
how to, 21-22
Slides, 202

Get Started button, 126

Get Your Page button, Google+, 325

GIF file format for logo, 35

Gmail
about, 3, 5, 6, 14, 41
add
account user, 68

signature, 65
app, 40-69
automatic reply, 66
benefits, 7
Contact Manager tool, 59
create a group, 61
customizing, 22, 64
default tabs, 52
email task list, 64
enable Hangouts app in, 242, 248
exploring, 42-43
features, 45
free data storage, 14
Google Tasks in, 62
Google+ users, 61
Hangouts icon in, 246
importing contacts, 69
inbox, viewing, 14
initiating video calls from, 18
Mail Fetcher tool, 67
make a new list, 63
managing contacts with, 41
marking messages, 57
original account user, 68
page, add Hangouts from, 245
People Widget Pop-up, 59
pop-up people widget, 43
regular vs Google Apps, 14
remove spam, 58
sample page, 40
Settings button, 57
signing in and out, 44
smartphone, connect to, 7
Starred category, 57
start a chat in, 251
storage, 21, 117
switching to, 67-68
synchronizing with Calendar, 43
Tasks feature, 43, 89
Google Analytics
account, 22
Google Apps, 10-38
about, 3, 5, 12
account

inclusions, 21
login name for, 23
signing up, 5
benefits of using, 7, 11
dashboard, 2
editions, 5
free trial, 8
getting started with, 21
list of, 6
platform independent, 24
who should not use, 13
Google Apps for Business
about, 5
cost per user, 21
signing up for, 25-28
Vault, 19
Google Apps for Education
about, 5
free use of, 21
Google Apps for Government
about, 5
cost per user, 21
Google Apps Marketplace
page, 6, 20, 34
Google Calendar, see Calendar
Google Chrome, see Chrome
Google Docs, see Docs
Google Drive button, 261
Google Drive, see Drive
Google Earth, 3
Google Effects, 262
Google Forms, 108
Google Groups for Business
app, 317-322
Google Groups, see Groups
Google Hangouts, see Hangouts
Google items, 274, 275
Google Maps Coordinate, 327
Google Maps Engine Pro, 327
Google Maps, 3
Google Marketplace, helpful apps, 327

Google Sheets, see Sheets
Google Slides, see Slides
Google Talk app, 242
Google Tasks in Gmail, 62
Google tools
about, 311
exploring, 310-327
Google Translate, 160
Google, account, setting up, 5
google.com, 3
Google+
business page, 323, 325-326
Circles, 61
description of, 323
enabling, 324
Hangouts built into, 242
page, learn about building, 326
Photos, 42, 117
premium features, enable, 249
government, cost per user, 21
green, going, 8
Grid view, Drive, 104
Groups
add welcome message, 320
creating, 319-320
delete a post, 322
enable, 319
home page, 318
inviting people to, 321
managing permissions, 322
start a new topic, 321-322

H

Hangouts
about, 6, 18, 241
answering a video call, 258
app, 240-265
adding, 245

install as plug-in, 247
archive, 255
blocking a user, 253
chat pane, 260
clearing window, 255
desktop app, 244
e-discovery, 298
exploring, 242-244
Fullscreen view, 259
Google+ account, 323
hardware requirements, 244
histories, 298
icon in browser shortcuts, 246
inviting others, 258-259
notes on Drive, 261-262
phone calling, 264-265
plug-in, 244
Screenshare, 259
start chat in, 252
using Vault with, 298
video
    call, 256-257
    conferencing, 240, 256
viewing files, 262
windows, 243
working with chat, 250
Hangouts on Air page, 256
hard drive crashes, 12, 100
hardware
    costs, 12
    requirements for Hangouts, 244
header, editing, 276
headers and footers, inserting, 142
Hello Fax, 165
Help button, 30
Help Center, 12
    adding storage, 117
    Drive, 104
    Vault, 301
help, finding, 31
hide menu and toolbar, 156
Hide Sheet, 177
hierarchy, using, 286

hijacked passwords, 13
hold, definition of, 305
Holds list page, 306
home page, Sites, 270, 271
horizontal lines, inserting, 142
HTML (HyperText Markup Language), 269
    format, 154

iCloud, 100
icon
    drag from bar to dashboard, 31
    in Gmail for Hangouts, 246
ideograms, 251
image
    formats, 212
    inserting, 141, 143, 185
    sizes, Sheets, 185
import
    calendar, 94
    contacts, 69
    slides, 209
inbox list in Gmail, 45
increased message size, 49
information
    density, Calendar, 75
    governance, 296
insert
    bookmark, 148
    content, 141-142
        in presentation, 211-216
    drawing, 145
    footnote, 147
    image, 143, 185, 212-213
    line, Slides, 215
    link, 144, 186, 213
    pictures, 51, 280-281
        into chat, 254
    shape, Slides, 215

text box, 212
video, 214
Insert menu, 142, 143, 183, 211, 274
Insert Photos icon, 51
Insert Table, 150, 216
install
    add-on, 165
    Chrome, 313
    Drive, 110, 125-126
    Hangouts app as plug-in, 247
instant messaging, 18, 243, 250
institutions, web-based apps for, 11
Internet
    Google synonymous with, 3
    unreliable access to, 13
Internet Explorer, 24, 312
interviews, 242
intranet site, 268
investment in other solutions, 13
invite
    new contact, 253-254
    others to events, 83
    people to Groups, 321
    users, 32
    to video call, 258-259
Invite People button, 256, 258
Is owner, 118, 119, 120
IT
    infrastructure, dealing with, 13
    maintenance, 7
    resources, 12
It's Not All Good
    arranging objects, 216
    blocking a user, 253
    Hangouts functionality, 245
    Internet connection, 13
    Quick Add feature, 84

security issues, 13
sharing files, 122
switching platforms, 13
templates, 134
transition and animation pitfalls, 222
translation tool, 160
viewing attachments, 50
web publishing, 164, 198, 235

item, remove from
web page, 284

J

Java applet, enable, 107

K

K-12 schools, free Google Apps, 5

keyboard shortcuts, 134, 135

keywords search
Chrome, 314
domain, 297
messages, 306

L

label
applying to email, 54
assigning to messages, 52
creating for email, 53
using multiple, 54

landing page, 285

layout of web page, change, 279

layouts, Slides, 205-206

learn more about Google+ page, 326

lectures, 242

licensed installations, 12

licenses
assigning, 299-300
changing, 301

Line button, 215

link
adding, 282
inserting, 51, 141, 144, 186, 213
sharing, 124

Linux system, using Google Apps on, 24

list
of shortcuts, 136
page, 286

List view, Drive, 104

lists
customizing, 221
numbered and bulleted, 139, 140, 220

live chat, 250

login
information, forgetting, 24
name for Google Apps account, 23

logo
adding, 31
uploading, 35

lost or stolen data, 12

M

Macintosh, using Google Apps on, 24

Mail Fetcher tool, 67

maintenance, IT, 7

malware
in attachments, 50
protection, Chrome, 313

manage
devices, 31
messages, 52
permissions, Groups, 322
presentations, 224
schedules, 7
spreadsheets, 187-190
tasks, 91
users, 33

Manage Licenses icon, 301

Manage Roles button, 33

Manage Site page, 274
editing page elements, 276, 277, 278

Managing link, 322

manually
add users, 32
enter a formula, 179-180
perform calculations, 183

Maps, 3

mark messages, 57

marketplace, shopping for apps, 34

masters, working with slide, 228

matters, Vault, 303-304

MBOX file format, 308

meeting
remembering, 15
setting up, 8
times, synchronizing, 71

memo, sending to a group, 61

Merge by MailChimp, 165

message
archiving, 56
assigning star, 57
chat, turn into video chat, 252
composing, 46
data, search, 306-307
deleting, 55
drag and drop, 56
forwarding, 48-49
holds, 296
managing, 52
marking, 57
moving, 55
reply to, 47-48
size, 49

messaging, 8

metadata tags, Vault, 307

microphone for Hangouts, 244

Microsoft Excel, see Excel

Microsoft Office, see Office

Microsoft Outlook, see Outlook

Microsoft PowerPoint, see PowerPoint

Microsoft Word, see Word

mini calendar, 72, 76

missing toolbar buttons, 218

mobile
device, adding Hangouts, 245
notifications, enabling, 95
phone
    access Calendar from, 96
    registering, 95-96

money, saving with Google Apps, 7

month calendar display, 74

monthly subscription, 12

More apps button, 257

More button, toolbar, 134, 172, 218

More Controls link, 31

More Fonts, 137, 219

move
files, 111, 116
mail from another account, 67-68
messages, 55

Mozilla Firefox, 24

multiple
files
    drag, 106
    upload, 105
labels, using, 54
rows, selecting, 177
text selections, 222
    formatting, 141
    music, storing, 99

mute sound in video call, 257

My Drive, 109
navigate folders in, 101-102

N

name already in use, 23

navigation
arrow buttons, Calendar, 76
Drive, 101-103
presentation, 237
subpage, 289

network via Google+, 323

new
folder, creating, 110
topic, start in Groups, 321-322

New Hangout, 253

New Slide button, 208

New Window, Chrome, 315

no ads for Education edition, 22

non-Google Apps file, opening, 113

Not Spam button, 58

Notepad, 308

notifications
by email, 230
enabling mobile, 95
receiving, 7
send by email, 158, 195

Notifications button, 30

numbered lists, creating, 139, 140

O

odt format, 154

office materials, spending less on, 8

Office suite, 4, 12
ingrained use of, 13

omnibox, Chrome, 312

on-the-record messages, 298

OneDrive, 100

ongoing costs, 13

online file storage, 100

open
chat pane, 260
document, 153
existing spreadsheet, 168
Google Docs, 130
non-Google Apps file, 113
presentation, 225
spreadsheet, 188

Open Link in New Tab, Chrome, 315

OpenDocument Format, 154

OpenOffice Calc, 17

Opera, 24, 312

operating systems, 7

operators, predefined search, 115

options, spell check, 161

organizations, web-based apps for, 11

organize
folders and files, 108
slides, 210
web content, 274
with Calendar, 71

Outlook
exporting contacts, 69
importing emails, 67
using with Gmail, 14

overlay
calendars, 78
others' calendars, 73
tasks, 91

ownership, understanding, 119

P

page
add or remove, 287-288
learn about building Google+, 326
level permissions, 291
location, specifying, 286
numbers and breaks,

inserting, 142
reordering, 286
reorganize, 290
setup, 162
view, 290

Paint Format button
using, 141

Paint Format tool, 222

paper clip icon, 50

passwords
resetting, 31
threat of hijacked, 13

payment plans, managing, 31

PDF Document, 154

People Widget Pop-up, 59

people, add to current chat, 253

perform
advanced sort, 193
calculations manually, 183
complex calculations, 181
spell check, 160, 232

permission
managing in Groups, 322
settings, 291
Calendar, 93
webcam, 143, 212

personal profile picture, 36

personalizing account, 31

phishing protection, Chrome, 313

phone calling with Hangouts, 264-265

photo album of video call, 262

Photo from Your Computer button, 254

photos
sharing, 18
storing, 99
using from Drive, 281

Picasa, 5
storage, 117
Web Albums, 42

picture
changing, 36
inserting, 51, 280-281
into chat, 254

pin a tab in browser, 317

pivot table report, creating, 191

place phone call in Hangouts, 264-265

Plain Text, 154

platform, switching to new, 13

plug-in
for Hangouts, 244
install Hangouts app as, 247

PNG format for logo, 35

pop-up
people widget on Gmail, 43
reminder, 87-88

posts, deleting in Groups, 322

PowerPoint, 17, 203
convert presentation from, 225
download presentation as, 238
import slides from, 209

PPTX (PowerPoint format), 238

practice page, Sites, 275

Preferences dialog box, 160
Slides, 231

preferences, setting in Drive, 127

premium features, enabling, 242

Present button, 214, 237

presentations
adding slide to, 208
app, access to, 6
collaborating on, 229
creating, 7, 17-18, 202-205
delivering, 236-238
downloading, 226

editing, 226
formatting, 217
inserting content, 211-216
managing, 224
options, 238
sharing, 17-18

preset filters, Drive, 108, 109

prevent automatic republication, 197

preview a file, 112

primary
calendar, 72
domain, 23
email address, 23

Primary tab, Gmail, 52

Print button, 162

Print Layout, 156, 157

Print Task List, 92

printing
and publishing
documents, 161-164
spreadsheets, 196-197
presentations, Slides, 233
without previewing, 234

privacy concerns, 235
web publishing, 164

Private, default setting, 118, 122, 123

privileges, understanding, 300

product demos, 242

productivity suites
about, 3, 4, 12
editions of, 21

professional slide shows, creating, 17-18

profile picture
changing, 36
for video feed, 257

program, opening from Web, 4

project
site, 268
website, make your own, 19

Promotions tab, Gmail, 52

Protect Sheet, 177

Public on the Web setting, 118

public video call, 259

Publish to the Web, 163-164

publishing
    presentations, Slides, 234-235
    stop, 197
    your calendar, 15

purchase plan, reviewing, 28

Q

Q&A forum, Groups, 318

Quick Add feature, 83-84

R

Recent, 109

reconfigure gadget, 284

register your mobile phone, 95-96

registered nonprofit group, sign up process, 26

registrar, domain names, 5

regular Gmail, free data storage, 14

Reload This Page button, Chrome, 314

reminders
    setting up, 15
    working with, 87-88

remote access of apps and files, 7

Remove Reminder button, 88

removing
    event, 81, 82
    site, 273

reorganize pages, 290

replace text in document, 156

reply to
    email from account, 68
    message, 47-48

report file, create and download, 309

Report Spam button, 58

Reports feature, Vault, 308

republication, prevent automatic, 163, 197, 234

requests, sending, 7

Research pane, 160, 231

Reset Styles, 139

resize rows and columns, 178

Resolve button, 159

Restore button on Drive, 114

retaining data indefinitely, 303

retention rules, setting, 302

Revert to This Version link, 278

review comments, 231

Revision History
    list, 278
    pane, 154

revisions to website, keeping track of, 278

Rich Text format (rtf), 154

right-clicking shortcuts, 111

rows, working with, 177, 178

run an audit report, 309

S

Safari, 24, 312

safeguarding data, 295

save
    button, no need for, 131, 169, 204
    filter view, 194
    money with Google Apps, 7
    style, 138
    video as file type, 262

Save to Drive, 50

schedule
    capabilities, 72
    coordinating, 83
    displays, 76
    events and appointments, 80
    managing, 7
    organize with Calendar, 71

Screenshare app, 259

search
    email messages, 14
    files, 114, 115
    fonts, 137
    functions, Vault, 296
    message data, 306-307
    operators, using, 115
    results, export, 308

Search bar, 30

Search box
    Chrome, 312
    Drive, 103

secondary
    domain, 23
    email address, 24

security
    issues, 13
    with Google Drive, 7
    with Vault, 21

select text, 136

Select Who Can Join button, Groups, 320

self-service online chat, 12

send comment notifications, 158

sent emails, copy of, 48

sequential data, entering, 171

server, administering a, 4

Set as Default button, 162

set up automatic email reply, 66

settings
    permissions, 291
    Groups, 322
    retention rules, 302

sharing files, 118
Talk/Hangouts, 250
visibility, 292
Settings button
using, 30, 104
setup
legal holds, 296
wizard, using, 29
Shape button, 145, 211
shapes, inserting, 215
share
files, 117-119, 120-121
folders, 117-119, 121
links, 124
files in the cloud, 98
settings, 119, 121, 122, 124
calendar, 15, 92-93
site, 291, 292
Share button on Drive, 121
Share Settings dialog box, 121, 122, 124
Shared with Me, 109
shared
calendar system, 6
workspaces, creating, 8
Sheets
about, 6, 7, 17, 167
adding, 175
app, 166-199
apply a filter, 193
blank spreadsheet, 166
Change Color, 176
chart preview, 184
collaborating, 194-195
comments, 194-195
copy
and paste URL, 186
formula, 181-182
create spreadsheet from, 170
data, 191
delete a spreadsheet, 190
exploring add-ons, 199
file formats, 185
formulas and functions, 179

getting started with, 168
insert
chart, 183-184
content, 183-186
images, 185
note, 187
integrated with Drive, 101
new spreadsheet from Drive, 107
print a spreadsheet, 196
publish a spreadsheet to web, 197-198
shortcuts, 172
menu, 176
sort data by column, 192
storage, 117
SUM function, 182-183
tracking and analyzing data, 167-199
view audit report in, 309
view options, 190
wrap text, 174
Shop Now button, 34
shortcuts
list, 136
menu, 111, 172, 176, 178
Sheets, 172
Slides, 219
Sync, 126
tables, 150
formatting, 217
Show Equation Toolbar, 156
Show Ruler, 156
Show Spelling Suggestions, 156, 157
sign in and out, 37-38
of Gmail, 44
Sign In to Chrome, 315
sign on and off, 11
Sign Out button, Google Apps, 38
sign up
for a domain, 5
procedure, 11
process, 25-28
sign-on page, Vault, 301

signature, adding to Gmail, 65
Site Location box, 272
site-level permissions, 291
Sites
about, 6, 7-8, 19, 267
app, 266-292
benefits to using, 269
comments, turn off, 289
content boxes, 279
creating websites with, 267-292
customizing page, 274
downside to, 269
edit page elements, 277
embed multimedia, 269
exploring, 268-270
format text, 277-278
free with Google account, 269
gadget, adding, 283-284
home page, 270
insert image, 280-281
item, removing, 284
layout change, 279
link, adding, 282
page, adding, 287-288
permission settings, 269
practice page, 275
sample home page, 266
search function, 269
share your website, 291-292
site, removing, 273
subpages, add links to, 289
templates, 269, 273
text, adding, 276
touring, 270
videos, adding, 282-283
website, building, 271-273
wiki page, building, 268
SkyDrive, 100
Skype, 242
slide
masters, working with, 228
shows, creating, 17-18

Slides
    about, 6, 7, 17-18, 201
    animations, 222, 224
    app, 200-238
    background, applying,
        207
    blank slide, 200
    collaboration, 229
    comments, 230, 231
    convert files from formats,
        225, 226
    fonts and font size, 219
    getting started with, 202
    images, 212-213
    import slides, 209
    inserting content, 211-216
    integrated with Drive, 101
    layouts, 205-206
    Line button, 215
    links, 213
    lists, 220
    organizing, 210
    Paint Format tool, 222
    presentations
        creating, 201, 204, 205,
            224-228
        delivering, 236-238
        printing, 233
        publishing, 234-235
    Shape button, 215
    slides, adding, 208
    speaker notes, 236
    storage, 117
    tables, 216
    text, 222
        boxes, 212
    themes, 203, 208
    toolbar buttons, 218
    tools, 231
    transitions, 222, 223
    video, 214
    view options, 227
    working with, 205-210
slow Internet connections, 13
smartphones
    Hangouts and, 241, 244
    managing, 31
    using web apps with, 4
smiley icons, 251
SMS (Short Message Service)

    texts, 95, 96
Snooze Notifications, 252
social network, Google+, 323
Social tab, Gmail, 52
software
    costs, 4, 12
    support, 12
    updating, 7
solutions, investment in
    other, 13
sort
    data by column, 192
    files, 116
    perform advanced, 193
    tasks by due date, 62
sound, mute in video call,
    257
spam filter, Gmail, 42, 58
speaker notes, creating, 236
special characters, inserting,
    147-148
Specific People option, 118,
    123
specify
    automatic substitutions,
        160
    view options, 227
spell checker, 159, 160, 161,
    231-232
spelling suggestions, 161
spreadsheet
    app
        access to, 6
        Sheets, about, 17
    blank, 166
    collaborating, 194-195
    create new, 7, 108, 168,
        169
    current vs entire, 189
    data, working with, 191-
        194
    downloading, 189
    enhancing, 167
    entering data, 171
    formatting, 172, 173
    insert content, 183-184

    managing, 187-190
    opening, 168, 188
    printing and publishing,
        196-197
    programs, 4
staff meetings, 242
star, assigning to message, 57
Starred category, Gmail, 57,
    109
start
    chat in Gmail, 251
    page, 286
    video call, Hangouts, 256-
        257
Start Publishing button, 163
Start Screenshare button,
    259
Stop Publishing button, 164,
    197, 235
stop publishing to web, 197
storage
    Drive, 7, 157
    Gmail accounts, 42
    online, 15
    per user, 21-22
    purchase additional, 117
    via upload, 99
Stream, Google+, 323
Styles button, 138
styles
    applying, 136, 138
    save customization, 139
subfolders, adding, 110
Submit a Template link, 133
subpages
    about, 286, 287
    add links to, 287, 289
subscription
    monthly or yearly, 12
    renewals, 31
    to special calendars, 79
suggestions, spelling, 161
SUM function, 182-183
support
    array of, 12

finding, 31

SurveyMonkey
getting, 327

Switch List button, 63

switch
to Gmail, 67-68
to new platform, 13
users, Chrome, 315
views, Drive, 104

symbols, inserting, 142

Sync shortcut, 126

synchronize
browser settings, 315
files, 101
meeting times, 71

syncing files, 124

system access, 12

T

Table menu, 150

table of contents, inserting, 142, 149

Table properties dialog box, 152

tables
custom colors for, 151
formatting shortcuts, 217
inserting, 141, 150
properties, 151, 152

tablets
Hangouts and, 241
managing, 31
using web apps with, 4

tabs, displaying email, 53

Take a Marketplace Tour, 29

Take a Snapshot, 143

take photo of video call, 263-264

Talk app, 242

Talk/Hangouts settings, 250

tasks
creating, 89
in Gmail, 62-63
list, email, 64

managing, 91

Tasks pane, 89, 90

team, creating workspaces for, 8

template
document, 130, 132-133
pages, 286
presentation, 204-205
sharing, 133
spreadsheet, 169, 170
using pre-built, 273

Template Gallery, 132, 165, 204

text
adding to web page, 276
chat, 14, 250
documents, creating, 16
editing on web page, 277-278
formatting, 222
selecting, 136

Text Box button, 145, 211, 212

theme
applying new, 208
choosing, 203

time
management, 72
zone setting, 31

Title Slide layout, 205-206

toolbar buttons, 134, 135, 218
additional, 146

Tools menu, 159, 160, 231

top-level pages, 286

topic, Groups, start new, 321-322

Tour of Admin Console, 28

touring Sites, 270

Track Changes, 165

tracking invites, Groups, 321

trademark symbols, inserting, 147

transfer ownership of file, 119

transitions
pitfalls, 222
setting, 223
working with, 222

translation tool, 160

Trash, 109, 113
list, retrieve item from, 114

TripIt, 327

Turn Google+ On button, 324

turn off comments, 289

turn tasks on or off, 90-91

tutorial, Google+ page, 326

Two-Sided check box, 163

txt format, 154

types of
accounts, exploring, 3
files, Drive, 101
interaction with files, 118
web page, 285-286

U

unavailable, show yourself as, 252

understanding
Google+, 323
ownership, 119

Undo button, 278

unhide a sheet, 177

universities, Google Apps free for, 5

unpin a tab in browser, 317

unreliable Internet connections, 13

unshare a file, 122

Untitled Presentation, 203

Update Roles button, 33

Update Table of Contents, 149

Updates tab, Gmail, 52

updating
software, 7
styles, 138

upgrades, 12
    to Google Apps for
        Business, 25
upload
    file to Drive, 105
    image to web page,
        280-281
    template, 133
    your company logo, 35
uptime guarantee, 21
URL (Uniform Resource
    Locator), 22
    availability of, 272
    copy and paste, 144, 186
    paste in link field, 214
    typing in Chrome, 314
usage stats, 30
Use This Template button,
    170
users
    access, editing, 122
    activity reporting, 19
    adding, 31, 32
    blocking, 253
    collaboration, 12
    information page, 33
    managing, 33
    signing in as, 37
    unlimited, 21
using
    numbers in formulas, 180
    setup wizard, 29
    web image, 281

V

Vacation Responder option,
    66
Vault
    about, 5, 6, 19-20, 295
    adding app, 297-299
    app, 294-309
    assign licenses, 299-300
    change licenses, 301
    collaborators, 305
    exploring, 296-297

export and audit data,
    308-309
extra cost of, 21
free trial, 297
Help Center, 301
holds, 305-306
matters, 303-304
metadata tags, 307
retention rules, 302-303
sample page, 294
search message data,
    306-307
sign-on page, 301
using with Hangouts, 298
verifying domain, 22, 27
video
    call
        answering, 258
        button, 252, 256
        invite others to, 258-259
        outside group, 259
        using apps during, 257
    chat, 14, 21, 244
    conferencing
        about, 8
        calls, 241
        Hangouts, 18
        sharing, 256
    meetings, Hangouts, 18
    storing, 99
    web page, add to, 282-
        283
    won't play, 214
view
    change in video call, 257
    exported data, 308
    multiple calendars, 78
    options, specifying, 190,
        227
    pages, 290
    revisions history, 154
    tasks with another calen-
        dar, 91
    your schedule with
        Calendar, 15
View Comments, Sheets, 177
View menu, 227-228
View Profile button, 36

viewer
    window, 112
    file types supported, 112
viewing
    documents, 156-157
    files on Hangouts, 262
    Gmail, 14
    items in Drive, 15-16
virtual hard drive, 100
virus protection software, 50
viruses in attachments, 50
visibility
    options for files, 118
    settings, 292
        changing, 123
voice chat, connecting via, 14
Voice app, 6

W-X

web browser
    choosing, 24
    updating, 25
web
    apps, 11
    camera for Hangouts, 244
    content, sharing via
        Google+, 323
    image, using, 281
    page
        about, 285
        creating with Sites, 19
        customizing, 274
        elements, editing, 276,
            277
        for domain name, 23
        html format
        upload image to, 280-
            281
    platform apps, access to, 4
    programming and
        upkeep, 269
    publish
        document to, 163-164
        spreadsheet, 197-198
    publishing pitfalls, 198,
        235

surfing, Chrome, 314

webcam
permission, 212
taking pictures with, 143
webinars, 242

website
access to tools for building, 6
add pages, 285-286, 287-
288
building, 271-273
creation, 7-8
removing pages, 288
week calendar display, 74

Who Has Access list, 119, 122

wiki pages
about, 268
creating, 19

Windows, using Google Apps
on, 24

word count tool, 160

word processing
access to, 6
app, 16
programs, 4

Word
documents, 154
viewing, 112

Wordpad, 308

WordPerfect Office, 4

working
remotely, 7
with chat Hangouts, 250
with comments, 159,
230-231
with formulas and func-
tions, 179
with reminders, 87-88
with rows and columns,
177

with Slides, 205-210

workspaces, creating shared,
8

Wrap Text button, 174

Y-Z

yearly subscription to Google
Apps, 12

Your domain only, 118

Your domain with the link,
118

YouTube
broadcast video calls on,
256
Google ownership of, 3
inserting videos from, 214
video, embedding, 275